The Best of
"THE PUBLIC SQUARE"

The Best of
"THE PUBLIC SQUARE"

BOOK TWO

Richard John Neuhaus

William B. Eerdmans Publishing Company
Grand Rapids, Michigan / Cambridge, U.K.

Wm. B. Eerdmans Publishing Co.

255 Jefferson Ave. S.E., Grand Rapids, Michigan 49503 /
P.O. Box 163, Cambridge CB3 9PU U.K.

Printed in the United States of America

10 09 08 07 06 05   9 8 7 6 5 4 3

Library of Congress Cataloging-in-Publication Data

Neuhaus, Richard John.

    [Public square. Selections]

    The best of The Public square. Book two / Richard John Neuhaus.

       p.   cm.

    ISBN 0-8028-4995-4 (alk. paper)

    1. United States — Religion — 1960-. 2. Religion and politics —
United States. 3. Religion and sociology — Unites States.
4. Religion and politics. 5. Religion and sociology.   I. Title.

BL2525 .N483   2001

291.1′7′0973 — dc21

                                     2001040309

www.eerdmans.com

Contents

Introduction

> *"The time has come," the Walrus said,*
> *"To talk of many things:*
> *Of shoes — and ships — and sealing wax —*
> *Of cabbages — and kings —*
> *And why the sea is boiling hot —*
> *And whether pigs have wings."*

"Inclusivity" is taken to be a very good thing these days. I do not claim to be as inclusive as Lewis Carroll. There is, for instance, nothing about cabbages or winged pigs in this book. But the reader may come to suspect that almost everything else is included in these little essays and asides. It really cannot be helped. The organization that publishes *First Things*, of which "The Public Square" is a monthly part, is called the Institute on Religion and Public Life. What of real interest is not included in "religion and public life"? Especially if you believe, as I do, that public life is mainly about culture, and at the heart of culture is morality, and at the heart of morality is religion.

I am a Catholic. There should be no doubt about that. But *First Things* is emphatically ecumenical and interreligious, the last term meaning mainly Christian and Jewish. To be Catholic is also to be lower case catholic. The book you have in your hands is not only catholic in its religious and cultural reach but is also catholic in the many subjects engaged. Theology, philosophy, politics, education, bioethics, law, marriage, child rearing, and much else get their turns — sometimes treated seriously (although never, I hope, ponderously) and sometimes treated whimsically (although never, I hope, frivolously).

These essays and asides (in the journal, the asides appear under the title "While We're At It") are drawn from the second five years of *First Things,* the journal having been launched on the world in March, 1990. The world did not ask for the launching, but the response has been nothing short of amazing. My colleagues and I had hoped that there would be a modest audience to sustain such a publication, but the number of readers continues to grow and grow. My economist friends tell me this is an example of "supply side economics." There is no demand for something until somebody supplies it, and then people discover that that is what they had been wanting for a long time. So it has been with *First Things* and "The Public Square." Some call it supply side economics. We call it the grace of God.

I thought about revising some of the items in this book in order to bring them "up to date," but then decided against that. There is a definite value in reading things in historical context, even if the context in this case is only five years. As I say in one of the essays, since 1984 when I published *The Naked Public Square: Religion and Democracy in America,* there has been a very clear pattern in what is aptly called "the culture war." A critically important part of that pattern is the growing awareness that we cannot intelligently address the great questions of public life without the wisdom transmitted and proposed by religious faith.

That awareness is undoubtedly a positive development. At the same time, we may be more aware of that truth because the problems confronting us are ever more perplexing and, too often, alarming. So you might well ask: Religiously, morally, socially, is our circumstance today better or worse than it was five years ago, or ten years ago when *First Things* was launched? You'll not catch me giving a clear-cut answer to a question like that. Leopold von Ranke, the nineteenth-century German historian, said God is equally present to every moment of history. I agree with that. Moreover, as a student of St. Augustine I believe that all of history is a confused entanglement between "the city of man" and "the City of God" until Our Lord returns in glory to straighten things out.

But I trust that the discerning reader will detect in these essays and asides — along with much that is troubling and even alarming — a note of hopefulness. Hopefulness, mind you, not optimism. Optimism is a matter of optics, of seeing what you want to see and not seeing what you don't want to see. Hope, on the other hand, is a Christian virtue. It is the unblinking acknowledgment of all that militates against hope, and the unrelenting refusal to despair. We have not the right to despair, and, finally, we have not the reason to despair. So I hope the reader will recognize that this is a book of honest hope.

For regular readers of *First Things,* this book is an invitation to revisit and savor again the kind of commentary that makes them regular readers of *First Things.* Others may take it as an invitation to subscribe, which they can do by writing (subscriberservices@pma-inc.net) or by visiting our website (*www.firstthings.com*).

"The time has come to talk of many things." While there may be nothing here about cabbages and whether pigs have wings, there is more than one reference to, among many other things, kings.

Richard John Neuhaus
Feast of the Annunciation
New York City

The Unhappy Fate of Optional Orthodoxy

I'll presume to call it Neuhaus's Law, or at least one of his several laws: Where orthodoxy is optional, orthodoxy will sooner or later be proscribed. Some otherwise bright people have indicated their puzzlement with that axiom but it seems to me, well, axiomatic. Orthodoxy, no matter how politely expressed, suggests that there is a right and a wrong, a true and a false, about things. When orthodoxy is optional, it is admitted under a rule of liberal tolerance that cannot help but be intolerant of talk about right and wrong, true and false. It is therefore a conditional admission, depending upon orthodoxy's good behavior. The orthodox may be permitted to believe this or that and to do this or that as a matter of sufferance, allowing them to indulge their inclination, preference, or personal taste. But it is an intolerable violation of the etiquette by which one is tolerated if one has the effrontery to propose that this or that is normative for others.

A well-mannered church can put up with a few orthodox eccentrics, and can even take pride in being so very inclusive. "Oh, poor Johnson thinks we're all heretics," says the bishop, chuckling between sips of his sherry. The bishop is manifestly pleased that there is somebody, even if it is only poor old Johnson, who thinks he is so adventuresome as to be a heretic. And he is pleased with himself for keeping Johnson around to make him pleased with himself. If, however, Johnson's views had the slightest chance of prevailing and thereby threatening the bishop's general sense of security and well-being, well, then it would be an entirely different matter.

So it was that some church bodies muddled through for a long time with leaderships that trimmed doctrine to the dictates of academic fashion and popular prejudice (the two, more often than not, being the same) while permitting the orthodox option as a kindness to those so inclined, and as testimony to the "balance" so cherished by placeholders radically devoted to the middle way. It was not always an entirely unattractive accommodation. In religion, too, sensible people prefer to be neither fanatic nor wimp. Considering the alternatives, and if one has the choice, it is nice to try to be nice.

Non-optional Orthodoxy

But then what used to be called orthodoxy came up against a new orthodoxy. The new liberal orthodoxy of recent decades is hard and nasty; compared to it, the old orthodoxy was merely quaint. The old orthodoxy was like a dotty old uncle in the front parlor; the new orthodoxy is a rampaging harridan in the family room. The old orthodoxy claimed to speak for the past, which seemed harmless enough. The new orthodoxy claims to speak for the future and is therefore the bearer of imperatives that brook no opposition. The choice of a few to live in the past could be indulged when the future was thought to be open and undetermined. Tolerating the orthodox was also a way of playing it safe. You never know: maybe the ways of the past would come around again. But the old orthodoxy that is optional is proscribed by the new orthodoxy, which is never optional.

The easy-going liberal tolerance that long prevailed was at home with accommodating preferences but uneasy about the question of truth. Not that it denied that there is a truth about this or that, but, then, who was to say what that truth might be? When the question of truth is bracketed — that is, when it is denied in practice — one can choose to be tolerant of a splendid array of "truths." Or one might decide that there really is no truth that makes tolerance necessary, and choose another course. The alternative to the course of tolerance is the course of power. Tolerance suspends judgment; the will to power acknowledges no reason for restraint.

In some churches, the new orthodoxy is most aggressively manifest in feminist and homosexual (or, as it is said, "lesbigay") agitations. These, however, are but the more conspicuous eruptions that follow upon a determined denial of the normative truths espoused by an older orthodoxy. Proponents of the new orthodoxy will protest, with some justice, that they, too, are committed to normative truths. These truths, however, are not embodied in propositions, precedent, ecclesial authority, or, goodness knows, revelation. They are experiential truths expressing the truth of who we truly are — "we" being defined by sex, race, class, tribe, or identifying desire ("orientation").

Identity Is Trumps

With the older orthodoxy it is possible to disagree, as in having an argument. Evidence, reason, and logic count, in principle at least. Not so with the new orthodoxy. Here disagreement is an intolerable personal affront. It is construed as a denial of others, of their experience of who they are. It is a blasphemous assault on that most high god, "My Identity." Truth-as-identity is not appealable beyond the assertion of identity. In this game, identity is trumps. An appeal to what St. Paul or Aquinas or Catherine of Siena or a church council said cannot withstand the undeniable retort, "Yes, but they are not me!" People pack their truths into what Peter Berger has called group identity kits. The chief item in the kit, of course, is the claim to being oppressed.

Nobody denies that there are, for instance, women, blacks, American Indians, and homosexuals beyond number who do not subscribe to the identities assigned their respective groups. This, however, does not faze those in charge of packing and distributing identity kits. They explain that identity dissidents, people who do not accept the identities assigned them, are doubly victimized — victims of their oppressors and victims of a false consciousness that blinds them to the reality of their being oppressed. Alternatively, identity dissidents are declared to be traitors who have been suborned into collaboration with the deniers of who they are. The proponents of truth-as-identity catch the dissidents coming and going. They say their demand is only for "acceptance," leaving no doubt that acceptance means assent to what they know (as nobody else can know!) is essential to being true to their authentic selves. Not to assent is not to disagree; it is to deny their humanity, which, especially in churches credally committed to being nice, is not a nice thing to do.

This helps explain why questions such as quota-ized representation, women's ordination, and homosexuality are so intractable. There is no common ground outside the experiential circles of identity by which truth is circularly defined. Conservatives huff and puff about the authority of Scripture and tradition, while moderates appeal to the way differences used to be accommodated in the early church (before ca. 1968), but all to no avail. Whatever the issue, the new orthodoxy will not give an inch, demanding acceptance and inclusiveness, which means rejection and exclusion of whatever or whoever questions their identity, meaning their right to believe, speak, and act as they will, for what they will do is what they must do if they are to be who they most truly are. "So you want me to agree with you in denying who I am?" By such reasoning, so to speak, the spineless are easily intimidated.

An Instructive Tale

Contentions between rival orthodoxies is an old story in the Church, and the battles that have been fought are riddled with ironies. An earlier round of the difficulties encountered by optional orthodoxy is nicely recounted by John Shelton Reed in a new book, *Glorious Battle: The Cultural Politics of Victorian Anglo-Catholicism* (Vanderbilt University Press). The Oxford Movement associated with John Henry Newman set out to restore to the Church of England an orthodox and catholic substance that it had presumably once possessed. By the middle of the 1840s, Newman and others came to the conclusion that the *via media* they had championed as an Anglican alternative to both Rome and Protestantism was in fact a "paper church," quite devoid of apostolic reality. After Newman and his companions left, the work of orthodox restoration was continued under the banner of "Ritualism" or "Anglo-Catholicism." It enjoyed the impressive leadership of such as John Keble and Edward Pusey, but in the public mind was more closely connected with sundry aesthetes and eccentrics for whom Anglo-Catholicism was, says Reed, a "countercultural" assault on the Victorian establishment.

It is a mark of the restorationists' success that they were soon perceived as a serious threat by the bishops at their sherry, and by Englishmen of consequence (their wives tended to be more sympathetic) who resented any departure from the unapologetic Protestantism of the national religion. In 1874, unhappiness led to parliament passing the Public Worship Regulation Act, which landed a number of Anglo-Catholic clerics in jail for short stays. Checked by this establishment opposition the ritualists, as Reed notes, did an about-face.

In their earlier restorationist mode, they had insisted that the entire church should conform to the normative orthodoxy that they claimed was constitutive of the Anglican tradition. By the 1870s, however, it had become evident that any steps toward uniformity would be at the expense of the Anglo-Catholics. Whereupon Anglo-Catholics became the foremost opponents of uniformity and enthusiastically championed ecclesiastical pluralism. All they were asking for, they said, was "tolerance and forbearance" for their way of being Anglican. In 1867, the Rev. Charles Walker was urging upon the Royal Commission on Ritual that peace could be found in the agreement "that the National Establishment embraces in its bosom two separate religions." Of course that appeal failed to carry the day, as is almost inevitably the case when previously tolerated options threaten the establishment.

Reed, an Episcopalian who teaches at the University of North Carolina, sums up the irony of Anglo-Catholicism: "A movement that originally championed orthodoxy had come to defend freedom; begun in opposition to religious liberalism, the movement now appealed to liberal values for its survival. Cardinal Manning, once an Anglo-Catholic clergyman himself, saw the irony, and maintained that 'Ritualism is private judgment in gorgeous raiment, wrought about with divers colors.' He declared that 'every fringe in an elaborate cope worn without authority is only a distinct and separate act of private judgment; the more elaborate, the less Catholic; the nearer the imitation, the further from the submission of faith.'" Reed adds, "Although some denied it, Manning had a point."

Defending Enclaves

It took a long time for Anglo-Catholicism to be thoroughly routed, but the job seems now almost complete. Among Anglo-Catholics in this country, many have left for Rome or Constantinople, some have joined up with groups of "continuing Anglicanism," and a few are determined to make yet another valiant last stand, despite a long and depressing record of failed last stands. In England there is the peculiar spectacle of "flying bishops," a kind of parallel episcopate ministering to parishes that are no longer in communion with their own bishops. That is generally conceded to be a transient arrangement.

Within the Episcopal and other liberal church bodies, it is still possible, here and there, to defend parochial enclaves of orthodox teaching and catholic sensibility. But those who seek safe haven in such enclaves frequently suspect that Cardinal Manning was right: there is something deeply incoherent about sectarian catholicity. There are numerous groups in this country — Baptist, Missouri Lutheran, Reformed, Pentecostalist — that maintain their version of orthodoxy in a way that is not optional. Setting aside the theological merits of their orthodoxies, such groups are sociologically secure; in their world, they are the establishment, and to that world the new and nasty orthodoxy of truth-as-identity is not admitted. Some of us may think such immunity comes at too high a price. But for those to whom sectarianism is no vice, and may even be a virtue, such withdrawal and disengagement seem like no price at all.

The circumstance is very different for those Christians to whom it matters to be part of the Great Tradition. One thinks especially of Lutherans, Anglicans, and those Reformed who claim the heritage of John Nevin and Philip Schaff; all think of themselves as "evangelical catholics" in ecclesial bodies temporarily separated from upper case Catholicism and upper case Orthodoxy. Anglo-Catholicism was the most impressively institutionalized form of this self-understanding. But, whether in its Reformed, Lutheran, or Anglican expressions, movements of normative restoration were compelled to settle for being tolerated options, and now it seems even that is denied them.

Almost five hundred years after the sixteenth-century divisions, the realization grows that there is no *via media*. The realization grows that orthodoxy and catholicity can be underwritten only by Orthodoxy and Catholicism. Perhaps more than any other single factor, the influence of Anglo-Catholicism among Protestants obscured this reality for a long time. It is a considerable merit of John Shelton Reed's *Glorious Battle* that it contributes to our understanding of why movements of catholic restoration, posited against the self-understanding of the communities they would renew, turn into an optional orthodoxy. A century later, an illiberal liberalism, much more unrelenting than the Victorian establishment, will no longer tolerate the option. It is very much like a law: Where orthodoxy is optional, orthodoxy will sooner or later be proscribed.

The Extremity of the Mainstream

In politics it matters a lot who gets described as "mainstream" and who as "extreme." And, of course, the media do the describing. Politicians who "defend a woman's right to choose" are mainstream. Those who would "ban abortion" are extreme. A new national survey by the Tarrance Group shows that only 13 percent of Americans favor unrestricted access to abortion through all nine months of pregnancy. That is the "mainstream" position. Fifty-two percent of Americans favor the outlawing of all abortions, or all abortions except the 1 percent (according to the Alan Guttmacher Institute) performed for rape/incest/life of mother. That is the "extreme" position. Go figure.

Almost any Republican who is "pro-choice" is described as a "moderate." The new thing is that it is now very widely recognized that, on abortion and much else, the mainstream media are far from the mainstream. "Moderate" and "mainstream" have become synonyms for the L-word that very few practicing politicians dare to use these days. In the last couple of months a number of books by academics have announced the revival of liberalism, but these volumes have about them a sweated tone of desperation. Of course such a revival will almost certainly happen at some point, but not for some years, I expect, and then liberalism redux may bear slight resemblance to the liberalism we have known.

Meanwhile, the increasingly marginal mainstream media will continue to depict as marginal the positions embraced by a majority of Americans. The consoling thing in all this is that the establishment media are not anywhere near so powerful as they, and their critics, claim. The next time you come across inflated claims about the omnipotence of communications in this "media age," prick the balloon with one word: Abortion. Twenty-three years ago, the establishment media, joined by almost every major institution in the country, unanimously declared that *Roe* had "settled" the abortion question. In fact, when the history of this period is rightly written, it will tell that *Roe*, more than any other single factor, radically destabilized our politics, with the result that a surprised and uncomprehending establishment frantically insists that the views of a small and declining minority really do, all appearances and election returns to the contrary, represent "the mainstream."

Maybe, they think, saying it often enough will make it so. That, combined with vesting their hopes in politicians of the left who campaign as conservatives, may restore the world that was before the "extremists" took over. What choice do such people have, except to admit that, just maybe, they got things wrong? Before doing that, the oracles who anchor the establishment networks and newsrooms will solemnly announce to the world that the American people have simply gone crazy. Not surprisingly, we are already getting books and articles reviving the contention that our constitutional order is in need of a major overhaul. The present system is simply ungovernable. And of course they're right: It is ungovernable, by them.

Islam Cornered

I am impressed by how often it happens; when I lecture on religion in American life someone will urgently point out during the Q & A that our society is now religiously "pluralistic" and it is therefore misleading to speak of religion in mainly Christian and Jewish terms. Then someone almost inevitably refers to Islam, frequently adding that it is the "fastest growing" sector of American religion. The someone is usually a secularist for whom the appeal to pluralism is one way of diluting the idea of a predominantly Christian presence in society, and of warding off the notion that ours is in any sense, even demographically, a "Christian nation."

One can well understand the fears associated with talk about "Christian America." But the claim that America does not continue to be a predominantly Christian society, in any sociologically meaningful sense of the term, runs counter to the facts. The appeal to the growth of Islam is especially misplaced. The numbers crunchers have arguments among themselves, but the best survey research puts the number of Muslims in the U.S. somewhere between 1.5 million (with half of those being American-born blacks) and four million. Of course, Muslim organizations, for understandable reasons, claim many more, but provide no credible data in support of their claims. Moreover, a distinctively Muslim public voice in American life — except on questions of Middle Eastern politics — is virtually nonexistent. With respect to American culture and domestic politics, the various Muslim organizations demonstrate that they are good Americans by reinforcing the Judeo-Christian moral tradition that is thought to be the baseline of our common life. (As for the fastest growing sector of American religion, that is, far and away, Roman Catholicism.)

As in the U.S., so also on the world scene. I have frequently suggested that, at the edge of the Third Millennium, Christianity — with the Catholic Church and evangelical Protestantism in the lead — is uniquely situated to be the culture-forming dynamic in world history. After the end of Marxism, Christianity provides the only coherent, comprehensive, compelling, and promising vision of the human future. This vision has been most persuasively set forth by this pontificate in encyclicals such as *Centesimus Annus* (on the free society), *Veritatis Splendor* (on the universality of truth), *Evangelium Vitae* (on the culture of life), and *Ut Unum Sint* (on Christian unity as a sign of human unity). In addition, there is the factor of the sheer magnitude of the growth of Christianity, which is highlighted in *Redemptoris Missio*'s view of the Third Millennium as "the springtime of world evangelization."

Of course this line of argument runs the danger of flirting with the unpleasantnesses associated with "triumphalism." Given the choice between triumphalism and defeatism, I'll take triumphalism any day, but that is not to deny that there are indeed real dangers in what is meant by triumphalism. In this connection, too, one encounters the claim that Islam represents a comparable or even greater world force to be reckoned with. There is much to be said for that claim. The history of the next century will in large part be shaped by the encounter between Islam and Christianity. Not for nothing has John Paul II very assiduously cultivated relations with various Islamic leaderships, as difficult as that is. And of course there are other world religions, such as Buddhism and Hinduism. But, unlike Christianity and Islam, they do not have and are not likely to develop assertive, culture-forming ambitions on a world scale. Shortly before his death in 1986, the French intellectual André Malraux is reported to have said, "The twenty-first century will be religious or it will not be at all." To the extent that is true, the drama will mainly be played out between Christianity and Islam.

On the Far Side of Modernity

Prescinding for the moment from the question of theological truth (which is, of course, the decisive question), in that drama Christianity most decidedly has the upper hand. Relative numbers are only part of the story. There are almost two billion Christians in the world (one billion of whom are Roman Catholics) and somewhat under a billion Muslims. More important than numbers is the fact that Christianity, unlike Islam, is positioned on the far side of modernity's secular alternatives to religion. Put differently, Islam has missed out on the last several centuries of world-formative history. Today it views itself, with considerable justice, as the "object" rather than the acting "subject" of world history.

These realities are helpfully laid out in a marvelous new book by Bernard Lewis, *The Middle East: A Brief History of the Last 2,000 Years* (Scribners, 433 pp., $30). Of course Islam is not limited to the Middle East, but, as Lewis notes, the Middle East is the birthplace of Islam and it is there that the consciousness of Islam continues to be effectively defined. In its first centuries, Islam had little to learn from the West ("Christendom") of the Middle Ages, being much farther advanced in most respects than the countries of Europe. But soon the West would pull far ahead in almost every field. The Ottoman Empire borrowed military techniques and cartographic information from the West, "but this information seems to have had little or no impact on intellectual life."

Lewis, the doyen of Western scholars of Islam, writes: "The literature available [to Muslims] on European history was minimal, and its impact infinitesimal. Such major movements as the Renaissance, the Reformation, the Enlightenment, and the Scientific Revolution passed unnoticed and without effect. Islam had its own Renaissance some centuries earlier, with significant effects even in Europe. There was no response to the European Renaissance, and no Reformation. All these ideas and others that followed them were seen as Christian and discounted accordingly. They were simply irrelevant — of no interest and no concern to Muslims."

There was one exception: "The French Revolution was the first movement of ideas in Europe which had a significant impact on the Middle East, and which began to change the processes of thought and action of its peoples. One reason for this is obvious. This was the first major upheaval in

Europe that did not express its ideas in Christian terms, and that was even presented by some of its exponents as anti-Christian. Secularism as such had no appeal to Muslims; if anything, the reverse. But a movement free from the taint of a rival and superseded religion, and opposed by all the traditional enemies of the Ottomans in Europe, was another matter. It could at least be looked at on its merits, and might even yield the elusive secret of Western power and wealth, about which Muslims were becoming increasingly concerned."

In 1699, Islam made its last major assault on Christendom, crawling away from Vienna in defeat and disarray. A little over a century later, Napoleon would establish himself in Egypt, and from then on, French, English, German, Italian, Russian, and American forces would humiliate Islam by demonstrating that the Middle East was more or less their object to be fitted to their designs. Christianity moves into the Third Millennium having transcended modernity in many respects, while Islam feels threatened by the consequences of the three centuries and more of world history that it missed. Islam, especially militant Islam, suffers from a profound inferiority complex that is not unrelated to its being inferior in the intellectual, cultural, scientific, and technological achievements that now, and will likely continue to, shape the future.

Lewis emphasizes that, while many in the West speak simply of "the West" and think of it in secular terms, to most Muslims there is no doubt that the West means Christianity. The crisis they face is understood as, above all, a religious crisis. When, for example, the Iranians speak of the United States as the "Great Satan," the reference is not primarily to military or economic power but to the Quran's description of Satan as "the insidious whisperer who whispers in the hearts of men." The perceived threat is not chiefly that of conquest or colonial domination but of apostasy. Western journalists conventionally talk about the Muslim fear of Western "secularization," and there is something to that, but, according to Lewis, in Muslim eyes even secularization is but another guise of Christendom's ascendancy.

And so at the edge of the Third Millennium, Christianity — with Catholicism and evangelical Protestantism in the lead — is positioned to be the chief culture-forming vision in world history. There are arguments against that proposition, the most impressive being that the global market, joined to technology, consumerism, and a debased (mainly American) popular culture, is shaping the future. And, of course, only the future will tell. But I think one thing is clear: If Malraux is right about the next century being religious, and I suspect he is, Islam is largely irrelevant to the American scene and is severely disadvantaged on the world scene. All this is no occasion for Christian triumphalism. An Islam that feels hopelessly cornered could be extremely dangerous. Therefore the cultivation of authentic dialogue with Islam is a matter of greatest urgency. Unfortunately, such a dialogue is almost entirely nonexistent today. Why that should be the case is a story for another time.

❧ Here they come again. The article is about addiction (to which, lest there be any misunderstanding, I am opposed). But then come the standard statistics about the cause of deaths: "In 1995 illegal drugs killed 20,000 Americans. Tobacco was responsible for 450,000 deaths; alcohol for more than 100,000." I am always bothered by these assertions, and not only because I like a good cigar and a Dewar's before dinner.

I know what it means to say that driving accidents kill 45,000 Americans per year. It means that, except for those who were terminally ill at the time, 45,000 people who otherwise probably had a long time to live were killed in driving accidents. Similarly with shootings, falls off high buildings, and electrocutions in the bathtub. But tobacco kills 450,000 people per year? Are we to suppose that they otherwise would have lived forever? There would seem to be no doubt that tobacco — more precisely, cigarettes — is not good for your health. Nor is being overweight, sexual promiscuity, jogging till you drop, or obsessive anxiety about your state of health. It may well be that in x number of cases cigarettes contribute, more or less, to the clinically determined cause of death. It may be that y number of people would have lived two or five or twenty years longer had they not smoked cigarettes. But that is very different from saying that cigarettes kill 450,000 people per year.

In his best-selling book, *How We Die,* Sherwin Nuland says we all die from the same cause: lack of oxygen to the brain. A thousand circumstances can contribute to that end, and innumerable, and often unknown, factors can contribute to each of those thousand circumstances. But the fact remains that — with or without cigarettes, alcohol, and drugs — the mortality rate is and will continue to be 100 percent. Understandably, people have a hard time accepting that. This is not a brief for adopting habits that are injurious to one's health and general well-being. There is a moral obligation to be a good steward of the physical self. But we should stop invoking statistics in a way that suggests we would naturally live forever unless "killed" by one bad habit or another.

It's bad enough that young people think they are exempt from the 100 percent mortality rule, but it's intolerable when a whole society turns so puerile. A seventy-six-year-old friend who is a chain smoker cites studies allegedly showing that cigarette smokers are significantly less likely to get Parkinson's or Alzheimer's. He says he would rather die of lung cancer, and hopes he is prepared to die of whatever finally does him in. Not dying at all is not an option. Maybe you have an argument against his view. I'm not sure I do.

Please. Spare me those letters pointing out that cigarettes, alcohol, and drugs can do great damage. I know, I know. My point here is about how we think about death, and how delusions of immortality can do great damage to our minds and souls. The pushiness of the health purists, including their manipulative use of statistics, pollutes the spiritual air, and is, I am sure, bad for our health. We should protest our having to inhale their second-hand fanaticism. I do not say it will kill us, but it can't be good for us. My point is not that we should light up, but, having come to terms with the constancy of the mortality rate, we would do well to lighten up.

Russia: Wilderness Years Ahead

For many evangelical Protestants in this country, post-Communist Russia is a vast mission field ripe unto the harvest. Russian Orthodoxy, however divided and dispirited by its years of subservience to political dictatorship, is strongly united in opposing the "invasion" by Western Christians. And, of course, it is not only the evangelicals who are resented. Much more deep-seated in the soul of Orthodoxy is a suspicion of the designs of Rome. As we have observed in these pages, there is today a sense of heightened expectation regarding the reconciliation of Rome and the churches of the East. But the obstacles to bringing together what was formally sundered in 1054 are still formidable.

A German writer, Barbara von der Heydt, has been examining the spiritual and cultural commotions in Russia and offers her findings in "Russia's Spiritual Wilderness" *(Policy Review)*. Since his return to Russia, the great Aleksandr Solzhenitsyn has been portrayed in the Western press as an ineffectual old man whose prophetic rantings have been largely ignored by the Russian people. In fact, the article by von der Heydt suggests, more people may be listening than those press accounts allow. Although not always so simply stated, Solzhenitsyn's message is simple: the past sufferings and present ills of Russia are attributable to the fact that "men forgot God." While Orthodoxy will have to play the primary role in any moral and spiritual rejuvenation of Russia, this requires that Orthodoxy itself undergo significant changes. Although generally unknown in the West, Orthodoxy has a glorious history of martyrs in this century. Under communism, many thousands of bishops, priests, monks, nuns, and lay people were killed for their Christian witness. The celebration of the Russian martyrs is a source of spiritual renewal, but at the same time it raises awkward questions about current church leaders who, with few exceptions, collaborated with the Evil Empire.

There are other problems. Von der Heydt spoke with Mikhail Dmitriev, a political reformer battling the nationalistic forces of imperial revanchism. "Despite his own agnosticism, Dmitriev claims that the only way to reform Russia, which he calls a 'profoundly atheistic society,' is to restore Christian values. But he makes the point that Orthodox values are pre-Reformation values, which are counter to markets and capitalism, condemning the accumulation of wealth and forbidding the taking of interest. 'The Reformation never reached Russia, and this is the attitude which controls their attitudes to economic behavior. Orthodox values are not compatible with real market values.' As reformers move ahead in the transition, some significant elements of the Russian Orthodox Church perceive a loss of Russian national identity in the westernizing reforms, and therefore oppose them. Dmitriev concludes Russia needs an infusion of Protestantism into Orthodox thinking on the market."

The Russian Orthodox are not likely to welcome the suggestion that they need to learn from Western Protestants. Yet, unlike both Protestants and Catholics in the West, Orthodoxy had no occasion to develop, either conceptually or practically, the ways of coping with the often troubling dynamics of democracy and the free market. Under communism, Orthodoxy was a fragile refuge from the world. Now it is being called upon to restore the moral character of a people who see only confusion, chaos, and the ascendancy of a gangster elite beyond the reach of any legal or moral authority. Von der Heydt's conclusion is sobering: "As daunting as the economic and political tasks are, reforming the character of the nation's soul is far harder yet. But in the absence of such a moral transformation, there can be no lasting economic or political reform. The destruction of the Russian soul was so devastating that it will take years for the country to find its compass. A free and stable Russia cannot emerge immediately. Indeed, it may take more than a generation. The children of Israel wandered forty years in the wilderness, unlearning the traits of slavery in Egypt before entering the Promised Land. Russians may be entering their wilderness years in their exodus from the slavery of communism."

Turning the Enemy into an Enemy of the Enemy

Ever since the Republican triumph in the November 1994 election, the *New York Times* editorial page has been frothing about the end of the world, or at least the end of the political and cultural world favored by the editors. Some of the hysteria is, although pathetic, not without its entertainment value. For instance, a lead editorial titled "Starving the Poor" and aimed at the Republican congressional majority's plans for welfare reform. Rather than speak in their own voice, the editors quote extensively from a statement made a month earlier by John Cardinal O'Connor in which he sharply and rightly criticizes the stereotyping of the poor for political advantage. Among other things, the Cardinal said, "It is increasingly rare for many of us . . . to believe that people can be poor, but honest; poor, but deserving of respect. Poverty is no longer blamed on anyone but the poor themselves.

Contempt for the poor has become a virtue." A touch hyperbolic perhaps, but it is surely a salutary caution, and a necessary reminder that a society is judged also by the way we respond to the needs of the most marginal and disadvantaged.

There is, however, something very odd about the *Times'* discovery of Cardinal O'Connor as a "compelling voice" for justice. The old axiom that the enemy of my enemy is my friend would seem to be at work here, even if the new-found friend was previously declared an enemy. During the ten years that he has been in New York, the *Times* has seldom — we were going to write "never," but maybe there was once — had a kind word for the Cardinal. It has on many occasions editorially lashed out at him and the Catholic Church for their putative bigotry and general obstructionism that got in the way of how the *Times* thinks the city and the world should be ordered. Indeed in the past decade a regularly repeated editorial theme has been the opposition of the Catholic Church in general, and Cardinal O'Connor in particular, to the course of putative progress.

But now, after November 8, 1994, the times they are a-changing. The editors write, "Given the savagery of the climate, it is useful to note what the Roman Catholic Church is saying in response. The church, through its efforts to feed and house America's poor, is intimately familiar with the problem of poverty. Of late, the church's most compelling voice has been that of the Archbishop of New York, John Cardinal O'Connor. . . ." My, my, and all this from the editors of the *Times*. They must be getting desperate. They are.

Desperate enough to trim a pastoral exhortation by the Cardinal to their own political purposes. Desperate enough to praise the Church for being "squarely on the side of the vulnerable," while excising the call for the protection of the vulnerable unborn — a call that the *Times* has routinely and stridently condemned as patriarchal indifference to the rights of women. Desperate enough to try to enlist a religious sanction for its politics, despite its thundering anathemas against the mixing of religion and politics by groups such as the Christian Coalition and its notorious editorial claim of some years ago that the Cardinal was, by criticizing policies approved by the *Times,* threatening "the fragile truce" that permits religious leaders to address questions of public moment. "Of late" the Cardinal has become a compelling voice. Of so very late. And, we can be sure, not for long.

The frothing and floundering of the *Times* in reaction to new ideas and new forces in our political culture is, as aforesaid, not without its entertainment value. In time, the editors may come to understand that the problem is not "the savagery of the climate" but the savagery of their reaction to a growing awareness that old social policies, apparently so compassionate, are often cruel in their consequences for the very people they are supposed to help. The editors say that "the country has a moral obligation to feed and protect those who cannot feed and protect themselves." In time, they may come to understand that "the country" doesn't feed or protect anyone. People and institutions do these necessary things. The editors may even come to understand that the most important institutions for doing these things are not governmental but the mediating institutions, such as family, church, neighborhood, and voluntary association. They may even get to the point where they add the term "subsidiarity" to their vocabulary. But all this will likely take the editors some time.

Meanwhile, we are sure that Cardinal O'Connor knows that his involuntary recruitment as the enemy of the enemies of the *Times* is very temporary. When next he violates the orthodoxies of the *Times,* as he inevitably must, it is certain that the editors will revert to type, and his "most compelling voice" will once again be the intolerably meddlesome voice of one who does not understand who is in charge of the city and the world. (*Urbi et orbi,* as Mr. Sulzberger might put it.)

A Pope of the First Millennium
at the Threshold of the Third

Hardly had heads stopped shaking in the publishing world over the astonishing sales of the new *Catechism of the Catholic Church* in the United States than along comes *Crossing the Threshold of Hope*. Knopf put out more than eight million dollars for the American rights and pinned its promotional hopes on the Pope's planned visit to this country in October. When the trip was postponed, executives at Knopf heard the sickening sound of millions of dollars going down the drain. In happy fact, however, *Crossing* immediately jumped to the top of the best-seller lists, with bookstores complaining that they couldn't get enough to meet the demand.

There is something funny going on here. If you believe the prestige press, what we have in this book are disjointed philosophical and theological ramblings by a reactionary old man who heads an authoritarian institution that is lamentably out of touch with most Catholics and the entirety of the modern world. Insight into what is going on here begins with not believing the prestige press. Another way of understanding what is happening is proposed by the book's author: "We find ourselves faced with a new reality. The world, tired of ideology, is opening itself to the truth. The time has come when the splendor of this truth *(veritatis splendor)* has begun anew to illuminate the darkness of human existence." Some may think that excessively sanguine. The Pope's hopefulness, however, is in no way to be confused with optimism. Optimism is merely a matter of optics, of seeing what you want to see and not seeing what you don't want to see. The hope in *Crossing the Threshold of Hope* is on the far side of a relentlessly realistic, indeed painfully bleak, understanding of the human circumstance. Which is to say that it is on the far side of the cross.

On the dust jacket, written in the Pope's hand, is "Be not afraid!" This, he notes, was the repeated greeting of the

Risen Lord to his disciples. (Here and elsewhere, one is struck by the vibrant employment of numerous biblical passages, making the book, among many other things, an intriguing study in the ecclesial interpretation of Scripture.) "Be not afraid!" is the abiding message of the Church to the world, as it was also the theme of Karol Wojtyla's sermon upon being inaugurated as Pope John Paul II in 1978. The plea of the book, reflected in the title, is that we must not stop at the threshold of hope and faith and love. Be not afraid to cross the threshold, for Christ, having gone ahead, is waiting to receive us on the far side of our fears. The book is philosophical and theological, to be sure, but most of all it is a testament to a profound piety forged in pastoral experience and prayer.

An Open-Ended Conversation

Some pages more than others, but every page evinces the intelligence, the warmth, and the passion of an extraordinary Christian soul. I read this book within days of having had a long and very lively dinner with the Holy Father, and all that we talked about has been much on my mind as I have gone back again and again to *Crossing the Threshold of Hope*. The best way I can describe the book is to say that it is very much like continuing an amiably earnest conversation over the dinner table for another ten or fifteen hours. It's not exactly *Everything You Wanted to Ask the Pope But Never Had the Chance*. It's better than that. There is a great deal that one might never have thought to ask but is essential to know if we are to understand this remarkable man and the faith that he proposes to us and to the world.

As most everybody knows, the genesis of the book was a plan to do an unprecedented worldwide television interview in October 1993, to mark the fifteenth year of this pontificate. The interview didn't come off, but the Pope was much taken with the questions submitted by the scheduled interviewer, Vittorio Messori, a noted Italian journalist. And so, in moments snatched between innumerable obligations, John Paul began writing down his responses to the questions, and, if you keep writing things down that way, pretty soon you have what could very well be a book. At least the Pope thought so, and Joaquin Navarro-Valls, the Holy See's press director, thought so, and Leonardo Mondadori of the Mondadori publishing empire thought so, and now it seems that pretty much the whole world agrees.

Promotional hype to the contrary, it is not "unprecedented" for a Pope to publish a personal book that has no official standing. This Pope has published several such books that have received little public attention. The new thing here is that he is responding directly to questions posed by a journalist, and they are questions of great interest to the general public. Another difference is the enormous financial investment that publishers have made in the book, combined, perhaps, with the reality of a world "opening itself to the truth." And, of course, while the book itself has no official status, it does provide invaluable insight into the thinking behind the many encyclicals, apostolic exhortations, and other official documents issuing from this pontificate.

In this commentary I will but touch on a few aspects of *Crossing* that bear upon matters of general interest, with particular reference to questions of concern to non-Catholics. Throughout the book there is a notable tone of modesty, both about his person and about the office he holds. To be sure, there is no trimming on the claims for the Petrine Ministry, but the accent is on the weakness and limits of Peter, and of the successors of Peter. Everything authentically Catholic, the Pope insists, must be understood Christocentrically, and Christ must be understood as the defining figure for all of humanity. He recognizes that the person of the Pope and the institution of the papacy are a puzzle and scandal for many. In response he cites Augustine, *Vobis sum episcopus, vobiscum christianus.* (For you I am a bishop; with you I am a Christian.) "On further reflection, *christianus* has far greater significance than *episcopus*, even if the subject is the Bishop of Rome."

Similarly Christocentric is the understanding of the Church. The institution of the Church is entirely at the service of the Gospel. He asserts that "the Church itself is first and foremost a 'movement,' a mission." "It is the mission that begins in God the Father and that, through the Son in the Holy Spirit, continually reaches humanity and shapes it in a new way." Elsewhere he suggests that the Church is a "protest movement," challenging all the principalities and powers opposed to the mission of Christ that is the Church. "What else are the sacraments (all of them!), if not the action of Christ in the Holy Spirit? When the Church baptizes, it is Christ who baptizes; when the Church absolves, it is Christ who absolves; when the Church celebrates the Eucharist, it is Christ who celebrates it: 'This is my body.' . . . All the sacraments are an action of Christ, the action of God in Christ." The foregoing is in response to Messori's observation that people are perplexed by the silence of God. In light of the continuing action of God in Christ, says John Paul, "it is truly difficult to speak of the silence of God. One must speak, rather, of the desire to stifle the voice of God."

Unity of Christians, Unity of Humankind

Repeatedly, the Pope returns to the question of ecumenism, and the connection between Christian unity and the unity of mankind. Those who have followed this pontificate with even moderate attentiveness know that there has never been the slightest question about the priority attached to ecumenism. On this score both traditionalist and progressivist Catholics have yet to catch up with the Pope. Traditionalists hesitate to cross the threshold and embrace ecumenism as an integral component of Catholic orthodoxy, while progressivists shrink back from the assertion that the only unity the Church can desire is unity in the truth. Divisions among Christians are a result of human sin, for sure, but John Paul suggests that something else, Someone else, has a hand in this. "Could it not be that these divisions have also been a path continually leading the Church to discover the untold wealth contained in Christ's Gospel and in the redemption accomplished by Christ? Perhaps all this wealth would not have come to light otherwise. . . ."

In this book and elsewhere, John Paul regularly makes reference to what the West has to learn from the Christian East, and it is no secret that the reconciliation of East and West is viewed as the primary ecumenical responsibility of Rome. But his reflections suggest that there is also a deeper understanding of the Gospel issuing from divisions in the West, between Rome and the communities that claim the legacy of the sixteenth-century Reformation. The healing of the breach between Rome and the Reformation requires an appreciation of a "certain dialectic" in how the Holy Spirit leads us into all truth. "It is necessary for humanity to achieve unity through plurality, to learn to come together in the one Church, even while presenting a plurality of ways of thinking and acting, of cultures and civilizations." Divisions, then, may have served a purpose, but that does not justify continuing divisions that do not serve the truth. "The time must come for the love that unites us to be manifested! Many things lead us to believe that that time is now here. . . ."

The charge that the Lord Jesus gave to Peter makes ecumenism imperative. "The Petrine ministry is also a ministry of unity," and that is entirely consonant with the Lord's command to Peter, "Strengthen your brothers in faith." John Paul thinks it significant that these words were said just as Peter was about to deny Jesus. "It was as if the Master Himself wanted to tell Peter: 'Remember that you are weak, that you, too, need endless conversion. You are able to strengthen others only insofar as you are aware of your own weakness.'" Since the Second Vatican Council the Catholic

Church has spoken many times about sins against Christian unity. But this note of repentance and confession is now struck with increased urgency.

At a consistory of cardinals in 1995, a draft program was proposed to prepare for the Jubilee Year 2000. The program reportedly emphasized the need for the Church to confess its sins, not only against Christian unity but also in events such as the Inquisition and the persecution of heretics and Jews. It is said the draft was not well received by many cardinals. If the Church is the Body of Christ, some worry, one must be careful in speaking about the Church being capable of sinning. While such cautions are legitimate, it will not do to speak merely about individual members of the Church sinning, as though the authoritative structures and institutions that define the Roman Catholic Church are not implicated in their actions. Some inexcusably bad things have been done by popes and cardinals and bishops and religious orders — all inextricably entangled with what is meant by the "Catholic Church." Beginning with his persistent reference to "the weakness of Peter," this Pope seems to be searching for the appropriate way to ensure that, at the threshold of the Third Millennium, the Church will be found on her knees seeking for herself the forgiveness she declares to others. For Christians and for the world, it is thought, there must be something like an act of universal repentance and absolution if we are to walk upright into the Third Millennium. What such an act (or acts) might be remains unclear, but this Pope clearly intends to be with us in crossing that threshold, and in a November letter he had more to say about how we might cross it more fully united as forgiven sinners. In that letter, John Paul said that the Church must "become more fully conscious of the sinfulness of her children, recalling all those times in history when they departed from the spirit of Christ" and thus "sullied the face [of the Church]."

No Salvation Outside Christ

The concern for Christian unity inevitably comes up against what some view as Rome's exclusivist claims to being, quite simply and without remainder, the Church of Christ. As is evident in a chapter of particular ecumenical interest ("Is Only Rome Right?"), that is not what the Catholic Church claims. "Outside the Church there is no salvation," John Paul suggests, is another way of stating the "revealed truth that there is salvation only and exclusively in Christ." Here he weaves a rich tapestry of biblical texts and the teaching of the Council that "The Church is in Christ as a sacrament, or a sign and instrument, of intimate union with God and of the unity of the entire human race." To be saved is to be brought into the most intimate life of God, "into the Mystery of the Divine Trinity."

This happens in the Church but that "cannot be understood by looking exclusively at the visible aspect of the Church." The Pope does not put it quite this way, but the implication is that, where this incorporation into the life of God happens, where salvation happens, there is the Church. The Church, he says, "is far from proclaiming any kind of ecclesiocentrism. Its teaching is Christocentric in all of its aspects, and therefore it is profoundly rooted in the Mystery of the Trinity." Christ and the Church, one is invited to think, are coterminous.

There are various levels and spheres of communion with the Church as it is most fully and rightly expressed in the Roman Catholic Church, but, in the final analysis, to say that there is no salvation outside the Church is another way of saying that there is no salvation outside Christ. This does not mean that only Christians can be saved. As the Pope turns to the question of world religions and the many who are not Christians, it appears that there are many who do not know the name of Christ who nonetheless are not outside Christ.

Asked why there are so many religions, John Paul refers, as he does regularly throughout this book, to the teaching of the Second Vatican Council. The several parts of that teaching must be kept in play. One part is that the "Church rejects nothing that is true and holy in these religions." Because truth and holiness are from God, all the many evidences of truth and holiness are of a piece, for God is one. In other religions can be found *semina Verbi* (seeds of the Word); their doctrines can "reflect a ray of that truth which enlightens all men," that truth being Christ. The Church "is bound to proclaim that Christ is 'the way and the truth and the life.'" Whatever truth and holiness is to be found anywhere finds its fulfillment in Christ, through whom God has reconciled everything to Himself. In considering the many ways of religion in the world, both past and present, we can affirm, says John Paul, that "Christ came into the world for all these peoples. He redeemed them all and has His own ways of reaching each of them in the present eschatological phase of salvation history."

As generous as he obviously wishes to be to all, the Pope offers rather sharp strictures with respect to, for instance, Buddhism and Islam. Buddhism, with its disdain for and detachment from the world, has some similarity to varieties of Christian mysticism, but such Christian mysticism "begins at the point where the reflections of Buddha end." The Christian goal is not nirvana but perfect incorporation into the life of the Triune God. Islam is similarly limited: "Some of the most beautiful names in the human language are given to the God of the Koran, but He is ultimately a God outside of the world, a God who is only Majesty, never Emmanuel, God-with-us. Islam is not a religion of redemption. There is no room for the Cross and the Resurrection. . . . For this reason not only the theology but also the anthropology of Islam is very distant from Christianity."

While the Pope stresses the requirement of respect for what is true and holy in all religions, it is when he comes to Judaism that respect is clearly joined to deep affection. Here are our "elder brothers in the faith," a phrase John Paul has employed innumerable times. In the chapter devoted to Judaism, he recalls childhood experiences in Poland and the unspeakable crimes of the Nazi period. As Pope he has met frequently with Jewish groups, and he was the first Pope to worship at the great synagogue in Rome. At one such meeting a Jewish leader said, "I want to thank the Pope for all that the Catholic Church has done over the last two thousand years to make the true God known." Some Jewish thinkers have suggested that Christianity is Judaism for the Gentiles, the way in which the God of Abraham, Isaac, and Jacob has, through Jesus, extended the covenant to the nations. While not subscribing to that formulation, John Paul proposes a heightened sense of alertness to the mysterious and continuing bond between Christian and Jew. Israel and the Church are "two great moments of divine election," and they "are drawing closer together." What is said about the unique relationship between Christianity and Judaism does not detract from but is based upon Jesus the Christ as the fulfillment of God's promise. "The New Covenant," says John Paul, "has its roots in the Old. The time when the people of the Old Covenant will be able to see themselves as part of the New is, naturally, a question to be left to the Holy Spirit. We, as human beings, try only not to put obstacles in the way." Twice he notes the significance of the fact that the Church's dialogue with Jews is conducted by the Pontifical Council for Promoting Christian Unity, whereas dialogue with other religions is under different curial auspices. This reflects a recognition that a singular measure of unity already exists between those who worship the God of Abraham, Isaac, Jacob, and Jesus.

John Paul is not much taken with the effluence of religiosities that appear under the banner of New Age. This, he suggests, is but another instance of the return of ancient gnosticism, the idea that liberation from the real world can be achieved by the adepts of a superior "gnosis" or "spiritual consciousness." The Pope observes, "Gnosticism never completely abandoned the realm of Christianity. Instead, it has always existed side by side with Christianity, sometimes taking the shape of a philosophical movement, but more often assuming the characteristics of a religion or para-religion in distinct, if not declared, conflict with all that is essentially Christian." Here and elsewhere, the heart of what is essentially Christian is Christ — the Word of God incarnate, redeeming the human project and drawing it to its completion in the life of the Holy Trinity. In this view, Judaism and Christianity — unlike Buddhism, Islam, and other traditions — understand creation and redemption in historical continuity; the accent of hope is not on salvation from the world but on the salvation of the world. In support, he repeatedly cites John 3:16, "For God so loved the world . . ."

To Keep Conscience on Guard

Speaking of salvation invites reflection on damnation. In some forms of piety to be found among both Protestants and Catholics, salvation is defined almost exclusively by reference to damnation. To be saved is to be snatched from hell, which is the destination of the generality of humankind. This is not the sensibility of John Paul, who, with early fathers of the Church and the continuing tradition of Orthodoxy, emphasizes the cosmic nature of a redemption that is directed toward the fulfillment of man in the life of God, indeed toward theosis or deification. Nonetheless the Pope is concerned about preachers and catechists who "no longer have the courage to preach the threat of hell. And perhaps even those who listen to them have stopped being afraid of hell."

He sympathetically recognizes that the undeniably biblical teaching about hell has been a problem for great Christian thinkers from Origen in the third century to Hans Urs von Balthasar in the twentieth. After all, it is clearly God's will that "all should be saved and come to the knowledge of the truth" (1 Timothy 2). Or, as John Paul puts the question, "Can God, who has loved man so much, permit the man who rejects Him to be condemned to eternal torment?" He answers, "And yet, the words of Christ are unequivocal." In Matthew 25, for example, Christ speaks clearly about those who will go to eternal punishment. So who is in hell? "The Church has never made any pronouncement in this regard. This is a mystery, truly inscrutable, which embraces the holiness of God and the conscience of man. The silence of the Church is, therefore, the only appropriate position for Christian faith. Even when Jesus says of Judas, 'It would be better for that man if he had never been born,' His words do not allude for certain to eternal damnation."

It is the case, however, that "there is something in man's moral conscience" that rebels against the loss of the doctrine of hell. After all, the God who is Love is also ultimate Justice. Reflecting on those who are responsible for creating "hells on earth," one must ask: "Can He tolerate these terrible crimes, can they go unpunished? Isn't final punishment in some way necessary in order to reestablish moral equilibrium in the complex history of humanity? Is not hell in a certain sense the ultimate safeguard of man's moral conscience?" Among some Protestants there is considerable anxiety that the Catholic Church teaches "universalism," the doctrine that all will ultimately be saved, or even Pelagianism, the heresy that it is possible to be saved without the grace of God in Christ. John Paul goes to some pains to clarify these questions.

He notes that ancient councils of the Church rejected the theory of a final apocatastasis according to which all would finally be saved and hell abolished. Yet one gathers he does not disagree with von Balthasar, who, in a famous essay by that title, asked, "Dare one hope that all will be saved?" The answer would seem to be that one may so hope — perhaps even that one must so hope — while not denying the abiding alternative to salvation, which is damnation. As for Pelagianism, his interviewer asks whether one cannot live "an honest, upright life even without the Gospel." John Paul: "I would respond that if a life is truly upright it is because the

Gospel, not known and therefore not rejected on a conscious level, is in reality already at work in the depths of the person who searches for the truth with honest effort and who willingly accepts it as soon as it becomes known to him. Such willingness is, in fact, a manifestation of grace at work in the soul. The Spirit blows where He will and as He wills (John 3). The freedom of the Spirit meets the freedom of man and fully confirms it." In sum, there is no salvation apart from the grace of God in Christ. Even those who have never heard of Christ are, if they are saved, saved because of Christ.

Behold the Man!

But this discussion may give the misleading impression that *Crossing the Threshold of Hope* is an exercise in systematic theology. There is theological reflection, of course, but in the main it is an unabashedly personal disclosure of how this Pope understands himself, his office, the responsibilities of the Church, and, above all, the strange ways of God with man. There is much on his devotion to Mary and why the typology of male and female is essential to understanding Christ and His bride, the Church. Some readers will find the most affecting parts of the book to be the autobiographical reflections, especially on his abiding concern for young people. He says, "As a young priest I learned to love human love." Such human love, rightly ordered, is on a continuum with the love of God, His for us and ours for Him.

This continuum of the life of God and the life of man is at the heart of all of John Paul's thinking. This is the humanism in his "prophetic humanism." He never tires of repeating that the revelation of God in Christ is the revelation of God to man but also the revelation of man to himself. Citing Blaise Pascal he says, "Only in transcending himself does man become fully human." *(Apprenez que l'homme passe infiniment l'homme.)* This truth is demonstrated by Christ in

His love that is perfectly ordered to the Father in the power of the Spirit. Thus Christ has "touched the intimate truth of man." "He has touched it first of all with His Cross. Pilate, who pointing to the Nazarene crowned with thorns after His scourging said, 'Behold, the man!', did not realize that he was proclaiming an essential truth, expressing that which always and everywhere remains the heart of evangelization."

John Paul is impatient with sociological analyses of spiritual realities. The Church does not march to statistical calculations but to the songs of Zion. At the same time, he does not shrink from offering his own assessment of the Church's circumstance at the edge of the Third Millennium. "If the post-conciliar Church has difficulties in the area of doctrine and discipline, these difficulties are not serious enough to present a real threat of new divisions. The Church of the Second Vatican Council . . . truly serves this world in a variety of ways and presents itself as the true Body of Christ, as the minister of His saving and redemptive mission, as the promoter of justice and peace." As the major transnational community, the Church is a force also in international affairs. "Not everyone is comfortable with this force, but the Church continues to repeat with the Apostles: 'It is impossible for us not to speak about what we have seen and heard' (Acts 4)."

Tom Burns, former editor of the *Tablet* (London), catches the feel of the book very nicely. "To write of John Paul II as a pontiff of the first millennium is not to say that he is an anachronism, but on the contrary that the radicalism of that time, when grace struck its roots into nature, when the blood of the martyrs was the seed of the Church, and mankind had to choose between stark alternatives, has come round full circle. The most modern of all popes recalls the most distant in time: 'Against the spirit of the world, the Church takes up anew each day a struggle that is none other than the struggle for the world's soul. . . . The struggle for the soul of the contemporary world is at its height when the spirit of the world seems strongest' — words that might have been spoken in the catacombs of ancient Rome." At the threshold of the Third Millennium, they are words of invitation to cross the threshold of hope.

❧ We almost got away with it. But now Texe Marrs, who runs Living Truth Ministries in Austin, Texas, has told his thousands of readers the real story behind "Evangelicals and Catholics Together: The Christian Mission in the Third Millennium." It seems that Charles Colson is a "closet Catholic" who was recruited by the Vatican to arrange for Protestantism's surrender to Rome. Neuhaus is a "Marxist heretic" who answers to "both the notorious *Catholic Order of the Jesuits* and the infamous Christian-bashing, *Jewish Anti-Defamation League.*" "When Rev. Neuhaus abandoned the Lutheran Church to become a Catholic priest, the Vatican and its Jesuits knew they had a potential winner. With Rome's guidance (and financial means!), they reasoned, Richard Neuhaus could be used to manipulate millions of gullible Christians into joining in a grand crusade to destroy Protestantism." In light of Marrs' revelations, we can see how sneaky Neuhaus has been in covering his tracks by pretending on occasion to be critical of the Jesuits and the Anti-Defamation League. "Colson and Neuhaus openly admit that they secretly worked for two years behind the scenes on this project. Their plan was to get the world's top evangelical and Catholic leaders to sign up and endorse the manifesto before expected opposition developed." (In retrospect, it was probably a mistake for Chuck and me to admit it publicly.) Those who want to know more can get *All Fall Down,* a special report by Mr. Marrs that reveals "the stunning facts about the greatest sell-out in the history of Christianity." It seems that Protestants have been recruited to work with Jews and Jesuits to bring "the whole religious establishment, under their supreme leader, the Pope, straight into the Great Apostasy." In addition to the real dirt on Colson and Neuhaus, the report "unmasks the Vatican connections" of some of the biggest names in Protestantism, including Pat Robertson, Billy Graham, Bill Bright, Robert Schuller, Richard Land, and Larry

Lewis. Oh yes, Marrs reveals that Neuhaus also publishes "a propagandistic magazine, *Things Considered.*" Don't say you were not warned.

✶ Nobody reads it anyway, a friend tells me, so what difference does it make? Maybe so, and maybe it's a small thing, but it should not go entirely unremarked. I can't be the only one who reads the annual presidential proclamations for Thanksgiving Day. This time President Clinton urged us "to lift ourselves closer to God's grace," noting that "ours is an unfinished journey." As to where we are going as a nation, he had this to say, "Our destination must be to create the means for every one of us to prosper, to enjoy sound education, meaningful work experience, protective health care, and personal security." The language gives a lift to the soul. The Lincolnesque ring of "meaningful work experience" puts one in mind of the first president to issue a proclamation declaring Thanksgiving a national holy day. President Clinton's proclamation concludes by urging "the citizens of this great nation to continue this beloved tradition." The 1994 proclamation breaks tradition, however, by not being dated. Past proclamations ended by noting that the document was given in a certain year of the founding of these United States of America and in a certain "year of Our Lord." That the 1994 proclamation is not dated at all may reflect simply an absence of historical consciousness. But whoever wrote it must have gone back to consult earlier proclamations, and the omission of the traditional conclusion must, one is inclined to think, have been deliberate. The "year of Our Lord" likely offended somebody's sense of what is appropriate in this "pluralistic" society. What about the Muslims, the Californicating New Agers, the Buddhists, the Confucianists, and the ACLUists? All might be "offended," as it is offensively said. To a certain mindset, pluralism is the enemy of particularity, requiring a denial of, or indifference toward, the differences that make most difference. The result is a dispiriting mix of the banal and mendacious. Authentic pluralism, of course, is the engagement of, even the celebration of, difference within the bonds of civility. But, as my friend says, we should not make too much of a Thanksgiving Day proclamation that almost nobody reads anyway. On the other hand, it's my job to bring such things to public attention. I don't know if the task is a "meaningful work experience," but I can thankfully say that it's not without its satisfaction.

The First Five Years

One doesn't want to make too much of a fifth anniversary, but neither is it nothing. Just surviving for five years is something. Most new journals do not manage that. *First Things* has not only survived but has flourished, and continues to grow in readership and by every measure of influence. I am grateful to editorial colleagues who do most of the hard work, to benefactors who have supported a risky venture, and, most particularly, to our thousands of extraordinarily devoted readers. If Our Lord continues to delay His return, there is every reason to believe that *First Things* will be flourishing twenty-five and fifty years from now.

Readers who were present at the creation will remember that this project was originally the Center on Religion and Society and was affiliated with the Rockford Institute in Rockford, Illinois. Under those auspices we published a monthly newsletter, *The Religion and Society Report,* and a quarterly journal, *This World.* In May of 1989 we went independent and reconstituted ourselves as the Institute on Religion and Public Life, combining what was done in the earlier publications in a new monthly journal that made its first appearance in March 1990. At the time, I told potential supporters that I expected *First Things* would have 5,000 paid subscribers in the first five years, and thought it possible that it might have as many as 10,000. I certainly did not expect that in 1995 there would be nearly 30,000 paid subscribers, plus newsstand sales and a controlled circulation to educational and other institutions. As the growth continues at an encouraging pace, I have stopped speculating about what may be the potential readership of a journal such as this. There is undoubtedly a limit, for this is definitely and designedly a publication for a particular kind of reader, and that will not change.

In this issue we republish the editorial statement of purpose that appeared in the first issue, "Putting First Things First." Five years later, we still affirm that statement wholeheartedly. Looking back on the first fifty issues, the editors believe that we have really tried to do what we promised to do. At the risk of immodesty, on some promises we think we have done very well indeed, better than could have been reasonably expected. Where that has happened, the credit goes chiefly to the large and varied company of contributors that *First Things* has attracted. Editors can encourage (and sometimes prod, provoke, and pester), but finally the journal depends on writers who have something important to say, know how to say it well, and want to say it to this audience.

For all that has been gratifying in the first five years, you should know that almost every editorial meeting includes intense questioning about how we can do better. The inaugural editorial says that "the key word is conversation," and notes that "a real conversation, as distinct from intellectual chatter, is marked by discipline and continuity." These five years have witnessed some remarkable changes that cannot help but have a marked impact upon the continuity of the conversation. In the really big picture, of course, there is always a certain wisdom in the adage, *Plus ça change, plus c'est la même chose.* But in the world measured by months and years, things happen. And some things have happened that have a bearing on what we mean by "Putting First Things First."

A few examples may suffice. The end of communism

and the consequent collapse of socialism as the ordering principle of social progress. Yes, there are still socialists around who have not gotten the news, but something definitive has happened, and our intellectual and moral discourse has hardly begun to take it into account. This is a weird historical moment. Now almost everybody says that *of course* communism was an evil empire and socialism is a dumb idea. But only a few years ago, most did not say that, and many insistently said the contrary. We need better to understand what happened and why in the great, and finally successful, contest with totalitarianism. For the sake of historical honesty, for the sake of the victims and the heroes and the heroines whom we must honor to maintain a hold on our own humanity, and for the sake of cultivating an idea of freedom more clearly ordered to moral truth. The end of this contest with totalitarianism complicates the meaning of freedom beyond yesterday's undeniable (although often denied) imperative of defending the free world.

For another example, in these five years there has been a marked change in thinking about church-state relations and, more generally, about the role of religion in public life. Our protest against "the naked public square" was then a distinctly minority position, whereas today there is a much more widespread recognition that church-state jurisprudence is a shambles, and that the democratic process requires the vigorous engagement of the religiously based moral convictions of the American people. I do not suggest that the ACLU has lost its punch or that there are not in the prestige backwaters of the academy extreme separationists still weaving their theories for a radically secularized public order. But, in the courts and other public forums, the ACLU now has impressive competition, while the political sea change of November 1994 has created a circumstance much more sympathetic to the public expression of arguments informed by religious tradition. So great is the change in the political climate that it seems likely we will have to pay more attention to the danger of uncritical enthusiasm for religion in public, especially when religion is promoted as an instrumental good for the achievement of sundry purposes public and personal. "We will not begin to solve our problems," a very major Republican figure announces, "until we give God a more important place in American life." The intention is laudable, no doubt, but if we are really talking about God, He is not awaiting a promotion by us. Such rhetoric suggests that we should perhaps move Him up from Number Seven to Number Two. Or maybe appoint Him the nation's Premier Role Model.

Five years later, the great change regarding abortion is that the Supreme Court is now isolated. It is obvious to all but the willfully blind that the *Roe v. Wade* regime imposed by the Court has not been ratified by the American people. The Court and the Court alone stands in the way of the political process seeking a way in which the unborn will be protected in law and welcomed in life. In its 1992 *Casey* decision the Court said that the country faces a "crisis of legitimacy" if the people fail to follow the Court in upholding the present abortion license. It is now evident that it is the Court that is caught in a crisis of legitimacy that is of its own creation. The unspeakable injustice of thousands of innocent lives taken each day with the blessing of the law continues to be the single greatest threat to the moral legitimacy of this political order. The second editorial in that inaugural issue was titled "Redefining Abortion Politics." We saw hope for change then; we see hope for change now. Even if we are wrong, this question will not let us go.

The more things change, the more things change. The now almost universal acknowledgment of the crisis of welfare and the poor as evident in the urban underclass. The near disappearance of mainline Protestant influence in the public arena, and the remarkable emergence of a conservative evangelicalism prepared to move from protest to governance. The striking steps toward rapprochement between Roman Catholics and evangelical Protestants in both faith and public responsibility. The astonishing vibrancy of this pontificate's assertion of Catholic social teaching. The slow, steady, and ever more secure building of a moral and even theological foundation of trust between Christians and Jews. The widespread recognition of the limits of statist solutions for social problems, and of the indispensable role of mediating institutions such as families, churches, and voluntary associations. These are among the notable differences between 1990 and 1995. Most of them, taken all in all, are differences for the better. There are other and less happy differences between then and now: the growth of the euthanasia movement, the slide toward eugenics and the manipulation of the human genotype, the looming war against immigration and, maybe, against immigrants.

The Familiar and the Abiding

In that very first issue we spoke about our society being embroiled in a Kulturkampf, a war over the definition of our common life. That struggle continues as, in various guises, the vaunted revolutions of the counterculture of the sixties are prosecuted on every front. We have published many articles on the polymorphous perversities of multiculturalism, deconstructionism, sexual liberationism, and other causes championed by the apostles of decadence and debonair nihilism. And we will undoubtedly publish more such articles as the occasion requires. But these revolutions are familiar now; they have long since lost their capacity to shock, and are fast losing their capacity to influence, at least outside the confines of the elite academy and what passes for the arts. In the larger culture, the counterrevolution seems to have begun in earnest. If so, the counterrevolution, generally described as conservative, will surely bring its own problems. It is a trustworthy maxim that everything human, given time enough, will go wrong. Familiar debates will be reconfigured, and on this question or that old allies will be opponents and opponents will become allies. The more things change, the more things change.

But this reflection on the first five years has dwelt too much on changes in public life. That opening editorial declared, "The first thing to be said about public life is that public life is not the first thing." I believe that even more strongly now, much more strongly now. It has to do with age, no doubt, and with having been rather rudely put on more intimate terms with mortality. My colleagues, younger and less scathed, share my determination that *First Things* will continue to put first things first. We will continue to publish arguments about the great transcendentals, the good, the true, and the beautiful, that are brazenly irrelevant to any social or political purpose. And we will publish articles that can claim no virtue other than whimsy, which is no little virtue. And so we hope to temper the sweated earnestness of the battles of the earthly city, knowing that this is not the city that abides. Putting first things first, we will for the next five years, and for however many years there are to be, take as our own the words that Eliot gave Thomas Becket:

> I have had a tremor of bliss, a wink of
>   heaven, a whisper,
> And I would no longer be denied; all things
>   Proceed to a joyful consummation.

Portnoy's Snit

If they understood what was happening, one might credit them with a measure of courage, or at least with a piquant contrariness. But the *New York Times* does not understand; the people in charge there do not, as it is said, get it. They are like the *New Yorker* movie critic who wrote in November 1972 that she did not believe Richard Nixon had been elected because she knew absolutely no one who had voted for Nixon. And so it is that the editorial page of the Sunday *Times* of December 11 led off with a long piece "In Praise of the Counterculture." The 1960s and its effluence were, we are told, a universal blessing. We would not have had the feminist movement, the gay rights movement, and a host of other improvements had it not been for the wonderful "Thoreauvian" dissenters of that era. That Thoreau was a humbug who is only kept in print by his capacity to capture the passing fancies of impressionable adolescents is neither here nor there to the editors of the *Times,* who apparently feel entitled to indulge their own impulse to throw an adolescent snit in protest against a nation that appreciates them insufficiently.

Outraged that Newt Gingrich — joined, it seems, by a majority of Americans — takes a rather dim view of "the counterculture," the *Times* lobs an in-your-face editorial at a nation that dared perpetrate an in-your-face election against the orthodoxies of the *Times* and its satellite worlds of correctitude. "In Praise of the Counterculture" could be read as the paper's letter of resignation from the world of power and influence outside Manhattan. If the country is going to get uppity with the *Times,* the editors sniff, the country can just go and find itself another newspaper to tell it what to think. On the other hand, it seems improbable that the *Times* will really withdraw from "the power and the glory" of directing the affairs of the nation and the world, or at least pretending to. But one never knows.

Anna Quindlen, for one, is not going to put up with it anymore. Writing her farewell column shortly before Christmas, she says, "I leave you with good tidings of great joy: Those who shun the prevailing winds of cynicism and anomie can truly fly." So there goes Ms. Quindlen flying far away from the ugly thing that America has become. But not before she thanks "a newspaper that stands for the very best that newspapers can provide," and offers us some final ponderings on what she called "the great issues of the day." The great issue of her final column is how she could remain such a wonderful person over all these years. "For more than twenty years I've been a reporter, a job that people say is sure to make you cynical and has somehow only left me more idealistic." It is with her, she explains, as it was with Anne Frank who, less than a year away from death in Bergen-Belson, wrote in her diary, "In spite of everything I still believe that people are really good at heart." Unlike Anne Frank, Ms. Quindlen is only going off to New Jersey, but the Republicans are in control there, too. She is generous in sharing with us what she has learned: "That is the most important thing I have learned in the newspaper business, that our business is one another." Brushing away a tear, one is comforted by the thought that others are left to carry on in the tradition of Anna Quindlen.

Columnist Frank Rich, for example.

President Clinton dismissed the Surgeon General Joycelin Elders for advocating, or seeming to advocate, the teaching of masturbation skills to the country's sexually challenged youngsters. In response, the Sunday *Times* of December 18 carried no less than two pieces in praise of masturbation. Frank Rich boldly and imaginatively entitled his article, wouldn't you know it, "The Last Taboo." (Incest was last year.) After the obligatory observations on Dr. Elders being a black and a woman (and we all know what America does to blacks and women), he lauds her for daring to speak "the dreaded M-word." Mr. Rich notes that sophisticated folk such as D. H. Lawrence, Woody Allen, and Philip Roth have given masturbation an honorable place in our high culture. *Portnoy's Complaint*, there are no doubt those who still remember, was largely about the bathroom fantasies of a boy who had big problems with his father.

Mr. Rich does not claim onanism is the most elevated form of sexual expression. He cites the observation of Mark Twain that "Of all the various kinds of sexual intercourse this has the least to recommend it." Among the problems with masturbation noted by Twain, "It is unsuited to the drawing room." With an entirely straight face, indeed with moral earnestness, Frank Rich continues in that idealistic vein for which Anna Quindlen was so admired by herself: "Perhaps these drawbacks are still troublesome today, but they are nothing next to such alternatives as unwanted babies or disease. That was the only point Joycelyn Elders was trying to make, and precisely because it cost her her job, this time it may finally get through." If we got him right, Mr. Rich finds it troublesome that masturbation is still thought to be unsuited to the drawing room, but if we encouraged a lot more of it there would be fewer unwanted babies and less disease. Dr. Elders said she wanted to educate the American people, and it appears she succeeded with a few, an inordinate number of whom are children of the counterculture working at what used to be called the nation's newspaper of record.

❧ Commentary on the dismal state of Catholic preaching is a commonplace. There are exceptions, of course, but the general picture seems not to be encouraging. The Second Vatican Council's emphasis on the importance of the homily (Catholics shy away from "sermon") in every Mass could not, of course, create instant competence for what was mandated. All kinds of homily services cropped up, some offering "hints" and "helps," and others selling complete texts that are sometimes read by priests verbatim. The quality of homily services ranges from the banal to the brilliant, with occasional slips into the heretical. For instance, a reader in Grand Rapids, Michigan, sends us the "Homily Helps" for Tuesday of the Second Week of Advent from a service published by St. Anthony Messenger Press. The text is Matthew 18 with its warning about offending against one of these little ones who believe in Christ. To the St. Anthony author, this suggests, quite inexplicably, a homily on the need for the Church to provide housing for the elderly. Which leads to this: "A fraction of the resources we devote to the unborn redirected to the end of life could result in facilities for the elderly that would be a model for the nation." One imagines Father, not yet fully awake, at the early morning Mass reading that and then thinking to himself, "What on earth did I just say?" Or devout Mr. McNaughton in the pew: "What on earth is he going on about now?" Then there was the homily service we glanced at while saying Mass in an upstate New York parish. The day was St. Matthias, celebrating the disciple chosen to take the place of Judas. The "homily suggestion" was that Our Lord's original choice of Judas "shows that God can make mistakes, too." We find ourselves hesitant to suggest that Catholic preaching would be greatly improved by burning all the homily services, but we are not quite sure why.

He Who Steals My Words . . .

When you steal from one author, it's plagiarism; if you steal from many, it's research. I wish I had said that, but it was in fact said by the noted wit Wilson Mizner (d. 1933). Plagiarism in its various forms seems to be getting renewed attention these days. A writer does a devastating article on the doleful effects of affirmative action in hiring and promotions at the *Washington Post*, and the *Post* management fires back that the writer is a charlatan and well-known plagiarist. She did admit to an error a while back in using some lines she found in her computer that she thought were hers but in fact had been borrowed from someone else. It is very doubtful that that qualifies as plagiarism. Since they were not able to refute the article, the *Post* editors were desperate to discredit its author. Among writers the charge of plagiarism is powerful; it is comparable to the potency in today's social climate of being accused of the sexual abuse of minors.

I've always been somewhat relaxed about this question of literary borrowings. After all, is it not said that imitation is the sincerest form of flattery? I assiduously make a point of attributing to the source anything I'm aware of borrowing, but mainly because I would be embarrassed to have somebody find me out. When people tell me that they've "stolen" something from me for a speech or newsletter, my response is that they're welcome to steal anything worth stealing. Not so with Dennis Prager, editor of *Ultimate Issues*. When people tell him that they stole something he wrote, he responds, "That makes you a thief, and you should repent." That seems a bit heavy, but Mr. Prager and others have prompted me to rethink the merits of their view.

There is the moral question of, among other things, property rights. The formidable Florence King has convincingly demonstrated that another Southern writer, Molly Ivins, has lifted her material without attribution, and changed material that she does attribute to Miss King. "If we had the right kind of laws in this country," said Miss King, "I'd challenge her to a duel over this." Miss Ivins, to her credit, has fessed up and apologized. Miss King is not entirely mollified. (It is a distinguishing mark of her writing that she is seldom mollified about anything.) In a letter to Miss Ivins published in the *American Enterprise*, Miss King notes that the *Washington Post*'s story on their little scrap talks about the Ivins "side" and the King "side" of the unpleasantness. Miss King writes, "How can there be a 'side' in this when everyone involved is either a writer or an editor? All of us, by definition, are on the same side — the word side. Every word I write is a piece of my heart, and I presume you feel the same way."

That is putting it too strongly. In my case it would mean that I have, after more than twenty books and probably two thousand published articles and reviews, quite lost my heart, for I cannot remember most of the words I have written. But there is that question of property rights. At a recent conference in Oxford, I ran across a fellow who has been giving his attention to plagiarism in the writings of Gilbert Keith Chesterton. GKC said some brilliant things about plagiarism, as he did about almost everything, but he seems to have been rather casual about his borrowings, and got through a stunningly prolific life without the bother of even one footnote. If one reveres GKC as much as I do, the Oxford don's research might seem to be a quibbling not untouched by sacrilege. Knowing that there's nothing new under the sun, it seems probable that few of us have ever written anything that is genuinely original, so why not celebrate someone like Chesterton who repackaged so very originally? On the other hand . . .

A Careless Corruption

King, Prager, and others are right: there is something corrupting in careless borrowing. Words are the only property that writers, qua writers, possess. And property is an integral part of personal identity and responsibility. While writers who write a great deal may not remember all their words, there are what might be called signature phrases that signal their public identity. Of course one is more aware of this in connection with writers with whom one is closely associated. "A rumor of angels," for example, is a signature phrase for Peter Berger. Similarly, "rights talk" signals Mary Ann Glendon. There are numerous other examples. Yet in books and articles I have run across authors using these phrases as though they had cooked them up themselves. That is not right for many reasons, and not least because, in the mind of attentive readers, it discredits writers who do it.

If one pays attention to the writing of one's friends, it is as nothing compared to the attention one pays one's own writing. I, perhaps immodestly, assume that I have a signature phrase or two. For instance, "the Catholic moment," "the naked public square," "politics is in largest part a function of culture . . ." (long-time readers can fill in the rest of the formula from memory), and so forth. One sees these phrases appearing without attribution, and it is not always amusing. In the book of a distinguished political philosopher, we are offered an extended discussion of religion and the First Amendment, and it concludes with this: "I would go so far as to describe this exclusion of religion from our common discourse as the creation of a naked public square." He did not have to go very far at all — only to the book of that title, which is not cited in his notes, and from which he also lifted, almost without change, entire paragraphs. I am not inclined to sue and, unlike Miss King, I'm not up to dueling, but, if it weren't for the flattery implied, I would just as soon people didn't do that sort of thing.

Corruption Convoluted

The embarrassment factor gets awfully convoluted. In a recent book, an author attributes one of my signature phrases to another writer, and then conscientiously notes in his critical apparatus that "the phrase is sometimes attributed to Richard John Neuhaus," even though the writer he is quoting, in the notes to the very text under discussion, attributes the phrase to me. So is there an element of sinful pride in my being a mite irritated? Of course. But beyond that, for people who write about ideas and their consequences, there is the not unimportant matter of getting the story right.

One more example and I'll get off this kick. A few years ago, a reporter for the *New York Times* made the interesting observation that, in the abortion controversy, pro-choice people talk about "rights and laws" while pro-lifers talk about "rights and wrongs." I thought that suggestive and developed it, with attribution, in these pages. Later, another writer whom I will call Smith used my developed version, without citing his source, after which yet another writer told me that the original *Times* reporter was plagiarizing from Smith. All this may seem trivial to more normal folk, but writers and editors cannot help but follow the fortunes and misfortunes of their words. And it happens that we sometimes lose track. The words and signature phrases of others end up in our own heads and seem so very at home that we come to believe they were born there.

It happens also that words insinuate themselves into everyday discourse in such a way that it never occurs to people that there is a source to be cited. When, for instance, presidents and other public figures go on about the naked public square, I confess to a slight twitch of proprietorial pride. Writers, poor souls, must take their satisfactions where they can. It's different when other writers do it, however. As Florence King says, we're on the same side — the words and ideas side — and there are rules to be observed. Unlike Dennis Prager, I am disinclined to call anyone a thief. But neither do I now say so insouciantly that, if it's worth stealing, go ahead and steal it. I have come to understand how important it is for people to publicly say thank you.

That assumes, of course, that you know that there is a source to be thanked. I fear I may be letting down the side when I entertain the suspicion that there really is nothing new under the sun, and some obscure nineteenth-century essayist may have written brilliantly about, for example, "the naked public square." It is even possible that years ago I read such a hypothetical essay and have quite forgotten where I got the phrase. So, just to be safe, to everybody on our side, to all the forgotten, misquoted, and unquoted scribblers in glory (and elsewhere): Thank you!

❧ Of course it's a lie, but the sheer brazenness of it elicits something akin to respect. It's this week's new Bible translation (it does seem there is one every week), which is, as is all too often the case, no translation at all. This one is called *The Inclusive New Testament* and is published by an outfit called Priests for Equality in Hyattsville, Maryland. Read what Anne

Carr, professor of theology at the University of Chicago, no less, says about it: "The text reads smoothly and beautifully, betraying no other agenda than a faithful rendition of the New Testament." Uh huh. Then read the allegedly faithful rendition of, for instance, Colossians 3:18f. But first recall the passage (Revised Standard Version): "Wives, be subject to your husbands, as is fitting in the Lord. Husbands, love your wives, and do not be harsh with them. Children, obey your parents in everything, for this pleases the Lord." And so forth. Now the same (so to speak) passage in The Inclusive New Testament: "You who are in committed relationships, be submissive to each other. This is your duty in Christ Jesus. Partners joined by God, love each other. Avoid any bitterness between you." And so forth. What to do when faced with a problematic text? Simply to say it is wrong might offend the faithful. Explaining how it really says what one wishes it to say takes effort, and may be unpersuasive. The much easier, albeit dishonest, thing is to rewrite the text and call it a translation. Professor Carr is the author of *Transforming Grace*. Watch for her next book, *Transforming Texts*.

Counting by Race

Many who have thought hard about race in America have now reached the conclusion that our original sin — or at least since the civil rights acts of the early 1960s — was to start counting by race. The usual way of putting this is to say that Dr. King had it right when he said in his great "dream" speech of 1963 that people should be judged not by the color of their skin but by the content of their character. Morality and the common good have a curious way of hanging out together, and Dr. King was right, both morally and in terms of public policy. As Glenn Loury, the distinguished black thinker at Boston University, has observed, once we start counting by race in order to benefit blacks, we invite those who do not have the interest of blacks at heart to do a complete count of the black reality, including much that in the recent past was not mentioned in polite company.

Of course we are told by voices on all points of the political spectrum that "color-blindness" is a naive ideal. What is naive and not at all ideal, however, is the idea that the government should continue to count by race. People cannot always be color-blind, and one can make the case that sometimes taking race into account is appropriate and necessary. But the government can and must be color-blind — as in "equality under the law." Part of the problem with governmental race counting is that the government can't do it and doesn't do it. How does the U.S. Census decide who is white and who is black? It doesn't. You do, by saying you are black or white or whatever.

Yet great interests are at stake in race counting. Government grants, voting districts, school transfers, and much else are determined by the race count. If your claim is contested, the "one drop rule" of any blood other than Caucasian gets you counted as a minority, with attendant entitlements. The 1990 census says 80 percent of Americans are white, 12 percent are black, about 9 percent are Hispanic, and nearly 3 percent Asian. Recognizing the arbitrariness of the count, census officials are talking about adding other categories, including "multiracial." Not surprisingly, minority activists strongly oppose this, fearing any dilution of their numbers and their consequent claim on benefits aimed at compensating them for their "disadvantage." This state of affairs, more and more Americans are realizing, is simply crazy; and dangerously crazy because it inevitably exacerbates the race consciousness that has so plagued our history.

The civil rights movement under Dr. King was largely successful in fighting malign race consciousness. The great mistake since then was to institutionalize a supposedly benign race consciousness that has generated new and potentially greater racial suspicion and hostility than we had before the Montgomery bus boycott of 1956. Jorge Amselle of the Center for Equal Opportunity, a Washington think tank headed by Linda Chavez, the former director of the U.S. Commission on Civil Rights, says, "You don't cure the problem of people treating each other differently because of race by having government treat people differently because of race. If you want a color-blind society, you have to have color-blind public policy." That puts it very nicely.

It may be that there will always be racial discrimination in America, and most of it not very "rational." Some have suggested that real color-blindness requires racial intermarriage almost as the national norm, but that doesn't seem to be in the offing. The census says that in 1990 there were 242,000 black-and-white couples, double the number in 1980, and up 375 percent since 1960. But that is still only 2.2 percent of the married population. The most basic discrimination in America, despite laws against it, is in housing — in the dynamics that determine where people live. And it may not be accurate to call this discrimination. Nobody has studied these matters longer or more intelligently than Harvard social scientist Nathan Glazer.

Then and Now

In the Fall 1995 issue of the *Public Interest,* Glazer notes that the overwhelming majority of blacks, both poor and affluent, live in overwhelmingly black neighborhoods. At the same time, the overwhelming majority of blacks and a majority of whites say they would like to live in an integrated neighborhood. One problem is that blacks define "integrated" as 50-50, while "whites have little tolerance for racial mixture beyond 20 percent black." It has been the case for years, both in the city and in suburbs, that anything above 25 percent black is the tipping point at which neighborhoods begin to become resegregated as black. The residential racial mix that people, both black and white, prefer inevitably will have a strong bearing on the racial configuration of neighborhoods.

Glazer invokes a demonstration by Thomas Schelling that he calls "elegant and decisive." "Take a checkerboard and distribute nickels and dimes on it at random, with ten percent of the coins nickels and a few spaces empty. Then move one coin at a time into an empty space, with only this rule: The nickel would like to have at least one of its neighboring spaces occupied by a nickel, and the dime would like to have one of its neighboring spaces occupied by a dime. In a relatively few moves, the nickels begin to concentrate in one section of the checkerboard. If the preference is for two neighboring nickels, or two neighboring dimes, the concentration will occur faster." Is this a result of prejudice or of preference, and how do you tell the difference? Experience counts. "It is not easy to separate out from prejudice the influence of fears that, with an increase in black occupancy, crime will increase, schools will decline, and house values will drop." People prefer not to live in neighborhoods where these things happen. On these matters, there is no difference between whites and blacks on what constitutes a "bad neighborhood." Those who can move out do move out. And the checkerboard effect remains relentlessly in play.

Glazer's is a melancholy reflection on what he hoped for thirty years ago and what he has learned since. "Government action can never match, in scale and impact, the crescive effects of individual, voluntary decision. This is what has raised group after group, this is what has broken down the boundaries of ethnicity and race (yes, race, when it comes to some races) in the past. But these effects have operated excruciatingly slowly when it comes to American blacks. They have operated to some extent, as we see by the greatly expanded number of blacks making middle-class incomes, by the creation of integrated middle-class neighborhoods. It is the scale that has been so disappointing. Why our expectations were so disappointed is still obscure to me, and all the research does not make it clearer. We have to go to the disaster that encompasses the black family, the failure to close educational achievement gaps, the rise of worklessness among black males, the increase in crime, and, behind all these, there are other factors in infinite regress.

"This failure leads many to propose larger-scale government action, unlikely as the prospects for such are in the present and foreseeable political climate. But even if that climate were better, it is hard to see what government programs could achieve. They would be opposed by the strongest motives that move men and women: their concern for family, children, and property. However wrong I was in expecting more rapid change to result from the civil rights revolution, a greater measure of government effort to promote residential integration directly was not the answer, and is still not the answer. The forces that will produce it are still individual and voluntaristic, rather than governmental and authoritative. To adapt the title of Glenn Loury's book, it will have to be 'one by one,' individual by individual, family by family, neighborhood by neighborhood. Slowly as these work, there is really no alternative."

Bliss It Was to Be Alive

I, too, look back. More than thirty years, to when I first began to march with Dr. King. The manifestos, the demonstrations, the vigils, the arrests and jailings, it all seems like only yesterday. Those of us on the cutting edge of the movement were called prophetic, and were praised for the sacrifices we made and the risks we took. Little did people know. It was the joy of being part of something grand and indubitably good. "Bliss was it in that dawn to be alive, but to be young was very Heaven." With Dr. King, I believed that what Gunnar Myrdal had called "the American dilemma" was turning out to be something like the redemption of the American experiment. I recall Dr. King saying over a leisurely lunch, "If we die tomorrow, we will know, and history will know, and God will know that we did our part." Heady stuff, that. But it was not yesterday. It was a long, long time ago.

The O.J. verdict, Farrakhan, and the widespread desire, even a palpable yearning, for a leader such as Colin Powell. The rubble of broken dreams, the stark terror of broken lives in the urban underclass. It is a very different time. Books such as *The Bell Curve* and *The End of Racism* add to our awareness that it is a different time. It is a time of candor when thoughtful people who do not have a racist bone in their body are exposing the lies of a civil rights establishment and its liberal claque that have no legitimate claim on the luminous moment that was the civil rights movement of Dr. King. It is also a dangerous time when permission slips are being issued to say things heretofore forbidden. The haters, white and black, are taking heart.

But for most Americans it is probably a time of disappointment mixed with relief. They feel that over these thirty years they have done what they were supposed to do, and it did not work out at all the way they hoped. So now they have decided that, unless they or their families are threatened by it, they are going to stop worrying about race relations in America. They have decided to stop even thinking about it. One feels one should argue against that decision, but it is hard to know just how.

For those of us who will not, maybe because we cannot, stop worrying and talking about it, several resolves are in order. When we speak about black America, and especially about the underclass, we must speak with respect for the humanity of others. The dope-pusher, the rutting teenager who is father of five and father to none, the thug who kills the Korean grocer, they are all, nonetheless, created in the image of God. That is not liberal sentimentality. That is hard-core Christian doctrine. People who want to get back to basics must want to get back also to that. As much as possible, we must think and speak in a color-blind manner. Social problems in America are human problems. They are not only "their" problems, they are also our problems. Yes, there are important differences in culpability. But as the late Abraham Joshua Heschel frequently observed, "Some are guilty, all are responsible." That maxim is not without its ambiguities, but the alternative is to accept the end of one nation under God.

If we understand that, we have no choice but to condemn and stigmatize as effectively as we can separatisms and racisms in whatever form. Pusillanimous academics who have been intimidated by radical shuffles must find the courage to challenge the racial separatism now so deeply entrenched at most major universities. People who say they are speaking "as a white male" or as an "African American female" are to be told in no uncertain terms that they have nothing interesting to say unless they are prepared to speak as themselves. They should know that, if they are to claim serious attention, they cannot demean themselves by reducing their identity to a contingency over which they have no control.

If we understand what is at stake, in every forum on every subject there will be zero tolerance of the abdication of personal responsibility. Nothing will do but a frankly moral condemnation of crime and vice, whether the vice be drug addiction or everyday sloth. The old excuses are out. Victim politics is finished. The American people have simply turned a deaf ear to all that. They've had enough, they've had more than enough. That seems harsh, and it is, unless joined to the hope that there is still a will to overcome the American dilemma, as in "We shall overcome."

If we want to overcome black-white hostilities, we will have to do it the old fashioned way: blacks befriending whites and whites befriending blacks, and learning to trust one another and work together. Undaunted by the checkerboard effect, we can do what we can do. As Loury puts it, change comes one by one and from the inside out. This is a different kind of affirmative action that can make a difference for the better. In many parts of the country, black and white local churches, one by one, can form real partnerships, and stick with it. Will the white churches usually be more affluent and therefore tempted to patronize the black churches? Maybe so, but so what? The temptation can be resisted, and the important thing is that what is done is done together as equals in Christ.

Not the End of Public Policy

Nor, despite all the public policy disappointments, are we bereft of political remedies. Leave it to others to argue that welfare reform is a fiscal imperative. Welfare reform is a moral imperative. Those who claim to speak for the poor but don't know any poor people stand exposed as the frauds that they are. Hundreds of welfare experiments in all fifty states must get under way, and must be carefully tested not — or not chiefly — by whether they save money or cut down the size of government but by whether they help people take charge of their lives and enter the mainstream of American opportunity and responsibility.

Then there is adoption. In recent years all kinds of policies and procedures have been put into place making interracial adoption impossible or extremely difficult. Such policies must be called what they are. They are racist. Hundreds of thousands of children have their lives blighted by being shuffled from place to place in foster care while millions of American couples yearn to adopt them. Couples pay many thousands of dollars to have people search out children in Asia and Latin America, while ideologically driven social workers and psychologists here at home tell us it is better for a child to die in a drive-by shooting than to have his "black identity" confused because he is adopted by white people. This is madness, and cruelty, of a high order.

And we can institute real school choice. Parental choice in education is a matter of simple justice, and for many poor parents it is a matter of survival. Government monopoly school systems in New York and every other major city are an unmitigated disaster. They cannot be fixed, they must be replaced. The monopoly is defended by what is probably the most powerful political lobby in America, the teachers' unions. Whatever the noble intentions and heroic efforts of many teachers, these unions are the enemy of the children of the poor. With very few exceptions, nobody in these major cities who can afford an alternative sends their children to the public school.

In New York City, it is generously estimated that one out of ten poor children beginning first grade will graduate from high school prepared for a real college education — "real" meaning not majoring in "black studies" or some other pseudo-discipline, and not dropping out in the first or second year. Ninety percent of the students in the parochial schools of the city — drawn from the same population — go on to college or technical training for a real job. The government school spends $9,000 per year per student, the parochial school considerably less than half of that. Middle-class and wealthy Americans have school choice. They pay tuition or move to where the schools are better. In opposing vouchers and other remedies, the government school establishment invokes the separation of church and state. What we need, what the poor most particularly need, is the separation of school and state.

Thirty years of mostly well-intended policies have turned upon us with a vengeance. It's not what we had in mind back then; it's not what we had in mind at all. But now we know where it started going wrong. It started going wrong when we tried to remedy malign race-consciousness with benign race-consciousness, when we started counting by race. So what is to be done? Perhaps just a few things in public policy, but those few things need urgently to be done. For the most part, it is a matter of one by one, from the inside out.

❧ "Experimenting with tradition since 1898." That's the entire message of an advertisement soliciting vocations to the

Franciscan Friars of the Atonement in Garrison, N.Y. Why would anyone want to give his life to experimenting with tradition? One might want to live tradition, transmit tradition, teach tradition, be faithful to tradition — but experiment with tradition? It says a great deal about the religious culture of our time when it is suggested that the most interesting thing to do with tradition is to experiment with it. Anyway, what kind of tradition can it be after only ninety-seven years, especially when all that time has been spent fiddling around with it? Not surprisingly, the friars are not overwhelmed by new vocations. On the other hand, religious communities that are not in a perpetual state of wondering who they are demonstrate a powerful capacity to attract the commitment of others. Jesus did not say, "Come follow me, and we'll try to figure out where we're going." The invitation to join the Atonement Friars in experimenting with tradition is not likely to appeal to people who have something better to do with their lives. And yet endowment funds elicited in the days when the community knew it had a tradition to serve will likely keep the advertisements running until the last friar to leave turns out the lights and the experiment is formally concluded. It's been going on for centuries. Inspirations bring communities into being, they grow uncertain, tentative, and experimental, and then they evaporate and die, while new communities are born by the rediscovery of traditions worthy of being lived. There is even precedent for communities only ninety-seven years old experiencing such rediscovery and renewal.

❧ Commenting on the 1992 *Casey* decision of the Supreme Court, we wrote in the *Wall Street Journal* that "lawless law is an invitation to lawlessness." David Smolin takes up that theme in an intriguing article in the *Baylor Law Review*. "Rev. Neuhaus represents the mainstream, rather than the fringes, of American theologically conservative theism. . . . Calling *Roe* and *Casey* and the Supreme Court 'lawless' is mainstream, rather than radical, among the one-third or more of Americans within the worlds of theologically conservative theism." We confess it is a discomforting experience to be called mainstream, even if mainstream of a one-third minority. But the more interesting part of Smolin's article is his view of the probable future facing what he calls the religious patriotism of the pro-life movement, and of "the religious right" in general. We are by no means prepared to say that he is right, but his conclusion bears pondering: "The difficulty with the religious right is that it cannot succeed. The religious right may succeed in preventing abortion from being mainstreamed as a social good; it may succeed in pushing America in a more libertarian, less regulatory, direction. The religious right cannot make America Christian or virtuous; at most, it can give individuals and groups more room to choose to be Christian or virtuous. The American people live within the cultural revolution as a fish lives in water; to expect politics to undo the cultural revolution is like expecting a baseball team to win the Presidential election. The cultural revolution is imbedded in the cultural forces of family breakdown, mass media, and 'secular' education, and therefore will not give way merely because of legislative decree or political leadership. The religious right lacks, at present, an adequate cultural strategy for combatting the cultural revolution. Thus, the time will come when the Christian Coalition, like the Moral Majority before it, will have to face up to its failure to achieve the goal of 're-claiming' America. The frustrated religious patriotism of traditionalist theists therefore must stem into other branches besides murder and impossible political dreams. In the end, there seem to be two primary options: either the religion will accommodate itself to the patriotism, or the patriotism will give way to the religion. Some will drift away from traditionalist theism to a religion that can accept *Roe* and still be proud of America. It may be enough, in the end, for many in the Christian Coalition to maintain a libertarian, rather than a moral, America. Few in the religious right seemed to notice that the country became, during the Reagan-Bush era, less, rather than more, moral, according to traditionalist Christian standards. Some may be satisfied to see politically conservative 'Christians,' or at least Republicans, in power and giving voice to virtue and God, even as the culture sinks deeper into moral depravity. In this way Christian patriotism will be tamed, as conservative Christians discover that America can be a great nation even with a 30 percent abortion rate and 50 percent divorce rate. Others, however, will cling to traditionalist theism; ultimately, they will have to reject patriotism. These traditionalists will look beyond the politics and even the laws of America, to the behavior of Americans: to our rates of abortion, divorce, murder, rape, theft, and illegitimacy; to the glorification of violence and sexual immorality in our media; to the constantly shrinking evidence of virtues such as patience, humility, generosity, faithfulness, honesty, kindness, and selfless love. If a significant portion of traditionalist theists reject patriotism, then traditionalist theists will join the underclass, and tribal Americans, as the newest of America's growing class of permanent political exiles. Once they accept that they are exiles, they will be peaceful; but they will no longer, as in years past, be willing to sacrifice for the country. Anti-abortion lawlessness is ugly, whatever one's position on abortion. It is but a passing thorn on a broad branch of disenchantment; no one can yet see what other thorns, leaves, or flowers that branch will grow."

Against Christian Politics

An election year does strange things to people. For instance, Father John Kavanaugh's helpful homiletical reflections in *America* are usually about the scriptural text for the Sunday. But he, too, succumbs to the quadrennial political itches when confronted by the Sermon on the Mount, and he offers to his preacher readers a little tract on "Christian Faith and Politics." Among the homiletical inspirations: "Imagine the irony of a Christian political movement that along with public prayer trumpets the priorities of military security, tax cuts for the well-to-do, and capital punishment." A bit uneasy about the hint of partisanship in that political swipe, he writes, "This is not a put-down of any particular political party, even though, at first sight, it may seem so." At first sight and at as many other sights as you may care to give it.

"A Representative [Henry] Hyde," Fr. Kavanaugh writes, "is very Christian in his defense of unborn babies, but I wonder what he thinks of capital punishment, capital gains, and military adventures." I cannot imagine that Hyde or any other sensible person is in favor of military "adventures," but I would not be surprised if he views capital punishment as a sometimes regrettably necessary means to protect society, and thinks capital gains taxes drag down the economy, thereby hurting everybody, especially the poor. Those positions are perfectly permissible in Catholic moral teaching. Support for killing unborn babies is not.

Protecting his nonpartisan credentials, Fr. Kavanaugh notes that Senator Ted Kennedy is "a great defender of women and the poor" but he criticizes Kennedy's support for abortion. The conclusion is inescapable: the Republican Hydes and Democrat Kennedys are more or less morally equivalent, except that the Hydes take a non-Christian position on a lot of things while the Kennedys fall short on only one. Never mind that Catholic teaching solemnly declares abortion to be an "unspeakable crime," while the points on which Fr. Kavanaugh disagrees with the Hydes are matters of prudential judgment on which people of equal Christian commitment might legitimately disagree.

If we take the Sermon on the Mount seriously, says Fr. Kavanaugh, we must all admit "how readily we compromise the revolutionary message of Jesus." Who would dare deny it? But then he leaves us with this edifying thought:

"Upon that admission, we might then discover a Christian politics that illumines the world far more brilliantly than the dim ideologies we guide our lives by." Admittedly, some ideologies are dimmer than others, but a "Christian politics"?

One is reminded of Fr. Kavanaugh's fellow Jesuit, the late Fr. John Courtney Murray. Asked by a politician how he could base his political philosophy on the Sermon on the Mount, Fr. Murray incredulously responded, "What on earth makes you think that a Catholic political philosophy is based on the Sermon on the Mount?" He explained for the thousandth time that a political philosophy has to do with the virtue of justice as discerned by reason and directed by the virtue of prudence. Similarly, the great Protestant teacher Reinhold Niebuhr devoted his life to warning against the dangerous sentimentality of a "Christian politics." Love compels Christians to seek justice also through politics, Niebuhr insisted, but we must never equate our penultimate judgments about what might serve justice with the ultimate truth that impels us to seek and serve justice in the first place. In sum, we must never declare our politics to be "Christian politics," thereby implicitly excommunicating those Christians who disagree with us.

We Have Been Here Before

I would not pick on Fr. Kavanaugh, who, as I say, usually does not ride his political hobby horse in public. But his mindset is representative of a widespread and growing phenomenon on both the left and the right — the religionizing of politics and politicizing of religion. In recent American history, it started on the left in the aftermath of the mainline churches' moral euphoria in having been so very right about the early civil rights movement of Martin Luther King, Jr. In the years that followed, that euphoria inflated the moral certitude of those churches, and their bureaucracies were soon pronouncing God's definite opinion on almost every question in public dispute.

That could not last very long, and it didn't. After a while the members of those churches turned a deaf ear to their leaders, and then began drifting away, leaving mainline Protestantism in a spiral of decline that has yet to hit bottom. Still on the left, something similar is happening in Catholicism as the bishops are inclined to generously loan their teaching authority to the church-and-society curia of the United States Catholic Conference. Analysts of the mainline declension of the last thirty years watch this Catholic development with an eerie sense of having been here before.

Of course the more publicly potent religionizing of politics is today on the right of the ideological spectrum. Conservative leaders regularly say that they are only doing what the religious left did for decades, indeed going all the way back to the Social Gospel movement at the turn of the century. They're right about that, and that's what should worry them. The conflation of Christian faith with a specific political agenda inevitably leads to the distortion of faith. The equally inevitable failure to achieve something worthy of being called "Christian politics" produces a crisis in which people will feel forced to choose between their politics and their faith. Devotion to "God and country" is a fine thing, but when the two are given equal standing, "country" will always fall far short of what people hope for, and they will then find themselves faced with the prospect of "God or country."

For organizations such as the unhappily named Christian Coalition, that prospect may not be far off. How many electoral setbacks will it take to undermine the relentless triumphalism necessary to sustaining such a political insurgency? When the disillusioned despair of achieving a Christian politics in a Christian America, "God and country" might very quickly become "God or country." Most will choose for God, no doubt, but we should not be surprised if there are others for whom the "Christian" in the Christian Coalition is subservient to the political goals of the enterprise. The more seriously Christian, on the other hand, may think it necessary to choose for God against further political engagement. The result could be a return to the political passivity that marked evangelical and fundamentalist Christianity during most of the twentieth century. Not inconceivably, profound disillusionment could also produce a much more radicalized "Christian politics" on the right, a politics aimed at dismantling what is believed to be an incorrigibly evil constitutional order.

The last possibility is more than hinted at in movements that go by names such as Christian Reconstructionism and Dominion Theology. Such movements, with their assertion that America must be refounded on the basis of "Bible law," claim relatively few adherents today, but they are waiting in the wings, alert to their opportunity when enough Christians decide that it is not possible "to work within the system." Once again, there is an eerie sense of having been here before. Except the last time, in the 1960s, these questions preoccupied a left that thought itself to be in revolutionary ascendancy.

A Different Victory

Do not misunderstand. I sympathize with most of the stated positions of the Christian Coalition. That is not the question. The question is the conflation of Christian faith and political agenda. I have even spoken at the annual "Road to Victory" conference of the Coalition. I pleaded that, while there may be welcome achievements from time to time, Christians are called to walk not the road to political victory but the way of the cross. The speech met with a great ovation, maybe because it's the kind of thing Christians are expected to say, but I have very limited confidence that most of those who cheered understood what I was trying to say. Afterward, one participant, on the edge of tears, said he felt betrayed. It was my writings, he said, that had led him to become politically engaged, and now I was telling him that he had made a mistake. That is not the point. That is not the point at all.

Psalm 146 warns, "Put not your trust in princes." Even when they are your princes and you think you put them on their little thrones. Especially when they are your princes, because that is when the temptation arises to invest your soul and your highest allegiance in their rule. No politics can liberate us from the limits of a fallen creation. We can probe and press at the limits, but the politics for which we were made, the politics that is the right ordering of all things, the politics of the Sermon on the Mount, will, short of the Kingdom, always elude us. Liberation theology — whether of the Marxist or the Reconstructionist variety — is idolatry.

Christian political engagement is an endlessly difficult subject. Our Lord said to render to Caesar what is Caesar's and to God what is God's, but he did not accommodate us by spelling out the details. Over two thousand years, Christians have again and again thought they got the mix just right, only to have it blow up in their faces — and, not so incidentally, in the faces of others. We're always having to go back to the drawing board, which is to say, to first things. Even when, especially when, we are most intensely engaged in the battle, first things must be kept first in mind. It is not easy but it is imperative. It profits us nothing if we win all the political battles while losing our own souls.

Alien Citizens

A very long time ago, when Christians were a persecuted minority of maybe fifty thousand in the great empire of Rome, an anonymous writer explained to a pagan named Diognetus the way it is with this peculiar people. Until Our Lord returns in glory, Christians do well to embrace the second century "Letter to Diognetus" as their vade mecum:

"For Christians cannot be distinguished from the rest of the human race by country or language or customs. They do not live in cities of their own; they do not use a peculiar form of speech; they do not follow an eccentric manner of life.

This doctrine of theirs has not been discovered by the ingenuity or deep thought of inquisitive men, nor do they put forward a merely human teaching, as some people do. Yet, although they live in Greek and barbarian cities alike, as each man's lot has been cast, and follow the customs of the country in clothing and food and other matters of daily living, at the same time they give proof of the remarkable and admittedly extraordinary constitution of their own commonwealth. They live in their own countries, but only as aliens. They have a share in everything as citizens, and endure everything as foreigners. Every foreign land is their fatherland, and yet for them every fatherland is a foreign land. They marry, like everyone else, and they beget children, but they do not cast out their offspring. They share their board with each other, but not their marriage bed. It is true that they are 'in the flesh,' but they do not live 'according to the flesh.' They busy themselves on earth, but their citizenship is in heaven."

It is an awkward posture, being an alien citizen. It poses irresolvable problems for both "God and country" and "God or country." Christians critically affirm their responsibility for the politics of the earthly city, knowing all the while that their true polis is the City of God. Loyalty to the earthly city is joined to an allegiance that others who do not share that allegiance cannot help but view as subversive. It is as with Thomas More on the scaffold, "I die the king's good servant, but God's first." And, had Henry only known it, Thomas was the king's better servant because he served God first. Like so many others over the centuries, Henry had a "Christian politics" that demanded a totality of allegiance that no alien citizen could render him.

Where We Are Left

Christians are commanded to love their neighbors, and politics is one way — by no means the most important way — of doing that. In a democracy, everybody is asked to accept a measure of political responsibility, and most do. For some it is their life's work, as in "vocation." Like everything worth doing, it is worth doing well. And, for those who are called to do it, even when they frequently fail, it is also worth doing poorly. Christians engaged in politics, we may hope, will bring to the task the gifts of personal integrity and devotion to the common good. But that does not make their engagement "Christian politics." It is still just politics. A Christian engineer who builds a really good bridge has not built a "Christian bridge." The merit of the project depends upon qualities pertinent to the "bridgeness" of the thing, although we may believe that those qualities are well served by the Christian conviction and integrity of the builder.

So where does this leave us with the Sermon on the Mount? Deeply troubled, for sure. It leaves us, against our sinful inclination, attending to a "preferential option" for the poor and the sorrowful, the meek and the persecuted. Attending to them not by politics chiefly but by politics also. That sermon depicts a way of living that Niebuhr variously called an "impossible possibility" and "possible impossibility," with the one never being entirely overcome by the other. Yet the never is not forever, for, above all, it leaves us alien citizens with an insatiable longing for that other polis He told us about, when all those around the throne and the angels numbering myriads of myriads declare with a loud voice, "Worthy is the Lamb who was slain, to receive power and wealth and wisdom and might and honor and glory and blessing!"

And then, around the throne of the Lamb, we will have reason to hope that all our efforts, including our political efforts, did not get in the way of, and maybe even anticipated in some small part, that right ordering of all things that is the only politics deserving of the name Christian. Until then, talk about "Christian politics" — whether of the left or of the right or of ideologies as yet unimagined — is but a refusal to wait for the Kingdom. It is the delusion that we

Christians are called to be or can be, in our exile from the heavenly polis, something other than the poor in spirit, the sorrowing, the meek, the hungry, the merciful, the pure in heart, the peacemakers, the persecuted — to be, in sum, something other than those whom the Sermon on the Mount calls blessed.

❧ There are no doubt readers who, in their pitiful naivete, assume that some cultural artifacts are inherently superior to others. Continuing on that risible assumption, they hold to the view that there is something like a canon of cultural greatness — in literature, philosophy, music, painting, and so forth. In the name of multiculturalism, the entirety of the progressive academy has for some years now been earnestly engaged in discrediting such outdated notions. Nonetheless, the academy's herd of independent minds is still capable of producing a new wrinkle on regnant ideas. For instance, Gary Taylor's new book *Cultural Selection* (Basic) goes into great detail to demonstrate that presumed cultural superiority is the product of political, military, and economic imperialism. In the course of his argument, he avails himself of Darwinian theory and the scientific language of biology. The result is sometimes striking. Many people, for example, might think that the world recognized Shakespeare as great because he is great. Mr. Taylor devastates such simplistic thinking. "Shakespeare was like a local parasite — attached to a species that eventually dominated its own niche and migrated out into others, taking the parasite along and introducing it into new ecosystems that had, often, no defenses against it." Wherever the English-speaking species has gone, the Shakespeare parasite has conquered. In fact, the reality is even worse than that, for the parasite has insinuated itself into numerous other languages suffering from immune deficiency. It would seem that the only defense against it is illiteracy, a defense greatly enhanced by the work of Mr. Taylor and critics similarly devoted to destroying the parasite's host culture. Since the parasite has so entrenched itself in other cultures victimized by the English-speaking disease, however, it seems likely that a hundred years from now an ascendant China, for instance, might reimpose Shakespeare upon what is left of Western culture. The battle against greatness never ends. It is a dirty job, but somebody has to do it. As Burke might have said, the only thing necessary for the triumph of greatness is for literary critics to do nothing.

🖝 "Out of the Whirlwind: Claiming a Vision of Progressive Christianity." We had mentioned earlier this national conference at Trinity Cathedral (Episcopal) in Columbia, South Carolina. According to news reports, "nearly one hundred" people showed up. Progressive is today's word for liberal, and it appears that participants huffed and puffed mightily to put some life into the poor thing. James Adams, for thirty years rector of St. Mark's Episcopal Church in Washington, D.C., presided, as inegalitarian as that sounds. "Here we are, a group of ninety people, gathered to talk about transforming an institution, the Church, that has a 1,900-year history of oppression and exclusion," announced Adams. It sounds like the kind of thing that should be killed, not transformed. But, considering the transformation the group had in mind, that may be a distinction without a difference. In the opening sermon, the retired Episcopal bishop of Atlanta, Bennett Sims, preached on Mark's account of Jesus healing a blind man. "We know that it was not the faith of the Nicene Creed that made him well. That fourth-century formulation actually may make some people ill," Sims said to laughter. "This is not to despise the Nicene Creed," he added. Of course not. "Though there are better ways to frame it without sacrificing orthodoxy," the bishop added. And this is just the group to do it. Dr. Frederica Harris Thompsett, academic dean of Episcopal Divinity School, asked, "How do you speak out in a post-Nicean way in a Nicean church? It probably means asking questions. The biblical prophets did." The prophets were famous for asking questions. That's no doubt why the symbol for Jeremiah is a question mark. Andrew

Getman of Washington, D.C., urged participants not to be nasty to conservatives. "Unless we can hear a conservative brother as someone who needs an arm around his shoulder and to be listened to, then that hurt can turn to violence." Which, being translated, means, Don't provoke the animals. Not everybody was happy with the meeting. Gene Robinson, assistant to the New Hampshire bishop, said, "I'm not so sure that the $500 or so we each spent getting here might not have been better sent to the Lambda Legal Defense Fund, which is fighting for us on gay and lesbian marriages." On the final afternoon, after extended small-group discussions, chair Adams offered a rousing call to arms: "I don't even want to identify what we have in common, because that would be divisive." One is reminded, for some reason, of the old question: What do you get when you cross a Jehovah's Witness and a Unitarian? Answer: Someone who goes around knocking on doors with nothing particular in mind. "Out of the Whirlwind: The Still, Small Sound of Expiring Air." But a measure of sympathy is in order. The basic mistake of the convenors was to think that people would pay their own way to a conference promoting "progressive Christianity" when expenses are covered for attending denominational meetings that do much the same thing.

Peddlers of an Unreal World

It's an argument I've been making for years, with little success: Social observers in general and religious folk in particular vastly overestimate the influence of the news and entertainment media. A Protestant friend who is a very successful writer routinely rails against our "post-Christian society." His supporting evidence is largely drawn from movies, television, and the papers. Recently a Catholic bishop told me that he was "scared to death" when a television executive told him that, given enough money and air time, the tube could make the American people think whatever its owners wanted them to think. Instead of being scared to death, he should have pointed out that this is arrant nonsense, the braggadocio that typifies overpaid egos who dominate a shrinking media market. Of course the media have a powerful and frequently malignant influence, but if they had only a small part of the influence that they (and their critics) claim, we would be living in a country that we would hardly recognize.

Were the television networks, the movie producers, and the editors of the prestige papers really in charge, there would be no pro-life movement, active euthanasia would be the uncontested law of the land, every school child would be indoctrinated in the joys of gay sex, home schooling would be prohibited, church schools would be run by state agencies, government day care for preschool children would be mandatory, churches would not be tax-exempt, and smoking anywhere would be a criminal offense. Certainly Reagan and Bush would never have been President, the Republican Party would be on the Department of Justice list of suspect organizations, and Ralph Reed would be in jail. That's just for starters.

Do I exaggerate? Maybe just a little. But imagine, on the basis of their record of advocacy, the America that would be created by Dan Rather, Peter Jennings, and Frank Rich of the *New York Times*. It is possible, of course, that were such an America to come into being, with all the authoritarian controls that would be required, those worthies would change sides and protest the oppression. In that case, many liberals might embrace conservatism as the "true" liberalism. No doubt the word "neoconservative" would be reinvented to describe them. But my point is that Rather, Jennings, Rich, and their ilk are not running the country. They make a difference, no doubt, but they are increasingly fighting to maintain their niches in media empires that are more and more out of touch with the American reality.

So who pushed my buttons on this subject? The other day I was speaking at Gettysburg College, a school in Pennsylvania with a vestigial Lutheran connection, and a professor took strong exception to my claim that ours is not a secular society but one that is maddeningly confused in its pervasive religiousness. All you have to do, he asserted, is to look at television, movies, and the big papers to see how thoroughly secular America is. But that's like determining what the weather is by reading weather reports rather than looking out the window, or reading sex manuals to understand sex. In the case of the media and social reality, the gap is considerably wider.

The Sunday after Gettysburg the professor's objection was on my mind as I was looking at the local publication that styles itself the world's newspaper of record. It is Palm Sunday and here is the television guide for Holy Week. Twenty-some movies and other programs are lifted up for special attention. These are among the items promoted for Holy Week: two polemics against white racism, an attack on the tobacco industry, three murder mysteries, one story about a serial murderer, a comedy about soap operas, a story on the sexual abuse of children, and a drama about vampire families in San Francisco. On Good Friday there is one movie that has what might be called a transcendent dimension — *Rosemary's Baby,* a story about the Devil's son born of woman.

You may object that it is not fair to judge all the media by the *Times,* and it is not fair to judge the *Times* by its weekly television guide. Perhaps, although it is generally acknowledged that the news media routinely take their lead from the *Times,* and the entertainment and culture business is heavily dependent on its judgment. As to whether the television guide is a good guide to the *Times,* the ten pounds of newsprint that Sunday had no other reference to religion other than a business story about selling palms to churches and an article in the Sunday magazine about a Catholic who has decided to become a Jew. Well, there was one other story, a rather sad one, that might count as religious. It was about aging homosexuals who regularly get together to reminisce, dance, and talk dirty in the basement of an Episcopal church in Queens.

Why They Do It

But stay with the television guide for a moment. No doubt, had I bothered to look through the many pages of listings, I would have found some religious services and maybe an old Cecil B. DeMille biblical epic being broadcast that week, but the interesting thing is what the editors chose to feature as being worthy of attention. None of the programs was related to, and some of them were grossly antithetical to, what is represented by Holy Week. Not so incidentally, especially in New York, the same week was Passover. The Lubavitcher hasidim bought two full-page ads urging the world to get itself ready for the return of the Moshiach, the late Rebbe Schneerson. So the *Times* collected well over $300,000 in ad revenue related to the week (including a full page of paid church notices) but, being a newspaper of scrupulous integrity, did not let that influence its studied indifference to there being anything noteworthy about Holy Week and Passover.

For those who by occupation or obsession (or a mix of both) monitor such things, the *Times* is as good a window as we have into the perversities of what passes for — because, unfortunately, it is — our high culture. How to explain that television guide? This is a city in which about 75 percent of the population is Christian and somewhat over 15 percent is Jewish. The majority of New Yorkers would be in church or synagogue at least once that week. Is it possible that the editors of the guide were not aware that it was Holy Week and Passover? It seems more than possible. Stanley Rothman and others have for years been giving us the research that demonstrates an enormous "religion gap" between the American people and the media elite. And I remember the reporter who told me he wanted to do a story that dealt with the influence of John Henry Cardinal Newman, only to be turned down by three senior editors who had never heard of Newman. In trying to understand the media, do not search for other explanations when ignorance will suffice. But *Rosemary's Baby* on Good Friday? I'm sorry, I think somebody knew exactly what he was doing.

At Mass on Palm Sunday morning, I looked out from the altar at hundreds of fervent worshipers and, knowing that the same thing was happening in hundreds of other places around the city, had no doubt that this, and not what the *Times* reported, is the real world. Of course what the *Times* and its media minions present as reality has real effects. Among other things, it makes that evangelical writer, that Catholic bishop, and that Gettysburg professor think that, as believers, they are fighting a rear guard action. It makes them feel marginal, when in fact it is the media that are increasingly marginal.

There is consolation in the fact that the *Times* is bought by less than one out of twenty people in the New York area, and the audience for television networks and movies has been declining for years. The people in charge know this. But as long as they can indulge their ideological urges and still make big money in a diminished market, they will continue to do what they do. They do damage, of course, but there is no cause for panic. More and more, they are playing defense, as more and more Americans stop taking them seriously. The critical thing is to trust your own experience and not let putative experts convince you that you do not know what you know.

The classic example from the social sciences is "the happy marriage syndrome." From the beginnings of survey research, people have been asked whether theirs is a happy marriage, and what percentage of marriages do they think are happy. With striking consistency, about 75 percent say they are happily married and that only 10 percent of Americans are happily married. The first they know from experience and the second they get from the news. All of the above notwithstanding, I would not be surprised if *Rosemary's Baby* got high ratings on Good Friday. If so, it demonstrates not that ours is a secular society but that, as aforesaid, it is maddeningly confused in its pervasive religiousness. There will always be those in the media who are bent upon offending and are not above exploiting confusion and depravity. But that's no reason to let them, including the old gray madam that is the *Times,* get away with the claim that they represent the real world.

A footnote: later in Holy Week, the federal appeals court in New York discovered a constitutional right to assisted suicide, a discovery promptly hailed in the *Times'* lead editorial. The big headline announcing the decision said the court "relieves anxiety of physicians." (Nothing was said about the anxiety of patients who may be killed rather than cured.) The Easter edition of the Sunday magazine had a long article on Episcopal bishops ordaining homosexuals, written by gay advocate Bruce Bawer. The lead editorial on Easter Sunday was a ringing endorsement of same-sex "marriage," beginning with the line, "Chances are that Americans will look back thirty years from now and wonder what all the fuss was about." At the rate it is going, chances are that Americans will look back thirty years from now and wonder why anyone paid much attention to the *New York Times.*

❧ The Council for Democratic and Secular Humanism, Professor Paul Kurtz founder and bishop, publishes *Free Inquiry.* A reader sends us a promotional letter he received in which the magazine lists all the important questions it covers in "preserving our freethought heritage." Included is this, "The rise of Richard John Neuhaus and why he bears close watching." I've been wondering about those people going through my garbage pails. Imagine, sneaky Humanists disguising themselves as the homeless. I can't wait until tomorrow. "Good morning, Professor Kurtz. Looking for free thoughts?"

❧ "I argue that in American culture, on the whole, language of the sacred, even language of God, can be pragmatically justified." That's a relief; religion is given another reprieve. Even language about God! — although only "on the whole," of course. The above bold assertion is offered by William Dean, professor of religion at Gustavus Adolphus College (Lutheran), in his new book *The Religious Critic in American Culture* (State University of New York Press). Dean is reviewed by United Methodist Philip Blackwell in the pages of *Christian Century*, who likes the book very much. Says Blackwell, "Many of us cannot in good faith subscribe to the claims of Christianity in a literal way, but we refuse to throw out the essential truths carried by the tradition. We are left to make something of the conventions of our faith." A convention is defined "as a social tradition that has developed through several generations. It is neither a claim to an objective and universal truth nor the exercise of arbitrary and subjective willfulness." It seems that the religious tradition that will come to the rescue of American culture has been developed over several generations, going back all the way to the ancients of the late nineteenth century. While its adherents do not subscribe to it in any literal sense and it is not "true" in any ordinary meaning of the term, it is nonetheless the bearer of "essential truths." Lest we suspect him of rigid adherence to an authoritarian tradition, Blackwell assures us that "conventions are revised continually by present interpretations." People who think the way he does, Blackwell suggests, are the answer to his question, "In a culture that has lost its bearings, who can speak a word of confident direction?" It would appear that another Great Awakening may be on the way, what with people like Dean and Blackwell who are sensitively revising the, er, essential, so to speak, truths, as it were, of religious conventions constructed by three or more generations of liberal Protestantism. Blackwell concludes: "At a time when people are so desperate for stability that they try to recreate a past that never existed, who can show a new way forward? In a public conversation where talk of the sacred often is embarrassing, cynical, or self-serving, who can reclaim the noble vocabulary of our shared conventions? Dean says that it can be done, and that it must be done quickly or we will lose the conventional wisdom that has brought us this far." The conventional wisdom that brought us to our present sorry pass has, in fact, lost its hold on more thoughtful Christians. Nonetheless, folk like Dean and Blackwell who are so desperate to believe that, in the absence of truth, their religion might still have some social utility will continue to console themselves with conventional nostrums such as "on the whole, language of the sacred, even language of God, can be pragmatically justified."

✹ And we have a winner in the Moral Equivalency Contest. The headline in the *New York Times* reads, "Amendment to Protect Flag Wins House Panel's Approval." The sidebar reads, "In the balance: a cherished icon and a cherished right." Ah yes, how to resolve the conflict between those attached to two grand old American traditions, saluting the flag and burning it.

Farewell to the Overclass

Egalitarian protestations to the contrary notwithstanding, every functional society has a class composed of those who wield concentrated political and economic power and who set its manners, or lack thereof. Within that class, different people do different things, and the most important thing that is done is the minting and marketing of the ideas by which people try to make sense of their lives.

Ruling class is the old-fashioned term, and happy the society in which the members of the ruling class wrap their preeminence in the language of equality and the goal of universal self-governance. In his last book, the late Christopher Lasch depicted the unhappy circumstance of our last several decades as a "betrayal of the elites." The elites, he said, have come to define democracy not in terms of self-governance but of upward mobility. In this view, the promise of democracy is the prospect of rising above the people to join the elites concentrated in government, the university, and the media.

We now have a quite new phenomenon in the history of the republic: two radically isolated sectors of the population, the underclass and the overclass. Both are in an adversarial posture toward the great majority of Americans, the overclass by virtue of ambition and unbounded self-esteem, the underclass by virtue of social incompetence and anomie. Between the two there is a fearful symmetry on many scores, but their service to each other is far from equal.

Although it goes back before the 1960s, the pattern then became more overt by which the overclass exploited the disadvantaged of the underclass to greatly expand their own rule. To be fair, they did not think they were exploiting the poor. And, in fact, the civil rights movement from the Montgomery bus boycott of 1956 through the rise of the black power movement in the early sixties was a rare instance in which elite advocacy on behalf of the disenfranchised and against entrenched custom enhanced the measure of justice in American life. That civil rights movement was, with considerable right, portrayed as a moment of moral luminosity, and the overclass has been basking in its afterglow for almost forty years. The principle seemed established for a time that the elites possessed their power, and were justly ambitious for more power, by virtue of their moral status as champions of the oppressed. The luminosity of that moment, however, was not sufficient to cast the light of moral legitimacy on all the causes that subsequently would be included in the great cause of all causes called Social Justice.

Upon consideration, most Americans declined the proposal that we should make permanent peace with communism (a.k.a. coexistence), were decidedly cool to the idea that marriage and motherhood are forms of slavery, deemed the drug culture a pathetic addiction, did not agree that religion in the classroom violated sacred rights, and persisted in viewing homosexuality as a perversion both pitiable and repugnant. They were unattracted by a cultural liberation that brought us crack houses, glory holes, and needle parks; and found themselves unable to follow the logic of replacing, by means of quotas, racial and sexual discrimination with racial and sexual discrimination. Most important, and despite the sustained barrage of decades of propaganda, Americans stubbornly refused to believe that the unlimited license to kill unborn children constituted a great leap forward in our understanding of human dignity. As if that were not enough, it had become evident by the 1970s that the social programs issuing from the civil rights movement had turned in very nasty ways upon the very people they were intended to help, resulting in an urban and chiefly black underclass of pathologies unbounded.

Clearly the moral mandate claimed from that now distant moment of luminosity had run out. The political notice that its date of expiration had passed was decisively given in the election of Ronald Reagan in 1980, although the notice was evident enough in the rejection of George McGovern eight years earlier. Mr. Clinton captured the White House, albeit with a minority of voters, because, like all successful presidential candidates after 1964, he ran as a conservative, and because George Bush apparently stopped running when apprised of the probability that he was not to be reelected by acclamation. But let us not be distracted by politics.

Isolated Enclaves

The fact is that we now find ourselves with two alienated classes. It is alienation that distinguishes today's overclass from the ruling classes of the past. A ruling class that discreetly disguised its role in deference to democratic sensibilities was by most Americans thought to be bearable and even admirable, especially as its privileges were thought to be derived from breeding and achievement. The overclass is something else. As the word suggests, it is marked by an overbearing quality; it presents itself as being over and against the American people but is quite unable to give any good reasons for its pretensions to superiority.

The encouraging thing is that an overclass cannot sustain itself as a ruling class because it offers no argument for its right to rule. Assumed superiority is not an argument. The overclass that emerged from the 1960s deconstructed the moral foundations of its current privilege by its relentless attack on all traditional justifications of privilege. Proponents of permanent revolution are hard put to call for a pause in the revolution in order to allow them to savor their triumph. They cannot recall from the political culture the passions and prejudices which they employed in overthrowing the establishment, and by which they are now being overthrown. Today's moment of populist insurrection is commonly called traditionalist, but it is in large part a continuation of the revolution of the sixties, now directed against the revolutionaries of the overclass who seized the commanding heights of culture.

Their perch on the heights is most precarious. In ways beyond numbering, Americans are railing at the governmental, media, and university elites, declaring that they have had enough and are not going to take it anymore. Rather than perching on the heights, it may be more accurate to say that these elites have retreated to protective enclaves in search of refuge against an angry and ungrateful populace. There they find solace among their own kind. In undisturbed caucus they propound the true socialism that has been betrayed by every socialism tried; their network anchorpersons sound nightly alarums against the ascendant fascism of Christian conservatives; and they churn out unreadable academic deconstructions of elitism, turning a blind eye to the elite that they are. Or the elite that for one shining moment — a Camelot, so to speak — they thought themselves to be. But now the enclaves are shadowed by the suspicion that they are only talking to themselves. Outside, the barbarians are taking over.

Why America Hates Harvard

The anti-elitist elite of the overclass finds itself in a galling quandary. It was no big news that Harvard hated America; the best and the brightest have always been prone to indulging a measure of contempt for the generality of mankind. The new twist is that America hates Harvard because Harvard despises what Harvard is supposed to represent — scholarship, honesty, and manners worthy of emulation. America is in rebellion against an overclass that has systematically trashed the values by which a ruling class can justly claim the right to rule. (Which, of course, does not stop many young Americans from wanting to join the overclass, also by way of Harvard.)

In addition to the inherent incoherence of anti-elitist elitism, the overclass attempted something quite new that has not worked and almost certainly cannot work. Looking back on the ruins of the glory that was Rome (his Camelot, so to speak), Gibbon, with a grandiloquence equal to his prodigious bigotry, blamed "the barbarians and religion." The same combination of barbarians and religion is blamed by today's overclass for its decline and impending fall. Both history and common sense suggest that there is no sustainable rule without religion. Not necessarily this religion or that, but religion in the sense of *religare*, of ideas and traditions that bind people together, that evoke the communal adherence we call loyalty. Being itself loyal to nothing, the overclass cannot evoke loyalty.

One cannot hold the commanding heights without commanding truths, and it was by the rejection of commanding truths that the overclass seized the heights in the first place. In the absence of truths, or even of the possibility of truth, the overclass, led by such as Richard Rorty, wanly sings the praises of "ironic liberalism," and tries not to notice that the choir gets smaller and smaller. They mint and try to market ideas that no sensible person would want to live by; their cultural coinage is rejected as being backed by nothing — literally nothing, as the debonair nihilists who issue it readily confess, indeed, as they incessantly boast.

So this is the new thing about the overclass: it does not so much want to rule as to be admired for having exposed the fraudulence of rule. At the same time, of course, it does want to rule. At least, if somebody must rule — and in the nature of things, somebody must — the members of the overclass, while denying in principle anything that might be called the nature of things, has a decided preference for ruling rather than being ruled. Especially if the alternative is the rule of barbarians and religion, meaning the American people.

Rulers of the past produced various warrants for their rule. There was, for instance, the divine right of kings. Gibbon and his philosophe friends contended that the religion of the Enlightenment provided a rationalist access to truth that superseded the dark ages before their arrival. More recently, Marxist masters were legitimated by putatively scientific appeal to the dialectic of history. Here in America, a ruling class that bore some similarities to the current overclass located its right to rule in its calling to reeducate the commoners. John Dewey and his acolytes recognized that Americans could not be weaned from religion except by a more attractive religion, and so Dewey proposed his Common Faith of Democracy, frankly presented as the religion of humanism, only to discover that Americans were incorrigibly attached to the antique truths of Sinai and Calvary. In bitter disillusionment, the heirs of Dewey resolved that, if they could not impose their religion, they would expunge religion altogether from our public life, and especially from the schools.

Whether called the knowledge class, the new class, or the overclass, today it is tottering, and it knows it. The campaign of liberation from the traditional meanings that give life meaning met with such popular hostility that some of the overclass had second thoughts. From out of one defensive enclave rode a paladin of high spiritual purpose (Hillary Rodham Clinton) proposing nothing less than a "politics of meaning." A puzzled populace, not knowing what was meant by meaning but recognizing the politics, politely declined the proposal. The politics may be disguised for the nonce, and there may be another election or two to be won, but the rule of the overclass is drawing to a close.

A generation that was born, nursed, and reared by the overclass, that never knew anything but the overclass, must finally fall back upon sounding a final trumpet for the nostrum that first roused it to political consciousness: The American people want change! The American people warmly agree. And so it was, future historians will note, that the overclass rode off into the sunset astride the weary old charger named Change, the very horse on which it had arrived.

❧ "We Are Church" is the conglomeration of leftist Catholic groups set on getting a million signatures to protest the oppression of a sexist, racist, phallocentric, eurocentric, authoritarian, etc. etc. church. Sister Maureen Fiedler is the national coordinator of the effort. (I take perverse pleasure in one reporter's comment on an encounter I had with Sr. Maureen on a network television program: "Neuhaus Romed while Fiedler burned.") She has sent a letter to Catholic schools suggesting that teachers enlist their students to get signatures for the protest, asking each signer to contribute one dollar. "Local groups that do the work receive 60 percent of the funds they collect!" For the mathematically challenged, she adds: "Collecting 1,000 signatures and $1,000, for example, means that your student group will earn $600 for local programs!" Apart from the unseemliness of exploiting children for her partisan games, this ploy does little to enhance the credibility of a signature campaign that is supposed to demonstrate massive discontent with church leadership. "So the kids in your school are really mad at the Church?" "Shucks no, we just needed new basketball jerseys."

❧ St. Ann's was a nice little parish church, says Helen Hull Hitchcock, and then it had the misfortune of being renovated. For Catholic churches, being renovated usually means running into the demolition program set forth in *Environment and Art in Catholic Worship,* a 1978 tract of doubtful authority that is treated by some liturgical experts as magisterial teaching far outranking papal encyclicals. Statues, stained glass, kneelers, and tabernacles — all must go in order to "facilitate interactive worship." This presupposes the interaction is between us very splendid people rather than between God and human beings in all their neediness. Father Avery Dulles once mentioned that he spoke in one of these renovated spaces and noted a big banner on the front wall, "God Is Other People." He said he very much wished that he had a magic marker with which to put a strong comma after "Other." As for St. Ann, Mrs. Hitchcock says it "has been expensively gutted, stripped, and transformed from a place of distinctively Catholic worship to a 'communal gathering space' — a multifunctional meeting room." She continues: "The justification for the literal iconoclasm in Catholic churches could hardly have been more clearly expressed by Cromwell's Roundheads after they had systematically beheaded every image in the Lady Chapel of Ely Cathedral or smashed all the stained glass windows at Canterbury, although Cromwell's soldiers were undoubtedly responsible for destroying far fewer sacred images than the liturgical 'experts' who imposed their views of renewal on the Catholic churches across America." Now it must be admitted that Catholic, and not only Catholic, churches frequently had an awful lot of schlock. "Environment and art in worship" is a very important subject. Critics of the liturgical and aesthetic experts sometimes confuse sacred space with cluttered space, and popular piety with vulgarity expressed in artistic trash. At the same time, Mrs. Hitchcock is right about the stripping of the altars that aims not at a cleaner or purer form but at a radically different understanding of worship itself. Among clergy the question is asked, What's the difference between a liturgist and a terrorist? Answer: You can negotiate with a terrorist. Having given up on negotiating, many are now in revolt against the alleged experts.

❧ Invoking the most frightful of alternatives to having to deal with women, Professor Higgins sings, "I'd prefer a new edition/Of the Spanish Inquisition." Edgar Allan Poe's "The Pit and the Pendulum" and Dostoyevsky's "Legend of the Grand Inquisitor" are among the many literary masterpieces that have indelibly imprinted upon our minds the Spanish Inquisition as what historians call the "Black Legend." Now here comes along Professor Marvin O'Connell of Notre Dame, writing in *Catholic Dossier.* He wants it understood that he is no apologist for the Spanish Inquisition, but he is one of those rare historians who suffer from scrupulosity when it comes to facts and he thinks some things should be set straight.

For instance, Isabella and Ferdinand wanted the Inquisition established in 1478 for what seemed at the time unexceptionable political reasons. It is ridiculously anachronistic, says O'Connell, to speak of the Inquisition in terms of "church and state," since there was only the state that, in centuries of conflict with the Moors, defined its aspiration to control the Iberian peninsula in terms of Christianity — as its opponents defined their imperial ambitions in terms of Islam. To be a heretic was not a religious offense but a political crime. In short, heresy was treason. That was also the case, it should be noted, in Elizabethan England where Catholics were persecuted and killed.

But in the modern lexicon of historical horribles, the Inquisition is right up there with the Gulag Archipelago and Auschwitz, and in its first decade and a half (technically, it lasted three hundred years) it was very cruel. A high figure for the number of people executed as heretics in that early period is two thousand. With tragic irony, almost all of these were *conversos,* Muslims and Jews who sought to escape expulsion by becoming Christians. The irony is that, had they remained Jews or Muslims, they could not have been deemed heretics. Of course not all *conversos* ended up at the stake. Historian William Monter, cited by O'Connell, writes that the New Christians "represent the first known large-scale and long-term assimilation of Jews into any Christian society. Although the process included many painful adaptations, some severe backlash, and even a decade of brutal persecution under the Inquisition, it ended with their general integration into Spanish society. Their descendents quietly flouted racist codes and contributed to the vibrant Catholicism of Golden Age Spain; St. Teresa of Avila was the granddaughter of a New Christian penanced by the Inquisition."

The Inquisition soon began to wind down. In the sixteenth and seventeenth centuries, when Spanish sovereignty extended from Italy to most of Latin America, on average fewer than three persons a year were executed by the Inquisition, which was set up wherever Spain ruled. O'Connell writes that, in a century in which mass atrocities have reached a quantitative and qualitative pitch that would have been inconceivable to Torquemada, "I think a measure of discretion would be appropriate when bemoaning the wickedness of the Spanish Inquisition." No letters of protest, please. Let the record show that I, with Professor O'Connell, think the Spanish Inquisition was a very bad thing, and I will do all in my power to oppose any attempt by the Supreme Court to bring it back.

❧ New Yorkers, or at least New Yorkers who live in Manhattan, are inveterate walkers. It is therefore not surprising that snippets of overheard street talk are a staple of conversation. For example, the other day two bedraggled derelicts brown-bagging Thunderbird or perhaps some more choice vintage while tottering against the fence of Gramercy Park on East 20th Street. Says the one to the other, "I didn't say it wasn't a good idea. I said you'd never get it funded." Which perhaps answers the question of what happens to failed directors of think tanks. It occurred to me that they might have been failed academics, but failed academics have tenure.

President Clinton and the White Race

"E Pluribus Unum." "Out of the one, many," as Vice President Gore translated it. That received some derisive comment, but nothing as compared with Dan Quayle's adding an "e" to the spelling of potato. Maybe that is because Gore's blooper was not a blooper. It accurately reflects the policy of this Administration. The term for that policy is multiculturalism — as in David Dinkins' "gorgeous mosaic," as in the comment of the White House aide who cheerfully announced that by the year 2050 there would be "fifty million Muslims in the United States." As, most notably, in President Clinton's San Diego commencement speech on race relations.

"Can we become one America in the twenty-first century?" Clinton asked. In answer, he lifted up the state of Hawaii, which "has no majority racial or ethnic group. It is a wonderful place of exuberance and friendship and patriotism." Lest anyone miss the point, he declared more flatly, "A half century from now, when your own grandchildren are in college, there will be no majority race in America." There are several assumptions here. First, that immigration will continue at well over a million per year, and involving mainly nonwhite populations. Second, that the birth rate of immigrants will far exceed that of the native born. Third, that this is inevitable, the American people having no say about it or else having agreed that this would be a good thing. Fourth and most troubling, that the current majority consists of a race called white people.

The polite term for this is racialism. The more common term is racism. Apart from Aryan militia circles, few nonblack, non-Asian, non-Hispanic Americans think of themselves as belonging to the white race. Clinton was criticized by many for not backing up his words in San Diego with an announcement of new policy initiatives. The alarming thing about the speech, however, was the resurrection of the idea of a white race, an idea from the era of Bull Connor that most of us hoped was definitively past. Pitting the "majority race" against nonwhite claimants to justice is a sure formula for exacerbating the tensions that Clinton says he wants to heal. It necessarily involves, among other things, the discredited and profoundly unjust policies of affirmative action and quotas that, not surprisingly, Clinton strongly defended in San Diego.

We have agreed in these pages with those who say we must regain control over immigration policies that are manifestly out of control. We have strongly disagreed when they say that race should be a factor in shaping immigration policies. No good can come from asking the American people, as some say they should be asked, whether they think it is a good idea that fifty years from now a majority of the population should be nonwhite. That is a racialist, if not racist, way of posing the question. Regrettably, albeit from the other side of the immigration debate, that is the way President Clinton has posed the question.

Multiculturalists and the champions of a white majority have in common the aim of raising race-consciousness, and in this they powerfully reinforce one another. To tell the majority of Americans, as Clinton did, that they should "celebrate" the prospect that in fifty years most Americans will not be like them is politically stupid and morally wrong. It is politically stupid because most people think that being like them is a pretty good thing. It is morally wrong because it invites the majority of people to identify themselves by race. The most long-standing and divisive struggle in American history — from abolition through the civil war to the civil rights movement led by Martin Luther King, Jr. — has been to overcome the racial mindset endorsed, however inadvertently, by Bill Clinton. Good arguments can be made for continuing to welcome a large number of immigrants to this country. But does the President really want to frame the public debate in terms of the proposal that a half century from now there will be no majority race in America? One earnestly hopes not.

Deep, Critical Reflection
on the Education Front

"Character education" programs in public schools come in for a drubbing by Alfie Kohn, writing in *Phi Delta Kappan,* a publication for professional educators. It seems these programs are "designed to make children work harder and do what they're told." "Even when other values are also promoted — caring or fairness, say — the preferred method of instruction is tantamount to indoctrination. The point is to drill students in specific behaviors rather than to engage them in deep, critical reflection about certain ways of being." No wonder Mr. Kohn is upset. There are few things more creative than a fourth grader engaged in deep, critical reflection about ways of being.

Character educators also encourage competition and give out awards for achievement. As Mr. Kohn complains: "When some children are singled out as 'winners,' the central message that every child learns is this: 'Other people are potential obstacles to my success.'" Even worse, character education fosters self-restraint. "This is noteworthy," Kohn writes, "because the virtue of self-restraint — or at least the decision to give special emphasis to it — has historically been preached by those, from St. Augustine to the present, who see people as basically sinful." I think he got the character educators there. The texts on character education, says Kohn, "describe religious dogma, not scientific fact." Scientific fact "supports the idea that it is as 'natural' for children to help as to hurt." Ask any parent.

Then Mr. Kohn gets to the heart of the matter: "Character education rests on three ideological legs: behaviorism, conservatism, and religion. Of these, the third raises the most delicate issues for a critic; it is here that the charge of ad hominem argument is most likely to be raised. So let us be clear: it is of no relevance that almost all of the leading proponents of character education are devout Catholics. But it is entirely relevant that, in the shadows of their writings, there lurks the assumption that only religion can serve as the foundation for good character. (William Bennett, for example, has flatly asserted that the difference between right and wrong cannot be taught 'without reference to religion.') It is appropriate to consider the personal beliefs of these individuals if those beliefs are ensconced in the movement they have defined and directed. What they do on Sundays is their own business, but if they are trying to turn our public schools into Sunday schools, that becomes everybody's business." The fact that leading proponents of character education (e.g., Kevin Ryan and William Kilpatrick) are Catholics "is of no relevance," but Mr. Kohn thought he would mention it just the same because "it is appropriate to consider the personal beliefs of these individuals." Now if only somebody somewhere along the line had "indoctrinated" Mr. Kohn and the editors of *Phi Delta Kappan* in the basics of clear thinking rather than letting them muddle toward adulthood in their befuddled engagement with deep, critical reflection about ways of being.

✮ Such self-discipline. It has been I don't know how many months since I've remarked on Father Richard McBrien of Notre Dame. In part because what he calls his "self-syndicated" column is hard to find these days. But dedicated readers send me one from time to time, and some are hard to resist. In this column, for instance, Fr. McBrien is taken with a writer who argues that "celibacy for Catholic clergy is fundamentally incorrect from a genetic perspective." "Genetically," Yamil Lara writes, "Catholics cannot afford to continue to practice institutionally mandated celibacy." "It is the extinction of our finest and the opposite of what our knowledge of genetics dictates." Fr. McBrien clinches the argument by citing a long list of high-achieving politicians, actors, and Protestant clergy who have given the world high-achieving children. So why aren't priests doing their duty to improve the race? Theologians and other ponderous types might object that viewing the priesthood in terms of genetic perpetuation is the very antithesis of the Catholic idea of the priest as an icon of eschatological disposability. Readers unaccustomed to such elevated reflections, however, might simply give a moment's thought to a world filled with little McBriens. Not that I believe terminal silliness is genetically transmitted.

✮ Here we have gone I don't know how many months without mentioning the National Council of Churches (NCC). The dear old thing managed to scrape up the money to hold another General Assembly, this time in Chicago. There were two big firsts among the speakers invited: the Rev. Don Argue, president of the National Association of Evangelicals, and Warith Deen Mohammed, head of Al-Islam, a black Muslim group. There was considerable uneasiness about inviting an evangelical Protestant, but, hey, that's what being ecumenical is all about.

The Best and the Brightest

Long before the Second Vatican Council, there was a liturgical renewal among Catholics. It was very different from what is called liturgical reform today. In the 1950s, I was attracted to the movement under the auspices of the sainted Monsignor Martin Hellriegel of Holy Cross Church in St. Louis. Father Michael Mathis was another early pioneer, and the Center for Pastoral Liturgy at the University of Notre Dame gives out a Michael Mathis Award, which this year went to Bishop Donald Trautman of Erie, Pennsylvania, the recently retired chairman of the national bishops conference committee for liturgy.

Receiving the award, Bishop Trautman launched a strident attack on critics of the current direction of liturgical reform, such as Joseph Cardinal Ratzinger, Msgr. Klaus Gamber, Fr. Joseph Fessio, and groups called Adoremus and CREDO. The tide is turning, Trautman declares, raising the question, "Is liturgical renewal becoming a dinosaur?" The critics say they want to "reform the reform," but Trautman does not credit their intentions for a moment. The proposals of the critics are "alarming." "They are indicative that the liturgical advances of Vatican II are in trouble — advances which the vast majority of Catholics have received positively."

While asserting that the people like the changes, he criticizes liturgists for failing to enlist the support of the people. "We have missed golden opportunities to reach the people in the pews," says the bishop.

On a college campus he recently saw a tee shirt with the message, "Join the resistance — support Vatican II." I have seen the same tee shirt. The bishop took it as a message of support for the changes since Vatican II. The young woman wearing the tee shirt I saw explained that she supports the understanding of Vatican II advanced by John Paul II and Cardinal Ratzinger, and urges resistance against those who have wreaked change and confusion in the name of "the spirit of the Council." Obviously, there are major disagreements about the meaning of Vatican II. But it obviously is not obvious to Bishop Trautman, for whom any criticism of his version of the reform is an attack on the Council.

In his speech, Trautman repeatedly calls for "full, conscious, and active participation" in the liturgy. A bishop of like mind announced a while back that, using a stop watch, he calculated that for fifty-two minutes of a Mass the people were not doing anything. Maybe they were praying or reflecting on the Word of God, which he clearly was not. But Bishop Trautman's particular passion is for "horizontal inclusive language" in Scripture readings and liturgy. Some readers may not be familiar with the terminology. As best I understand it, vertical language goes up and down, and horizontal language goes sideways. The bishops are now adopting "moderate horizontal inclusive language," which sounds like a diagonal compromise.

"I say to you," Trautman said at Notre Dame, "addressing women using male language denies women their own identity." No doubt some women have told him that, although a recent national survey, reinforced by pastoral experience, suggests that there is little popular support for, and considerable opposition to, what is called "inclusive" language. Here, too, it seems that those who presume to speak for "the people in the pews" have not effectively reached them. The

bishop has a point with the *Catechism of the Catholic Church,*
which in its excessively literal translation ends up with an
overuse of "man" and "men" that is simply bad English. He
cites a *Catechism* passage that says priests should "give themselves entirely to God and to men." He comments, "Given
homosexual behavior in our society, this is not the appropriate language to promote celibacy." A really keen sensitivity
to sexual innuendo, however, might give the bishop pause
about his enthusiasm for "horizontal" language regardless of
gender.

Inclusive Fundamentalists

Panicked at the prospect of his cause becoming a "dinosaur," the bishop seizes upon any argument at hand. The
possibility that people may think the *Catechism* is promoting homosexuality "is an example of why exclusive language is unacceptable." He also makes much of the fact
that Tyndale publishers recently put out an inclusive translation of the Bible. "If Bible scholars from the fundamentalist tradition . . . employ gender-inclusive language and
our revised edition of the lectionary offers only a tokenism,
there is a serious loss to God's people," says Bishop
Trautman. "It is no secret that many Roman Catholics are
entering fundamentalist churches today. How can the Roman Catholic tradition fail to keep pace even with the
evangelical tradition in offering inclusive language?"

Even with those fundamentalists and evangelicals. How
backward can we Catholics be? In his grasping for an argument, however, the bishop gets quite muddled. I do not want
to believe for a minute that he believes that Catholics are becoming fundamentalists because they want gender-inclusive
language. Fundamentalists are as enthusiastic about gender-
inclusive language as Bishop Trautman is about the Tri-
dentine Mass. The Tyndale experiment is a nonevent. The
big development on the Bible translation front is that the

publishers of the New International Version (NIV) — which is by far the most widely used translation among Protestants — recently announced that they are definitively shelving any plans to dabble, even ever so cautiously, with inclusive language. The earlier suggestion that they might do so met with massive protests. If Catholics are becoming fundamentalists, it is more likely in order to escape the "reforms" promoted by Trautman & Co.

He laments that the "reformers of the reform" now have the upper hand in the Church. "There is a dismantling of the renewal taking place before our very eyes," he declares. But then he offers the consolation that the reformers of an earlier day were also given a hard time, only to be vindicated later. "Why do we hurt our best and brightest?" he plaintively asks. Speaking of the best and brightest, he immediately adds, "By God's providence there are similarities between Father Mathis and myself." Ah, the lot of the unappreciated. A prophet is not without honor . . .

In fact, there is much to approve in changes made since the Council. Although there are no doubt some who would like to, Catholics cannot and should not simply go back to the way things were. In his undiscriminating defense of the liturgical establishment, however, Bishop Trautman dismisses critics as reactionaries. There is a big difference, however, between antiquarianism and respect for tradition, continuity, and patterns of popular devotion. That earlier liturgical renewal was one of *ressourcement,* of reappropriating the fullness of the tradition in order to complement and, where necessary, to correct liturgical practice ossified by mistaking mystification for mystery. That was the renewal embraced by Vatican II. Then came the agitations of those who mistook reform for perpetual innovation.

In the 1960s, I was the token Protestant on the board of the National Liturgical Conference. It used to attract ten thousand or more participants to its annual liturgical weeks. By the end of the sixties, the liturgical week (it may have been the last one) attracted a ragtag crowd of hippies manqué under the slogan of e. e. cummings' "damn everything but the circus." What passed for the avant garde of liturgical reform had in fact become a disheveled and depressing circus of preening self-indulgence and uncritical celebration of everything in the cultural marketplace that presented itself as liberation from putatively stifling tradition.

Bishop Trautman cites the great liturgical scholar Josef Jungman in his support, but there is a great disjunction between Jungman's work and the liturgical establishment of today. Many of the pioneers, such as Martin Hellriegel, became vocal critics of the liturgical revolution, and for their troubles were derisively dismissed as old-timers who had lost touch with "the spirit of the Council." In fact, and although they did not use the phrase, they were the first advocates of the "reform of the reform." After thirty years of changes big and small, why are some so panicked by the suggestion that it is time to reevaluate what has happened and where we ought to go from here? Of course there are on the margins a few people who think Vatican II was a mistake and would repeal everything, both legitimate and illegitimate, done in its name. But they are just that, on the margins and certain to stay there. They in no way represent what is meant by a reform of the reform.

So many good things have been done since the Council, and so much that is doubtful or wrongheaded. The reform of the reform is nothing more than a proposal that we try to sort them out. Bishop Trautman is right in sensing a widespread and growing uneasiness with the direction of liturgical change. But his strident depiction of those who disagree as enemies of the Council and persecutors of the "best and brightest" can lead only to sterile polarization, and a deepening of the suspicion that the liturgical establishment holds in contempt both the tradition of the Church and the sensibilities of the faithful who, despite all, persist in their faithfulness.

❧ The Endless Search for the Mainstream Department. Professor Douglas Jacobsen of Messiah College in Pennsylvania writes in the April issue of *Interpretation* that Protestantism is in need of a new center. The two-party model (liberal and evangelical) will no longer do. Jacobsen's new center, it says here, "must be based on inclusiveness rather than exclusiveness. Its net must be spread as widely as possible, to as many people as possible. It should be a meeting place of many varieties of Protestants." I don't want to be a spoilsport, but I wonder if the new centrism isn't what used to be called liberalism.

A More Real World

The day Mother Teresa died, an editor at *USA Today* asked for an op-ed piece, which I did. In it I quoted her words upon receiving the Nobel Prize for peace (see below). The next day a more senior editor called to say they couldn't use it. "We had in mind," he said, "more on the role of the media and less on abortion." In other words, they didn't want a piece on Mother Teresa.

She was a most improbable celebrity. Less than five feet short and craggy-faced, she was born in, of all places, Albania, and followed God's call to live with and for "the poorest of the poor," the street people of Calcutta. And there she died at age eighty-seven. Not a very promising career path toward becoming one of the best known and most loved people of the century. But, of course, that was not her goal.

In the same week Diana, Princess of Wales, was killed, and inevitably comparisons were made. The media frenzy and orgy of bathos were tasteless in the extreme, but it is fitting that she was mourned. Striking, however, were the commentators, many of them secularist to the bone, who went on about her having been "canonized" as a "saint." It is strange how even the Church's enemies reach for the Church's vocabulary when their words fail them. It was "the week of two saints," according to one news program. Comparisons need not be invidious, but the contrast could hardly be sharper. Diana was killed at age thirty-six in the company of a wealthy playboy who, it was intimated to the press, she intended to marry. Born into British aristocracy, she had married into the royal family, and loaned her publicity to approved causes. And yes, she was beautiful.

The other woman was vowed to a life of poverty, chastity, and obedience; her only beauty was her laughter and her eyes (what laughter! what eyes!); they reflected the joy of doing, as she put it, "something beautiful for God." It is no criticism to note that we probably never would have heard of Diana had she not married Prince Charles. Like some dissident Catholic theologians, she owed her celebrity entirely to the institution that she trashed. At the same time, we should never have heard of Mother Teresa. The whole point, after all, was to hide her life away in the lives of those whom the world is glad enough to forget. The unwanted, the unneeded, the unloved. Mother Teresa's goal, she often said, was not to be successful but to be faithful. But astonishingly successful she was, in a curious way. As wise as a serpent and as innocent as a dove, she employed that success in the service of the truth that she served.

A Fool for Christ

The rumor got out about this little nun in India doing something beautiful for God, and it was spread far and wide, notably by the late Malcolm Muggeridge of BBC. Over the years she would become a spiritual magnet, and today the Missionaries of Charity count more than four thousand sisters and novices, four hundred priests and brothers, and hundreds of thousands of lay volunteers, all serving the poorest of the poor in a hundred countries. The mighty of the world, who pride themselves on their realism, heaped honors upon her, often in lieu of heeding her words. Against the world's realism Mother Teresa did not propose anything so flimsy as idealism. She called us to a different realism, a more real world, a world where life is found when lost in service to others. It is easy to live in a dream world where we fantasize that we are royalty. Much harder, and infinitely more rewarding, is the real world where the royal family is composed of those whom Jesus called "the least of these," and of those who find life in surrendering life to their care.

Mother Teresa became what the apostle Paul called "a fool for Christ," and it is not surprising that some thought her simply a fool. To the powerful and worldly wise who believe an over-populated world is filled with millions of expendable people who never would be missed, she was a bothersome naïf who insisted on the dignity of every life, destined from eternity to eternity. She was a rebuke to politicians and ideologues who claim to speak for the poor but are not on speaking terms with poor people. "If you don't know them, you don't love them and don't serve them," she said. She had no grand schemes for ridding the world of poverty, which all too often are schemes for ridding the world of poor people. In defiance of elites who dismiss charity as a "band-aid solution" and demand that charity be replaced by justice, she called her order the Missionaries of Charity, knowing that charity is but another word for love. She knew that justice without love is deadly.

Mother Teresa was not a social worker who happened to be a nun. For her, people were not clients or cases. In those she served she saw the face of Christ — and it did not matter whether they were Christian or Hindu or Buddhist or bereft of any sustaining faith. She believed with them and for them. Her business was not to deliver services but to transform lives. For her, even the most wretched life was transformed by transcendent hope. There is, she insisted, no such thing as a life not worth living. She stood at the entrance gates and the exit gates of life, bearing witness that all is gift, all is grace. In the words of Rabbi Abraham Joshua Heschel, "Just to be is a blessing. Just to live is holy."

Some, including some Catholics, derided her as dreadfully old-fashioned. The Missionaries of Charity were pathetically out of step with the progressive directions pioneered by so many religious orders in recent decades. And her "authoritarian" leadership was an embarrassment. Those who confuse the authoritative with the authoritarian were scandalized. Mother Teresa did not deny that she had bowed to authority. It was the authority of the one who said, "Come, follow me" — with all you have, with all you are, all the way. And, like Mary, who is the Mother of us all, she said, "Let it be." And it was. It was for her, and it is for thousands who have followed in her following him. In our time, and in all times, submission is a scandal. Mother Teresa scandalized the world, and she scandalized many in the Church. As was the case with the Lord she followed, she forced the question of whether she was right or whether she was crazy. One way of avoiding the question was to turn her into a celebrity.

It has been said that a celebrity is someone who is well known for being well known, but there is more to it than that. One might say she was an accidental celebrity, but more than accident is involved. In a world captive to wealth and glitter and power, her witness kept alive the rumor that there is a radically different measure of human greatness. And even those whom the world counts great half suspected that she was right. She was greatly honored by those whose measure of greatness she challenged. They were even willing to overlook her violation of their conventional wisdoms. Upon accepting the Nobel Prize for peace in 1979, she declared: "To me the nations with legalized abortion are the poorest nations. The greatest destroyer of peace today is the crime against unborn children."

She said much the same at a big prayer breakfast in Washington with Mr. Clinton and his courtiers in attendance. They listened, or feigned to listen, with faces fixed and, perhaps, teeth gritted. Afterwards, of course, all rose in a standing ovation. "She is a saint, after all, and allowances must be made," some no doubt said to themselves, before turning their attention again to what they call the real world. Mother Teresa agreed with John Paul II that the great contest of history is between the "culture of death" and the "culture of life," and that the culture of life is simply, and demandingly, the way of unconditional love for those whom Jesus called "the least of these." Those who bestowed the honors partly hoped and partly feared that this strange little nun was right.

The unborn, the dying, the radically handicapped, the lepers, those afflicted with AIDS — all those who are shunned by the sleek and strong because they smell of neediness and death — live along the fault lines of society. Mother Teresa understood that a people is judged not by the successful whom we celebrate but by those along the fault lines for whom we care. The message she embodied, and the message of the thousands of sisters all over the world who joined her in the Missionaries of Charity, is disturbingly countercultural. It is disturbing because it demands a response not simply of admiration but of emulation. That's the way it is with saints. Also with the saint whom a cynical world, not quite knowing what to do with the radical innocence of faith, turned into a celebrity.

Christians know better. Or at least we should. And sometime soon — perhaps in the lifetime of some who are reading this — she will be formally beatified, canonized, and raised to the honors of the altar. Little children will ask whether you ever saw her. And you will answer, "Oh yes. That laughter! Those eyes! What joy!" And another generation will listen for the voice that says, "Come, follow me," and will throw away their lives, and thereby find their lives, in doing something beautiful for God.

❧ "Collective Spirituality Behind Youth Crowds for Pope?" asks the headline of a story in *Religion Watch*. We don't usually use the word "collective," but some Christians, the Apostle Paul included, do think Christianity is a corporate thing, as, for example, in "Church." The report is based on a sniffishly dismissive article in the *Tablet* (London) on how the Pope manages to attract crowds of hundreds of thousands and even millions all over the world. "The Pope believes in a powerful, visible, and obedient Church. The large assemblies of Catholics who congregate during his pastoral visits are the best expression of this muscular Christianity. . . . It is interesting to note that those who organize the youth days are the trusted 'Pope's legions': Opus Dei, the Focolare, Communione e Liberazione, charismatics, and the rest, while those who attend are often the vast mass of drifters, of semi-believers, those who seek the warmth and emotion of a mass meeting, whether it be Woodstock, a Billy Graham rally, or St. Peter's Square." In fact, events such as the recent world youth gathering in Paris are organized by the local church, but more interesting is the reassurance that properly liberal *Tablet* types would not be caught dead attending, never mind helping to organize, such gatherings of the great unwashed. "Charismatics and the rest" is a particularly nice touch. It has even been rumored that this pope has approved of eating with tax collectors and sinners. The more decorous Catholics of England cannot help but be nervous about what their Anglican friends will think of them.

⚜ Singin' them old third-way blues. For people who don't have a scorecard it must be explained that the new name for capitalism is neoliberalism. This is the usage among leftist intellectuals all over the southern hemisphere or what used to be called the Third World. And among their friends in the West who were so bitterly disappointed by the failure of real-world, existing socialism, a.k.a. communism. The vicissitudes of history, however, have not dissuaded them from their earnest search for a "third way" between socialism and capitalism, namely, neo-liberalism. Among Catholics of the left, the complaint is that the capitalist neoliberals have hijacked Catholic social teaching, with the help of a none-too-alert Pope who in the 1991 encyclical, *Centesimus Annus,* said the free economy is the way to go. "A theology of liberation is more needed today than ever — but a renewed liberation theology in a different form than previously," Father Peter-Hans Kolvenbach, Father General of the Society of Jesus, told a Swiss news agency. He and others have discovered that the global economy of neoliberalism has not benefited everyone equally. There are still poor people, he sadly notes. He says that the earlier liberation theology of the 1970s and '80s had become "exhausted." That is to say, Marxism was discredited by the very history to which it appealed for vindication. But that older liberation theology should not be forgotten, since it was "deeply rooted in the Gospel and real life of the People of God." Fr. Kolvenbach said that a French Jesuit, Fr. Jean-Yves Calvez, is "working on proposals for a new papal encyclical on problems of marginalization, unemployment, and social rejection." But the proposed new encyclical will not deal only with the problems being experienced by the Jesuits. It will also address what is described as the more general crisis of society. The older liberation theology was sharply criticized by the Congregation for the Doctrine of the Faith in 1984 and 1986. Nothing daunted, Fr. Kolvenbach says the third way is now being set to a new tune and "is undoubtedly needed in developed countries too, although not in any sense a copy of the Latin American theology." He does not say whether the Pope has been informed about the new encyclical that is in the works. In preparing new encyclicals, the Jesuits operate on what the intelligence community calls the NTK ("need to know") principle. In the old days — back when "jesuitical" meant crafty — they didn't even explain their secrets to the news media.

Science, Greed, and Justice:
An Unbeatable Combination

News reports of the last several months freshly impress upon the mind the bright prospects for the human future now that science, greed, and justice have joined forces against the wickedness of the cigarette industry. Documents recently released powerfully reinforce the allegation that the millions of dollars spent on advertising by R. J. Reynolds had the clear purpose of increasing sales. Not only that, but increased sales now have been definitely linked to the actual use of the product. Moreover, recent studies indicate decisively that most users also inhale. The evidence against the tobacco companies does not stop there. Internal memos have come to light showing that tobacco executives have conspired to make a product that is more attractive to the customer. Of course the industry denies any intention to give customers what they want or to encourage a demand for its product.

Members of Congress have declared themselves shocked by revelations that the industry, not content with having sold trillions of cigarettes in the past, is clearly planning to maintain and even expand its market in the future. A whistleblower in the industry has leaked to the House Committee on Protecting People from Themselves conclusive documentation that the tobacco companies have engaged in market research, which is paid for by profits made from selling cigarettes. It is now revealed that the strategy of the tobacco giants is premised upon the finding that younger people have, on average, a longer future than older people. There is no doubt, say members of the committee, that the industry's market plans for the future are geared to the people who are more likely to be around in the future. Said committee chairperson Elsa Comstock, "This new evidence provides the smoking gun we've been looking for. The industry's strategy is to give people a choice, and then hope they will choose to buy its products. In all my years in Congress, I have never seen such a flagrant attempt to stay in business."

New legislation is almost certain to require the manufacturers to include in their advertising stronger messages discouraging the purchase or use of their product. Support for such legislation is reinforced by scientific research of recent years showing that cigarette smoking is unhealthy. This is a dramatic change from the widespread assumption of the past hundred years or more that smoking cigarettes is a remedy for respiratory problems and one of the surest ways to extend life expectancy. In the view of scientific experts, the recent findings vindicate what used to be the minority opinion of those who referred to cigarettes as "coffin nails" and who otherwise challenged what were commonly viewed as the health benefits of smoking. "Seldom in history," said former nanny general Dr. Ever Kook, "have we witnessed the power of science to so radically reverse a popular misperception."

The recent negotiated settlement with the tobacco companies, now being considered by Congress, has put the industry on the defensive. Some antismoking legislators have expressed concern that the industry's future profits may be in jeopardy, thus imperiling the settlement's requirement that the companies pay anti-tobacco lawyers and state governments more than $500 billion over the next twenty years. With that concern in mind, Vice President Albert Bore has proposed that the domestic price of a pack of cigarettes be quadrupled, which, it is acknowledged, would pose no deterrent to the affluent but, in the words of Representative Comstock, "would punish the poor for their filthy habit."

The proposed legislation would also secure the interests of lawyers and state politicians by providing trade incentives for the marketing of cigarettes abroad. "There are more than five billion suckers out there," noted Vice President Bore, "and, fortunately, American brands, thanks to our technological edge, are the smoke of choice." Prospects are especially bright in poor countries where life expectancy is not so high in any case. The Vice President also observed that their smoking is less a threat to the ecosystem than "the danger of their becoming rich and wasteful like the rest of us." I. M. Swindler, who receives $15 million per year as chairman of Lawyers for Social Justice, says his group strongly backs the proposed measures as "an eminently fair arrangement for all the parties who matter."

✹ Thanks to an alert reader in Florida, I have here the venomous gushings of Steve Gushee, an Episcopal minister, who writes a religion column in the local tabloid. The Rev. Gushee is much exercised by Catholic bishops who are considering the reintroduction of meatless Fridays. "Can weekly confessions, fasting before communion, and knuckle-knocking nuns be far behind?" (Dare we hope?) The Second Vatican Council worked a revolution, according to Gushee. "Many discovered for the first time that religion was not meant to control their life but unleash it for unlimited growth." There you have it, *aggiornamento* as slipping the leash. Bernard Cardinal Law of Boston favors the fast, which prompts Gushee to write, "But Law is the kind of religious conservative who thinks the Spanish Inquisition was enlightened evangelism. . . . Some churchmen just can't get accustomed to the freedom and joy their faith proclaims." Nor others to the humility and charity that it enjoins.

What Then Is To Be Done?

What an awful tangle we're in about race. Forget our serially sincere (Jim Nuechterlein's fine phrase) President's ballyhooed dialogue on race. Multicultural effusions about the wonderful new world when there will be no majority or minority and we'll all be amalgamated into the gorgeous mosaic on the far side of the prescribed therapy of black accusations and white self-denigrations for the sins of slavery and racism — all this demeans a subject about which most Americans are surprisingly ready to get serious. If, that is, it seems believable to them that there is a purpose in raking over these questions again, if it seems there is something to be done.

There are other recent and more important twists in the racial tangle, such as Professor Glenn Loury's going very public in a number of forums about his disillusionment with conservatives because they basically don't care about black poor people. Loury of Boston University is a cherished contributor to this journal and has been celebrated as one of the most influential black intellectuals (yes, the adjective is unavoidable in this connection) in America. Predictably, those on the left, both black and white, have been quick to react to Loury's break with loud chortles of we-told-you-sos. Somewhat earlier, Loury and his friend Robert Woodson, who works with community initiatives in the inner city, very publicly disengaged themselves from the American Enterprise Institute because of its association with Charles Murray and Dinesh D'Souza, both of whom have written controversial books deemed to be less than sensitive to blacks as victims.

On the right, the editors of *National Review* do try to be sensitive to what they take to be the need of Loury and others to maintain a remnant of credibility among blacks by continuing to support affirmative action, albeit in a sharply modified form. The editors conclude: "Still, there is no excuse for conservatives to be (unconservatively) rude to Professor Loury — though his references to Charles Murray and Dinesh D'Souza are less than genial. There is no doubt that Professor Loury and Robert Woodson are indeed conservatives; but they might reflect upon the option of resisting cultural intimidation."

In the same issue of *National Review* is a long review essay by John J. DiIulio of Princeton University discussing four new books on race and making some of the points he has also made in these pages. Of particular interest is his evaluation of *America in Black and White* by Stephan and Abigail Thernstrom (Simon & Schuster), a recent scholarly work that documents in great detail the progress that blacks have made in recent decades. DiIulio does not deny the progress, but he takes the Thernstroms to task for slighting all that remains to be done, and for ignoring the crucial component in the possible doing of it. He writes of the book that it "makes nary a mention of the religious life of black Americans, rich or poor. But the evidence is growing that the only people who are now doing something to make inner-city blacks part of 'one nation, indivisible' [the Thernstroms' subtitle] are those who seek 'one nation, *under God,* indivisible.'" Actually, the Thernstrom book does make a passing reference to religion in reporting the growing number of blacks and whites who belong to racially integrated churches, but it is very much in passing.

A Jewish Factor

Passions are running high in these disputes, and I have been caught in the crossfire, trying, irenic soul that I am, to hold friendships together. The circumstance is complicated by what might aptly be called a Jewish factor. It is not coincidence that some of the conservatives whose alleged unconcern most offends Loury and others happen to be Jewish, and are usually called neoconservatives. Jews tend to feel, with considerable justice, that they have historically sided with the black cause, that in recent years they have been singled out as the objects of frequently vicious black hostility, and that, in any case, there is really not much more they can do to be helpful. As is regularly pointed out, it is very dispiriting to be told that the national expenditure over thirty years of five trillion dollars to eliminate poverty and racism has only exacerbated the problem of poverty and racism. Some may conclude, not entirely unreasonably, that enough is enough.

There is another aspect of the Jewish angle, however. It is the ascendancy of the view, ably promoted also by DiIulio, that religion is the key to anything good happening among the black poor. There are relatively few black Jews, and it is understandable that Jews who are not black are inclined to think that, if DiIulio and others are right about the centrality of religion, doing something about the plight of the black underclass is chiefly a job for Christians, both white and black. Of the Thernstrom study DiIulio writes: "The tragedy of the book is that the authors are virtually silent about our moral obligation to do something — not talk, not debate, but *do* something — about those black Americans — who, to white Christians, are brothers and sisters in our Lord Jesus Christ — who have yet to make the climb."

He continues: "When it comes to motivating black and white Americans to respond, up close and personal, to the plight of inner-city blacks, debating 'racial injustice' is a sickly, sorry substitute for promoting religious morality and 'justification,' the Christian doctrine of the sanctification of the human person through the gift of God's life, which enjoins us to accept our social and economic fellowship with others, especially those whom Christ commanded His followers to love first, last, and always: society's poor, its children, its prisoners, its fallen, its feared." Protestants should overlook the muddled treatment of justification and sanctification. DiIulio is a Catholic, and you know how they are. But his point is clear enough. Both the motivation and the means for *doing* something are emphatically Christian.

The gist of the argument is convincing, I believe, but that doesn't mean that doing something is entirely up to committed Christians. DiIulio concludes by making very concrete public policy proposals to address the problems of poverty and race, including getting rid of affirmative action based solely on race, releasing nonviolent low-level drug offenders from prison, permitting prayer in the public schools, and changing tax laws to encourage contributions to inner-city community organizations.

Glenn Loury's anti-conservative blast and the contention over the Thernstrom book are forcing an urgent question. It is not enough to say that what has been tried hasn't worked as we hoped, and may have made some things worse; nor is it enough to expose liberal fatuities about remedying the "root causes" of poverty and crime. DiIulio writes: "So what if brain-dead liberals continue to make silly arguments about the overall condition of blacks and the state of race relations in America? So what if most young black males who go to prison are justly convicted? What is our endgame here? More debate about race à la President Clinton's commission on the subject? A continuation of our de facto three-part national urban policy: abortion (favored by liberal elites), incarceration (favored by conservative elites), and suburbanization and gated communities (favored, it seems, by almost everyone who can afford to move)?"

Explicit commandment, moral intuition, and simple self-respect combine in compelling the belief that there must be another way. Just believing that is prelude to doing something. The something in question is centered in religion that is both motive and means, and extends to public policy tasks that should claim the attention of all Americans. Who knows? Even Mr. Clinton's dialogue on race — if or when it moves beyond the old rancorous mix of invective and utopianism — might contribute to such a happy change.

❧ Poor dear old Yale. It just can't understand the petty intolerance of its infatuation with tolerance. Readers are familiar with the law school's refusal to let the Christian Legal Society recruit there because it "discriminates" against non-Christians. (See my exchange with Dean Anthony T. Kronman in the August/September 1997 issue.) Now there are the "Yale Five," Orthodox Jewish students who want to be exempted from Yale's requirement that for two years students live in coed dorms. The Yale Five say that boys and girls in the same bedrooms and bathrooms is a circumstance that violates their religious and moral convictions. Among the most fatuously smug and narrow-minded of the defenses of Yale's refusal to allow an exemption from its rules is offered by David Denby, writing in the *New Yorker:* "Temptations must surround the orthodox of any faith when they leave family and community and enter the world," writes Mr. Denby. Indeed, he suggests, it is the solemn duty of the university to provide temptations. One of the Jewish students said, "We cannot, in good conscience, live in a place where women are permitted to stay overnight in men's rooms." To which Denby offers the presumably knock-down argument, "In that case, [he] should avoid living in big-city apartment buildings as well." Boys and girls living and sleeping together is Yale's elevated aspiration toward educational excellence. "Living in a coed dorm for two years is now part of the known Yale experience," writes Denby, "just as taking certain required courses, like the Literature Humanities and the Contemporary Civilization courses at Columbia, is part of the life of other schools." The "just as" is worth noting. Dormitory rutting, it seems, is right up there with Matthew Arnold's maxim about the best that has been thought and said. Mr. Denby is the thorough traditionalist in defending the coed dorm tradition of, say, the last twenty years. "The experience of confronting both new ideas and people who think differently from oneself has traditionally formed the heart of a liberal education." How else are Orthodox Jews to know that some people are lewd, immodest, and prone to engage in sexual intercourse outside of marriage if Yale does not see to it? Nobody ever said that the educational mission of the university is easy. Denby concludes, "In this society, existence is rarely free from jostling: we all, every day, find our deepest convictions offended, even traduced by *something.* In that respect, the Yale Five, whether they get their way or not, will have to take their chances along with the rest of us." Why, of course. It's part of "entering the world." *Our* world, in which they must become like us (or at least like David Denby). It is the new world of secularism's oppressive tolerance. And to think it was only fifty years ago that Bill Buckley could raise such a ruckus by suggesting in *God and Man at Yale* that maybe the university was less serious than it should be about transmitting the Christian heritage.

✺ *Nicotine Theological Journal* is not just about smoking, although the editors do keep returning to the subject in order to tweak religious liberalism about one of its most adamantly held dogmas, the unmitigated evil of tobacco. *NTJ* is published by the Old Life Theological Society and is "dedicated to recovering the riches of confessional Presbyterianism." The current issue takes a skeptical view of the Southern Baptist boycott against Disney. They note a Jerry Falwell publication with the headline, "Walt Disney Would Be Ashamed." So why, the editors wonder, are Christians obliged to honor the sacred memory of Disney? In addition, they note, Disney's involvement in so many enterprises has not overlooked the Christian market. Just south of the Magic Kingdom in Orlando, for instance, is a new Disney development called "Celebration." It's for people who want the morality of the 1950s combined with "all the neat gear you have today." "By subtly conflating 1950s-style wholesomeness with Christian virtue, it is luring white, middle-class, pro-family values citizens to *live* in a theme park. No longer is Disney content to get them for a week a year. It wants to buy their whole souls. (Oh yes, there will be churches in Celebration. The first to go up will be a Presbyterian (USA) Church. But when will the first Southern Baptist Church be built? And what happens when from the pulpit its pastor urges a Disney boycott?)" The issue also includes some comment on the FT question about "the end of democracy," and seems to come down on the side of David Bovenizer, whose letter to FT suggested that democracy ended with Lincoln. Although the editors insist that their publication is not "a Reformed version of *Cigar Aficio-*

nado," the issue does conclude by returning to a subject of more than incidental interest. J. Gresham Machen, that stalwart opponent of theological modernism, wrote to his mother during his last semester as an undergraduate at Princeton: "The fellows are in my room now on the last Sunday night, smoking the cigars and eating the oranges which it has been the greatest delight I ever had to provide whenever possible. My idea of delight is a Princeton room full of fellows smoking. When I think what a wonderful aid tobacco is to friendship and Christian patience I have sometimes regretted that I never began to smoke."

❧ Britain's New Labor government has a few tried and failed ideas of its own. Albert Mohler, president of Southern Baptist Seminary in Louisville, brings to my attention that Her Majesty's Government promoted a first-ever Sexual Awareness Week. An official explained, "Young people are less likely to have early sex if there is good communication about the subject at home. We are emphasizing that sex is fun and talking is the key to a healthy sex life." Right. "It's really fun, kids, so don't do it." I can't help thinking that it's a sad commentary on the younger generation when they have to be instructed to take an interest in sex. What's really interesting, however, is the assertion that talking is the key to the thing. "Brits do it verbally." It's downright kinky.

❧ Here's a site on the Internet inviting folks to join an "Ecumenical Dialogue on Women's Ordination," sponsored by one Luis T. Gutierrez. The invitation cautions that the discussion must be conducted "in a spirit of Christian charity." "No flaming is allowed from either side of the issue." Then this: "IMHO [in my humble opinion], the male-only priesthood is *not* of divine will. However, our goal is to seek the truth in charity, with proper respect toward those who are in apostolic succession, and following the model of community discernment given to us in Acts 15. May God's will be done." Acts 15 on the Internet is an intriguing idea. In that chapter

Peter and James speak the mind of the Church, and we read, "Then it seemed good to the apostles and the elders, with the whole church," to support the ministry of Paul to the gentiles. The apostolic letter in the same chapter puts it yet more strongly, "For it has seemed good to the Holy Spirit and to us . . ." One imagines the conclusion of the proposed dialogue on women's ordination, assuming such dialogues can ever conclude: "It seems good to 241 people accessing our website that women should be ordained, while 183 say the Church is not authorized to ordain women. Since there is no recorded hit by the Holy Spirit, the motion is carried that women should be ordained." Mr. Gutierrez says, "IMHO, the male-only priesthood is *not* of divine will." At least for a Catholic, such an opinion is hardly so humble. The opinion flatly holds that the Pope is wrong, as is the Congregation for the Doctrine of the Faith, which, with the express authorization of the Pope, declares that the Church's teaching on this matter is infallible. One may say one has difficulty understanding that teaching, or that one thinks the teaching has not been adequately explained, or even that one hopes that in the future there will be some presently unforeseeable development of the teaching that will, in a manner consistent with the teaching, allow what is now disallowed. The last hypothetical is a reach, to be sure, but arguably within the range of assent to the Church's authoritative teaching. What is neither honest nor constructive, at least for faithful Catholics, is to claim to be seeking God's will while rejecting the Church's authoritative discernment of God's will. It does not help at all to describe that rejection as a humble opinion.

 Conversations with God, books one and two, has turned into a publishing sensation, with spin-offs of tapes, videos, and a veritable industry of promotion. Neale Donald Walsch's nom de mike as a talk-show host was Bob White until God decided to take him into His confidence. God typically wakes him up at 4:20 a.m. and Walsch grabs his yellow legal pad and furiously writes down the words from on high. This is revelation-lite. In response to the age-old problem of theodicy, for instance, God is most reassuring: "In truth, there is nothing evil." "I do not love 'good' more than I love 'bad.'" In addition, God tells us to "stop making value judgments." Asked why he was chosen to receive these messages, Walsch responded: "I think it's just a few who allow themselves to feel worthy of being chosen and therefore experience the fact that they've been chosen. I was inspired to write these things, and now over a million people have said by their purchasing and their thunderous response to these books that they have found value in that material. So I'm deeply grateful and, I have to say, very humbled." When P. T. Barnum estimated one per minute, the American population was much smaller.

Sin and Risk Aversion

Dorothy Rabinowitz of the *Wall Street Journal* has done a great service in recent years by exposing the hysteria that seizes whole communities when someone accuses a teacher or nursery school of sexual abuse. Here and there all over the country, like witch hunts of old, the madness suddenly breaks out and hundreds of people are harassed, arrested, and sometimes jailed for years on the flimsiest of evidence. It is frightening, and, of course, many lives have been ruined. Naturally, there are lawyers and experts, usually psychologists of one sort of another, who make a living out of all this.

From the peanut gallery: Well yes, but what about the abused kids whose lives are ruined? A good question. We dare not belittle the seriousness of the sexual abuse of children. At the same time, sexual abuse is subject to wildly different definitions, and there is something terribly wrong when parents and other adults are afraid of the legal repercussions in the most innocent gestures of affection.

So why do I mention this? (Warning: Now it gets controversial.) In recent months I have received or been shown letters from a number of clergy, Protestant and Catholic, who are in jail for sexually abusing minors, male and female. Not surprisingly, some claim they were railroaded, and the studies of Rabinowitz and others make that all too believable. Guilt or innocence aside, however, there is another and profoundly disturbing factor here. A common lament of these clergy is that their bishops and fellow clergy have completely cut them off. One priest says he has not heard from or been visited by a priest for three years. "Risk aversion," another says, is the order of the day, as bishops follow the advice of lawyers who tell them to keep their distance. Are these letters self-serving? Probably so. But one bishop tells me they ring true to him, although he maintains close contact with the one priest in his diocese who has been charged with abuse. A Methodist supervisor says, "I don't care what he's done, he's one of ours."

Catholics in particular should understand that a priest is still a priest, as in "You are a priest forever in the order of Melchizidek." Nowhere does the Bible say we should visit those in prison, unless they're in for child abuse. I was discussing this with an acquaintance and mentioned the words of Jesus, "When I was in prison you visited me." To which he immediately responded, "But Jesus would never be in prison for something like that!" So he would be in prison for insider trading?

The Diocese of Dallas has been hit with a huge $120 million judgment for its negligence over a period of years in letting a Father Kos get away with interfering with young boys. It appears the responsibility rests chiefly with the predecessor to the current bishop, but that in no way lets the diocese off the hook. In order to distance the diocese from the sleazy business, it has announced that it is appealing to

Rome to nullify the priest's ordination on the grounds that he, in order to be ordained, lied to the diocese about his sexual proclivities. Some may think that good public relations, but critics point out that the diocese is responsible for priestly formation and screening candidates for ordination. In addition, it is noted that the last time Rome nullified an ordination was forty-seven years ago.

An official of the diocese says the purpose of the appeal is to make emphatically clear that Fr. Kos is "isolated from the Catholic Church." There is something disturbingly un-Catholic about such an expression. I have no idea whether this Fr. Kos is repentant or not, but even if he isn't, isolating someone from the Church is not my understanding of the Catholic way. Many years ago, G. K. Chesterton responded to an anti-Catholic critic who charged the Church with tolerating a vast horde of criminals, prostitutes, and other unsavory types who hang on to its fringes. That is a fact, said Chesterton. "They cannot get the Church's sacraments or solid assurances, except by changing their whole way of life; but they do actually love the Faith that they cannot live by. If you explain it by supposing that the Church, though bound to refuse them absolution where there is not amendment, keeps in touch with them and treats their human dignity rather more sympathetically than does the world, Puritan or pagan, that also probably refers to a real fact. It is one of the facts that convince me most strongly that Catholicism is what it claims to be. After two thousand years of compromises and concordats, with every sort of social system, the Catholic Church has never yet become quite respectable. He still eats and drinks with publicans and sinners."

Whether sinners are on the fringes or presiding at the altar, the Church is still the Church. A priest's betrayal of his office is a terrible thing, and crimes must be punished. More terrible to contemplate, however, is a Church that, for reasons of institutional risk aversion, isolates sinners from the redeeming love of God in Christ, which is the only reason for the Church's existence in the first place.

❧ I don't often have occasion to comment on the *Tuscaloosa News*, even though it is owned by the *New York Times*. In fact, I don't think I've ever commented on the *Tuscaloosa News*. But here's an editorial railing against that Judge Roy Moore of Etowah County, Alabama, who displays the Ten Commandments in his courtroom. The editorial deplores his "rabid supporters" and cheers fifty-two Alabama clergy who, it says here, condemn the "style of Christianity [that] weighs too heavily in favor of a single religious mindset." "Rabid" seems something less than civil, and one has to wonder about styles of Christianity that do not come down strongly on the side of Christianity. We are told that the fifty-two clergy are from "well established religious backgrounds: Baptist, Presbyterian, Episcopalian, Jewish, Hindu, and others." I confess to being curious about the "others" that come after Hindu on the list of religions well established in Alabama.

❧ Martin E. Marty of the University of Chicago cites Max Scheler's observation that the apostate is one "who is engaged in a continuous chain of acts of revenge against his own spiritual past." Marty offers as examples Thomas Cranmer, Malcolm Muggeridge, and Methodist theologian Thomas Oden. Cranmer persecuted those who held the views he would later embrace; after a long life of lechery, Muggeridge was converted to the faith and spent his remaining years excoriating lechers; Oden is sharply critical of the theological liberalism he once espoused. Marty comments: "Cranmer turned often, Muggeridge cannot turn again, and Oden is likely to stay put this time — while the rest of us try to unlearn what they taught us so eloquently before their various turns." I doubt that Marty was ever taught by Oden and, while he has been around for a long time, he surely did not sit at the feet of Cranmer. As for learning lechery from Muggeridge, I don't believe it for a moment.

❧ The godfather of liberation theology is generally considered to be Gustavo Gutierrez of Peru. While his work of thirty years ago launched the movement, Gutierrez has a record of distancing himself from some of the movement's more bizarre excesses. He has tried to remain within the boundaries of Catholic theology, demonstrates great respect for popular piety, and adamantly resists the Europeans and North Americans who would make Latin America over in their own image. In sharpest contrast is the North American feminist theologian Rosemary Radford Ruether, who has for many years served as a cheerleader for whatever radicalisms are playing on the fringes of the left. Ms. Ruether recently visited Peru and says she was disappointed to learn that Gutierrez was not in good standing with her "womynist" networks. "Gutierrez has insisted that feminism is alien to the 'Latin American reality' and is a diversion from the primary concern of liberation theology for the poor," she writes. Then this obituary: "Gutierrez deserves our tribute as founder of a movement that has reconnected theology with social justice. It is sad to see him bowing to the stranglehold of a rightist church while those who are partly his heirs move on to broader theological reflections on the realities of their society." As always, Ruether is confident that "the future clearly belongs" to her favored radicalisms of gender, ecology, and "indigenous spirituality," even if indigenous folk like Gustavo Gutierrez must be left behind. If the Latin American reality doesn't want the future she has in mind for it, all the worse for the Latin American reality. Needless to say, Ms. Ruether is a passionate opponent of cultural imperialism.

❧ Be glad you don't live in Murphy, North Carolina. Wal-Mart has the only real record store there, and to get the really vile and filthy stuff you have to travel 50 to 150 miles to Gainesville or Atlanta in Georgia. This is in a big front-page above-the-fold story in our parish newspaper that bemoans the censorious tyranny by which big chains are squelching freedom of speech and artistic creativity. Thirteen-year-old Adam McLean complains of the albums he buys at Wal-Mart, "They blank out all the words they think are bad. I hate it. It doesn't sound the same." For instance, a Nirvana song title has been changed from "Rape Me" to "Waif Me." Surely this violates the constitutional right to be raped, and who knows what horrors may be involved in waifing. Wal-Mart and other guilty parties also routinely remove the word "nigger" from songs, thus denying young people the benefits of elevated racial consciousness. The Blockbuster chain does the same thing with movie videos, asking producers to edit out or change particularly scatological, pornographic, or violent scenes. Sometimes this is done without the permission of the movie's director. Chuck Warn of the Directors Guild of America complains, "But the movie goes out with his or her name on it. It can be very damaging to someone's career." One can imagine how crushing this must be to the aspiring purveyor of smut. One talent scout told the *Times* "on condition of anonymity" (you can see how oppressive the climate has become) that one band he knew had omitted a song with obscenities so that its album would not have to carry a parental advisory sticker. So there you have it: now even parents want a say in what their children listen to. An industry spokesman declares that musical groups are now "in the position of singing what's on your mind or selling your records. The music industry is now hostage to a group of retailers that don't care a whit about music or the music industry." Artistic purity encounters crass commercialism! The story concludes with Nina Crowley of an industry association saying that all this is "creating a chilling effect." "Some of these kids are wondering if they are going to have to change what they do if they want to make any money." Our confidence in the idealism of youth is such that we are sure that they, unlike Wal-Mart and Blockbuster, will rise above such base motives as making money. This great country would not be where it is today were it not for those who are prepared to pay the price for the defense of adolescent swinishness. It is a comfort to know that we can count on the *Times* to stand by the martyrs who brave the slings and arrows of outraged decency.

❧ "For some Christians the Bible is always authoritative. They are called fundamentalists. For others, however, Jesus Christ is authoritative." So the Rev. Michael Morse of the United Church of Christ writes in the *Washington Post*. He continues: "To treat the Bible literally leads to all kinds of serious distortions and cruelties. To treat Jesus seriously leads one to the inevitable conclusion that he believed in lifestyles filled with equality, mutuality, compassion, commitment, responsibility, a sense of partnership and love. There is plenty of room in those lifestyles for gay persons, even for gay marriages." Jesus was a real sweety.

❧ The headline of a Reuters story, "An Early Mass Celebrated by Mother Teresa." The story continues, "Mother Teresa, who returned home last week to continue recovering from heart surgery, led a Christmas Mass yesterday at her Calcutta mission." I hope nobody tells the Pope.

❧ Nobody has ever suggested that modesty is Norman Mailer's strong suit. He has now written an "autobiography" of Jesus, *The Gospel According to the Son*. Random House sends out an interview with Mailer in which he says he felt up to the challenge of speaking for Jesus because his own status as a celebrity has endowed him with "a *slight* understanding of what it's like to be half a man and half something else, something larger" (emphasis his). Mailer goes on: "'Obviously, a celebrity is a long, long, long, long way from the celestial,' he said, 'but nonetheless it does mean that you have two personalities you live with all the time. One is your simple self, so to speak, which is to some degree still like other people, and then there's the opposite one, the media entity, which gives you power that you usually don't know how to use well. So the parallel was stronger than I realized.'" According to Michiko Kakutani of the *New York Times*, in Mailer's account God the Father and Son "are fond of self-dramatization, and both tend to feel put upon by their public responsibilities. . . . In trying to describe Jesus and God as accessible novelistic characters, Mr. Mailer has turned them into familiar contemporary types: he has knocked them off their celestial thrones and turned them into what he knows best, celebrities." One gathers that the book conveys a *slight* understanding of what it's like to be half repulsed and half something else, like bored.

✵ "By their fruits ye shall know them" is subject to sundry interpretations. An interpretation of more than usual interest is offered by Episcopal bishop Walter C. Righter, who ordained actively gay Barry Stopfel and was subsequently tried for heresy and acquitted. According to the *Sunday News Journal* of Wilmington, Delaware, "Righter said Stopfel's ministry proves he merited ordination. 'He had a Christmas offering this year of $26,000. That's the highest offering of any church on the East Coast. What's that to be afraid of?'" Cash box and case closed.

Abraham Joshua Heschel

I first met Abraham Joshua Heschel in 1965, when he was fifty-eight and I a kid of twenty-nine. The occasion had to do with defending protestors against the Vietnam war, which led to the formation of Clergy and Laity Concerned About Vietnam (CALCAV). We hit it off in a big way, and ours became an intense intellectual and spiritual friendship until his death in December 1972. We both loved to argue, and mainly we argued about the connections and conflicts between the Jewish and Christian ways of being children of Abraham. I thought he was too enamored of what I viewed as an excessively easy pluralism. He thought I was too insistent in my Christian particularism. For hours beyond number we went back and forth, often in his book-crammed office high in the tower of Jewish Theological Seminary, he smoking his cannon-sized cigars and I puffing on my pipe until the air was so thick we had to open the window even in the dead of winter. (He quit the cigars after a minor heart attack a few years before he died.) Of course I learned much more than he did from these exchanges. Heschel was a very learned man, and a great soul.

His books are still in print (e.g., *The Earth Is the Lord's, The Sabbath, Man Is Not Alone, God in Search of Man*) and I warmly recommend them. Since his death twenty-six years ago, something of a Heschel cult has sprung up. In fact, it had already sprung during his lifetime. On the twenty-fifth anniversary of his death, the first volume of the biography by Edward Kaplan and Samuel Dresner appeared, *Abraham Joshua Heschel: Prophetic Witness* (Yale University Press). It has been admirably and admiringly reviewed by Rabbi David Novak, one of Heschel's star students, in these pages (October 1998). It is also reviewed in *Commentary* by Jon Levenson of Harvard, a frequent contributor to this journal, under the title "The Contradictions of A. J. Heschel." While Levenson, too, admires Heschel, he has some big problems.

Heschel came from a dynasty of hasidic rabbis in Poland, took his doctorate at the University of Berlin, succeeded Martin Buber as head of the *Lehrhaus* in Frankfurt, and, after escaping Nazism to America, became the most read and most influential Jewish theologian of his time. He was a devoutly observant Jew who believed there are many ways to the truth. Kaplan and Dresner say it is a wonder that he was able to "reconcile" the different worlds of which he was part. Levenson is not sure that he did. "The question of the authority of *halakhah*, traditional rabbinic law in all its specificity, is the most obvious point of division between the traditionalist world of Heschel's origins and Jewish secular modernity. But it is, or should be, a no less troubling point of division between the world he grew up in, and whose basic religious dictates he continued to follow, and the world of religious but non-Orthodox Judaism in which he spent his entire professional life both in Germany and later in the United States." Levenson's conclusion is that "it was not out of the reconciliation but out of the *collision* of the several worlds in which he traveled that his most profound reflections on Jewish theology and spirituality were born."

It is for others to figure out the "contradictions" in Heschel's way of being Jewish. I am interested here in another question about Heschel's thought that Levenson raises, a question that was at the heart of our friendly but intense disagreement. He notes that at the University of Berlin Heschel immersed himself in the emerging fields of aesthetics, phenomenology, and psychology (a combination in which another Polish thinker of the time was also deeply immersed — Karol Wojtyla, later to be Pope John Paul II). From this he developed his crucial understanding that God is always the *Subject* and man the *object* of divine action; the initiative is always with God. In Heschel's case this was combined with the dominant liberal Protestantism of Berlin that pitted the prophetic against the priestly, and the authentically spiritual against the religiously institutionalized. As Levenson observes, this "very dubious dichotomy . . . was a staple of Protestant biblical studies and was, moreover, often linked to anti-Jewish (and anti-Catholic) polemics."

Truth in Tradition

I think Levenson is on to something here. I want to say this very carefully, but I did at times discern a liberal Protestant streak in Heschel's thinking. In connection with my insistence on the particularity of Jesus as the Christ, he thought I should be more accommodating, like our mutual friends at Union Theological Seminary (across the street from Jewish Theological). Union was and is a bastion of liberal Protestantism. I will leave it to Levenson and others to worry about whether there was a contradiction between Heschel's leanings toward liberal universalism and his being an observant Jew. But from a Christian perspective, Heschel's uneasiness with my particularism reflected a suspicion of the incarnational.

His passionate fear, shared by liberal Protestantism, is that religiosity should somehow try to take God captive. It is a legitimate fear but, when unrestrained, leads to other equally grave distortions. There is a lovely phrase in Christian theology: *Finitum capax infiniti* — the finite is able to hold the infinite. Heschel said he believed that, but I am not sure how he did. It is precisely on the possibility of the incarnational that another Jewish theologian, Michael Wyschogrod, has made such valuable contributions. (See my discussion of Wyschogrod in FT, January 1997). Among all the reasons that I am sorry Heschel died so early is that we never got a chance to discuss Wyschogrod in this connection. Not to mention related contributions by David Novak and others. Serious theological engagement between Christians and Jews has, thank God, greatly advanced in these twenty-five years.

Make no mistake, however. Heschel had a great appreciation of the embodiment of truth in tradition. He was fond of telling the story of a woman who approached him in the synagogue, complaining that the service did not say what she wanted to say. "Madam," he responded, "you have it precisely backwards. The idea is not for the service to say what you want to say but for you to want to say what the service says." As many long-suffering congregations know, I am fond of using that in homilies.

Heschel was a great soul in a time of spiritual cripples. He looked like a prophet. It was not only little children who said that he looked like what you think God may look like. He was something of a showman, and he knew it. He knew so much, he understood so much, and he wrote like an angel. I count it among the very great gifts of my life that he was my friend.

❧ According to the *Guardian* of London, the Holy See was playing a nefarious role at the Cairo+5 conference of the

United Nations by opposing, among other things, access to abortion as a human right to be guaranteed in international law. In the story, Frances Kissling of Catholics for a Free Choice is quoted as saying that the Holy See's representatives are "working with countries such as Argentina and Guatemala, which support their views." Apparently working with the member states of the UN is against the rules. Not only that, but the Holy See is also "mobilizing conservative organizations within the U.S. which are not necessarily Catholic to lobby delegates." Lobbying delegates? That is going too far. Says Kissling, "They planed and bused in over a hundred young people — mainly from Utah, which is heavily conservative and Mormon." The Vatican is bankrolling the Church of Latter-Day Saints! The plot thickens. Clare Short, Britain's secretary for international development, shares Kissling's outrage at the insidious cooperation with Muslim states. "The Holy See is in an unholy alliance with reactionary forces deeply unholy, and I speak as a fully signed-up ethnic Catholic, as I learned to call myself in Bosnia," says Short. I didn't know you could sign up for that. Maybe there's a form, "Ethnicity: Catholic." Ms. Short adds, "There's this alliance trying to find governments which, for one reason or another, they can bully into adopting a position to obstruct this growing, informed international consensus." Possibly the Holy See is threatening them with a cut-off of IMF loans, or maybe a nuclear bomb. It is all wondrously silly, of course. Not only the *Guardian* but the *New York Times* and other media gave vent to their angry astonishment that anyone should challenge what they declare to be the consensus of the enlightened. It is also wondrously encouraging, and I trust that Archbishop Renato Martino, who represents the Holy See at the UN, is gratified by his press, which is an indicator of his effectiveness.

Bill Clinton and the American Character

This is the long-promised reflection on what "the Clinton affair" does or does not mean for the state of the republic. It is of course an interim reflection, since people will be trying to sort this out for many years to come. But for now at least some of the dust has settled and the main outline of the story is clear enough. I mean, of course, the story surrounding the White House intern, which, admittedly, keeps bumping into other stories. For the next little while we are stuck with a President who, beyond reasonable doubt, is guilty of perjury, tampering with witnesses, and obstruction of justice, and who probably is a rapist. That we are better off stuck with him rather than having removed him from office was, many thought, the clinching argument of Dale Bumpers, former Senator from Arkansas, during the Senate trial. "If you have difficulty because of an intense dislike of the President, and that's understandable, rise above it," Bumpers exhorted the Senators. "He is not the issue. He will be gone. You won't. So don't leave a precedent from which we may never recover and almost surely will regret. . . . After all, he's only got two years left." That the impeached President was not the issue in an impeachment trial was among the more curious assertions in this curious affair.

But it is true that the public contention was about more than Bill Clinton. For a year and a half we have been treated to seemingly endless discussion about what all this means for our constitutional order, our political culture, and, inevitably, "the American character." In this reflection, it is the last question that is of particular interest. This "journal of religion and public life" does not understand public life primarily in terms of politics as that term is ordinarily used. It should not be surprising, therefore, that in this space President Clinton has seldom been mentioned since his election in 1992. In fact, in more than seven years he has been mentioned about ten times, mainly in connection with his statements and actions relative to abortion. So we have hardly been obsessed with the man.

This is not to suggest, however, that I have not had definite views about him. Permit me to begin with a personal word about how I understand his sinking of our political culture in apparently bottomless mendacity. When he started running for President he was known as a "New Democrat" — meaning a liberal mildly mugged by reality — and I was inclined to see him as among the less bad of a bad lot of Democrats. Until I came across an old video of the program, I had quite forgotten that at the beginning of January 1993, I had done an extended one-on-one interview with Robert MacNeil of what was then the *MacNeil/Lehrer NewsHour* about the impending Clinton presidency. Asked by Mr. MacNeil what I expected, I answered: "I think what I expect, and maybe what I wish as well, is that he will continue on a trajectory [of] trying to move the Democratic Party into, if not the center, at least into conversational distance with most Americans. I think he has taken the lessons of the 1972 McGovern debacle very much to heart and he could have a real opportunity, especially when he speaks of a new covenant with America, to engage in a new kind of political discourse."

Few may remember now, but a "new covenant" with the American people was a major theme of the Clinton campaign of 1992. Because he received only 43 percent of the vote, I noted, "he knows he has to reach out in trying to rebuild trust in a deeply confused and conflicted society." "That would be a very significant contribution. There is reason to believe he might do that. There is a lot of reason to believe he might not. We have to hope for the best now with Bill Clinton; we have to hope that what he did in order to secure the nomination, which is understandable, is not the last word. He had to really lock himself in tightly to pretty extreme interest groups on issues such as abortion, school choice, homosexual rights construed as civil rights. Now the question is, now that the party is his, can he move to make the American people, this deeply conflicted people, his constituency in something like a covenant, in something like a conversation that can elevate the politics of our time."

In that interview, I referred to our "culture war" — a term I had been using since the late 1970s — and said it was very sad that Clinton had made the economy the central issue of the campaign, and that George Bush had allowed him to do that. "That's not what Americans are most disturbed about today," I said. "They are disturbed about What kind of people are we? And what kind of people are we going to be?" Was I hopeful, MacNeil asked, that Clinton is prepared to lead in addressing these questions, to which I responded, "Of course. The alternative to hope is despair." MacNeil: "Do you think he is, then?" I said, "I want to hope he is. I hope he takes advantage of what now clearly is an opportunity that no Democrat has had since McGovern." After elaborating on that at some length, the interview concluded with my saying: "I think that, and this now is a dreadful scenario and it's the flip side of what I said earlier, if President Clinton were to move vigorously to get passage of the [pro-abortion] Freedom of Choice Act in Congress and if he then, as he at times said he would, put Justices on the Supreme Court for whom it would be necessary to pass the litmus test of *Roe v. Wade,* we would have a divide, a conflict of morality in our public life, much more intense than anything we have seen since the nineteenth-century conflict over slavery. It's a frightening prospect."

I tried, then, to put the best construction on Clinton's election, but I'm afraid that did not last long. As I said, I had quite forgotten about the MacNeil/Lehrer broadcast, which is not surprising, since a few days later, on January 10, 1993, I was hit with an emergency cancer operation which I barely survived. Some days later, after I had been removed from the intensive care unit, I was lying in the hospital bed, plugged with tubes and surrounded by friends. We were watching a Clinton news conference following his inauguration, at which he announced that he was rescinding the Reagan-Bush executive orders that placed pitifully modest restrictions on government support for abortion, and said the military should be open to gays. In words that have been frequently quoted back to me since then, I painfully raised my head from the pillow and announced — in what I am told was an oracular tone — "Mark my words. We are watching a man stumbling through the rubble of a ruined presidency." I have never had a moment's doubt about the accuracy of that pronouncement. Nobody could know all the ways he would stumble, nor how sordid the rubble would be, but whatever promise this presidency held was ruined from the beginning.

Keeping His Word

The Clinton news conference was on the anniversary of the *Roe v. Wade* decision, the very day that tens of thousands were marching in the streets of Washington to give life a chance. There was nothing in Clinton's words about his famous propensity for feeling their pain, nor even the slightest gesture of ambivalence about the slaughter of the innocents. Completely absent was any reference to a "new covenant," or reaching out to create a "national conversation" about who we are and intend to be. For Clinton, it seemed, the thousands of marchers, and the majority of Americans who are morally troubled by abortion, did not exist. Those who believe the defense of the innocent is the great moral cause of our time were undeserving of even passing acknowledgment. In tones of unctuous self-righteousness, Clinton declared himself the champion of the presumably self-evident justice of a "woman's right to choose." It is the only promise that he was to keep.

The gays did not get what they wanted with the military, and on other major issues — for example, welfare reform, crime, and free trade — Clinton would prove himself to be what liberals call a "moderate" Republican. As for foreign policy, there, too, he is stumbling through ever deeper rubble. His only ambitious and unabashedly liberal proposal, the effort to socialize medicine led by his wife, went down in flames before it even came to a vote. Although pundits persist in calling him a successful politician, there have been few successes apart from presiding over the enactment of Republican policies. Only on abortion has he kept his word. Also in foreign policy, the one consistent element has been the effort to establish abortion as an internationally mandated human right. In the history books he will be most accurately described as The Abortion President.

Not all readers will agree, and I do not wish to overplay it, but I believe that abortion is the lie of which all his other lies are the excretion. It is said that, if one can lie about this, one can lie about anything. To be sure, many people are less than honest about abortion, but the discussion then turns to what ought to be done about it. Honest people can disagree about that. Honest people cannot deny what is done in abortion. With Bill Clinton, that adamantine denial leaves no room for the slightest suggestion that there might be legitimate cause for moral uneasiness. What is so striking is that this is the one uncompromised and uncompromisable position of his presidency. Never once in all these years has this famously lip-biting practitioner of welling empathy publicly acknowledged even a twitch of uncertainty about the unlimited abortion license imposed by *Roe v. Wade*. The dogmatic assertion of a right to kill the helpless and innocent is a lie so wild that it cannot be — to use the Clinton term of art — compartmentalized.

Of course there have been many other lies. His friends and political allies have said that he is a remarkably good liar. Obviously, that is not true. A good liar does not have a reputation for being a good liar. The other lies, big and little, have been self-serving and opportunistic, as is also the abortion lie. Maybe, as many who have known him claim, he was a liar from the start. His perception of reality, they say, has always been subservient to ambition and desire. In some perverse way, Clinton may, at least most of the time, believe what he says. After meeting with Clinton early in the presidency, my colleague James Nuechterlein described him as "serially sincere." Clinton seems to be persuaded, it is observed, that he really means whatever he is saying at the time. I don't know if that is right. Did he believe what he was saying when, in January of last year, he told the American people he had never had any kind of sexual relationship with Miss Lewinsky? If so, we are dealing here not with an extraordinary capacity for compartmentalization but with a species of autism — an absorption in self-centered subjectivity securely insulated from reality. The external referents by which truth and falsehood are determined are made irrelevant by virtue of what appears to be a self-blinding that has brought about the spectacle now evident to all, that of a man stumbling through the rubble of a ruined presidency.

The President We Deserve?

But what does this tell us about "the character of the American people"? After all, they elected him, and did so twice. Not by a majority, to be sure, but by enough to secure his claim to the office, and securing that seems to be his main goal and achievement. The failure of the political process to remove him from office has been turned by some into an indictment of the character of the American people. The people, we are told, got the President that they deserve. In 1976 Jimmy Carter campaigned by promising America a government as good as its people. Now it is said that America has a government, or at least a President, as bad as its people. That, I believe, is a conclusion not to be lightly accepted.

Shortly after the Lewinsky scandal broke, I wrote in this space: "If, as almost all informed parties seem to believe, Mr. Clinton has during his term of office had sex with one or more women other than his wife, and if he has directly looked the American people in the eye and lied through his teeth in denying it, and if the American people know this and still allow him to continue in office, I promise critics who say I have an excessively hopeful view of the American character that I will engage in an agonizing reappraisal of my position." Obviously, I have some explaining to do, and it will take some little doing. I trust it will not be excessively agonizing for the reader.

A most doleful conclusion about the American character was announced by Paul Weyrich, President of the Free Congress Foundation, on February 16, 1999, and has been the subject of widespread commentary. Weyrich is an old war-horse of conservative causes and in the late seventies he was the one who suggested to Jerry Falwell the name "moral majority." Now he has concluded that it was all a dreadful mistake. "What Americans would have found absolutely intolerable only a few years ago, a majority now not only tolerates but celebrates." Until now, he says, "we have assumed that a majority of Americans basically agrees with our point of view." "I no longer believe that there is a moral majority. I do not believe that a majority of Americans actually shares our values." The United States "is very close to becoming a state totally dominated by an alien ideology, an ideology bitterly hostile to Western culture." We must now face the fact, he says, "that politics itself has failed." Conservatives must now "secede" and form "some sort of quarantine" from the general culture. Paraphrasing the sixties slogan, "turn on, tune in, drop out," Weyrich urges conservatives to turn off, tune out, and drop out — in the hope that they can "find places, even if it is where we physically are right now, where we can live godly, righteous, and sober lives."

It is hard to know how to take Weyrich's statement. Within weeks he was back at his old political stand, touting Republican presidential candidates, just as though politics had not failed after all. But he says he is deadly serious about his announcement of the end of politics. If so, it is depressing that he labored for more than thirty years under the deadly delusion of there being a moral majority that already agreed with his positions and was only awaiting the opportunity to give that agreement effective political expression. That was not the case and is not the case, and is probably never going to be the case. Most people most of the time are thoroughly indifferent to politics, which is probably just as well. For most who do pay attention, politics is mainly entertainment, much like following baseball. The public contention for moral truth is always a minority vocation; it is a task to be pursued, in St. Paul's words to Timothy, "in season and out of season." To say that politics has failed is to say that the American experiment has definitively failed. There have been and are today societies in which politics — free deliberation and decision about how to order public life — is precluded. It is the better part of wisdom to know that, in whatever form, it could happen here and may be happening here — as, for instance, in the judicial usurpation of politics. But the claim that it has happened here, that politics has failed, is an apocalyptic excitement to be kept on a tight leash.

There are other religious and political conservatives saying, in effect, that for thirty years they tried to wake up America and have now concluded that it can't be done. This is the message of columnist Cal Thomas and Michigan pastor Ed Dobson in their book *Blinded by Might*. In fact, Dobson, after a stint with Falwell's Moral Majority, invoked a pox on politics many years ago, and it is hard to know how seriously to take Thomas on this score. He, too, is back to his old political stand in his syndicated column that runs neck and neck with George Will's in being the most published in the country. But after the failed impeachment effort, the Weyrich-Thomas-Dobson line seems to be gaining ground. To the extent that they are issuing a caution against the dangers of politicizing religion and are underscoring the limits of what can be achieved through politics, their statements should be welcomed. But it is more than that. It expresses a painful deflation of political expectations that can only be explained by a prior and thoroughly unwarranted inflation. In addition, it purports to know much too much about the character of the American people.

Enter the Neo-Puritans

Last October Andrew Sullivan set the party line for one liberal reading of what has happened to conservatism. In a *New York Times Magazine* article, "Going Down Screaming," he depicted conservatives as embracing a neo-Puritanism that increasingly rails against a decadent culture. This journal, he said, is "the spiritual nerve center" of a new conservatism of "moral righteousness" (he meant self-righteousness, of course) that sounds increasingly like a twisted replay of the radicalism of the sixties. Alan Wolfe is a sociologist at Boston University who directed interviews of two hundred suburbanites and concluded in *One Nation, After All* that America is a country of more or less happy liberals. He, too, has had fun with the Weyrich-Thomas-Dobson claims, noting the similarity with sixties radicalism, and suggesting that we may be witnessing the breakup of the alliance between economic conservatives and the "moral regulators" in the Republican party. Both kinds of conservatives, he says, subscribed to a "new class theory" which claimed that sundry elites were radically at odds with the values of most Americans. The Clinton affair, he says, gave the majority a chance to take a stand against the "relativism" of the elites. "But the opposite happened. As the President's popularity held steady and even grew, conservative moralists decided that the problem was not Bill Clinton but the large majority of Americans who wanted him to remain in office. Faced with its first test, the new class theory failed."

New class theory was and is a good deal more sophisticated than Alan Wolfe suggests, but that is another argument. I cite him only to illustrate the uses to which some liberals are putting what they take to be conservative despair of the American character. Columnist William Safire is a conservative of a strongly libertarian bent, and he reaches similar conclusions. He is puzzled that so many are so fanatically loyal to a rascal like Clinton. (Forget that George Stephanopoulos, Dee Dee Myers, and a host of other associates do not seem to be terribly loyal. The White House calls them the "commentraitors.") On the basis of his admittedly unscientific reading of responses he has received, Safire suggests that, if people feel they have to choose between Clinton and the neo-Puritans, they'll take Clinton. "There we have a snapshot of . . . this President's remarkably solid support. The loyalists' Clinton: not a reckless predator of women but a victim of an elitist-moralist plot; not a breaker of solemn oaths but a breaker of moral chains; not a cornered con man but a hero to all who feel hunted. Is this the new, much different, Silent Majority?"

Among conservatives, Paul Gigot of the *Wall Street Journal* offers a vigorous riposte to the claim that the failure to remove Clinton is an indictment of the American people. "Those who know Paul Weyrich," he says, "understand that he will focus on the hole in any donut. But now he sees a hole and calls it an abyss." Gigot recounts the conservative successes of the past twenty years, from winning the Cold War to welfare reform to the ascendancy of school choice. He cites data suggesting that only 40 percent thought Clinton's offenses did not deserve impeachment, but more were worried about the disruptive effect of removing him from office, many of whom found the prospect of Al Gore as President "scary." "This narrow definition of political self-interest," says Gigot, "may be regrettable, but it isn't irrational or morally corrupt." I note in passing that editor James Nuechterlein and the former editor of *Commentary,* Norman Podhoretz, both indubitably conservative, also opposed removing Clinton from office because it would be too disruptive and polarizing. But this is a Catch-22 situation. If sixty-seven or more Senators had voted to remove him, the action obviously would not have been dangerously polarizing. The prospect of removal was so polarizing only because Democrats (including some who publicly said he was guilty as charged) marched in partisan lockstep toward a predetermined acquittal.

To return to Paul Gigot's analysis: "Voters weren't saying

they share Mr. Clinton's morals. They were saying this President isn't much worse than most politicians, all of whom they mistrust. Throw in the public's ambivalence toward sexual harassment charges, and Mr. Clinton's survival seems preordained. The miracle is that he got himself impeached." Of the readiness of Weyrich and others to throw in the towel, Gigot says, "This tendency always exists on the religious right, which cares more about salvation in the next world than in this one. They tuned out at least once earlier this century, after the Scopes trial." One rather hopes that they care more about salvation in the next world, and one notes that Weyrich, although his constituency is largely evangelical Protestant, is an Eastern Rite Catholic. But Gigot's point stands. There is in fundamentalist-evangelical Christianity, as among some Catholic traditionalists, an apocalyptic temper conducive to hyperbolic renderings of both successes and defeats. It is a very unconservative conservatism.

"Conservatives," Gigot concludes, "used to understand that all political change is slow, that in fact it ought to be slow, and that the task of political persuasion is never done. Russell Kirk, who forgot more about American culture than Mr. Weyrich remembers, liked to say that 'There are no lost causes because there are no gained causes.' Conservatives can't save America by becoming anti-American." (Actually, it is Kirk quoting T. S. Eliot, but that point, too, stands.) Similar arguments are made within the worlds of evangelical Protestantism. Charles Colson, for instance, writing in the mainline evangelical publication, *Christianity Today:* "On all sides I hear battle-weary evangelicals talk about abandoning cultural engagement and tending our own backyard instead. I can't imagine anything more self-defeating, or more ill-timed, for two reasons. First, it is unbiblical. Scripture calls us to bring Christ's redemption to all of life; despair is a sin. Second, to leave the cultural battlefield now would be to desert the cause just when we are on the verge of making a historic breakthrough. I believe John Paul II is exactly right in predicting that the year 2000 will usher in 'a great spring-time for Christianity.'"

Colson cites a number of evidences that "the tide is turning in the culture war" — including declining rates of divorce, abortion, births to unwed teens, people on welfare, and crime. As to ideas, it is clear that the false gods have failed. "The only remaining 'ism' is postmodernism, which is not an ideology but . . . the admission that every attempt to construct a comprehensive, utopian worldview has failed. It is a formalized expression of despair." Knowing his evangelical audience, Colson's conclusion is not untouched by the above-mentioned hyperbole: "The dawn of the new millennium is a time for Christians to celebrate, to blow trumpets and fly the flag high. To desert the field of battle now would be historical blindness, betraying our heritage just when we have the greatest opportunity of the century. This is the time to make a compelling case that Christianity offers the only rational and realistic hope for both personal redemption and social renewal." No dropping out there.

An Obituary for Outrage

Among conservative intellectual heavyweights, few carry more weight than William J. Bennett. Seven months into the Monica Lewinsky phase of the continuing chronicles of the Clinton scandal, he published *The Death of Outrage: Bill Clinton and the Assault on American Ideals.* The book is an exemplary instance of the venerable genre of the jeremiad, made more effective by his fair-minded statement of opposing arguments. Bennett's conclusions, however, offer naught for our comfort. "What explains this seeming public indifference toward, and even acceptance of, the President's scandals? The explanations most often put forth include very good economic times; scandal fatigue; the fact that a tawdry sexual relationship makes people queasy; the President's hyperaggressive, relentless, and effective spin team; the inclination to withhold judgment until more facts are known or give the President the benefit of the doubt; the fact that there are few leaders in any realm (religious, business, and the academy among them) who have articulated the case against the President; and the fact that Republican leadership — the Loyal Opposition — has been quiescent and inconsistent in its comments about the Clinton scandal, apparently afraid of voter backlash. These are plausible explanations. And still. I cannot shake the thought that the widespread loss of outrage against this President's misconduct tells us something fundamentally important about our condition. Our commitment to long-standing ideals has been enervated. We desperately need to recover them, and soon. They are under assault."

Bennett wants to resist the thought, but he is inclined to believe that this is a moment of truth about who we are as a people. "When rocked with serious, credible allegations of grave misconduct and violations of law, the President retreated for as long as he could to a gilded bunker, obstinately and 'absolutely' unwilling to rebut troubling allegations made against him. And the history books may describe how a diffident public, when confronted with all the evidence of wrongdoing and all the squalor, simply shrugged its shoulders. And, finally, that William Jefferson Clinton really was the representative man of our time, when the overwhelming majority of Americans no longer believed that presidential character mattered, and that no man, not even a President, was accountable to the law."

Seven months later, after the impeachment and Senate acquittal, Bill Bennett publicly opined that he had been forced to the conclusion that his most doleful analysis had been vindicated, that he has for years been wrong about the American people, that maybe he was simply out of touch. In a *Wall Street Journal* article he reviews again the arguments offered to exculpate the American people, and he finds them wanting. "These wishful assertions do not square with reality," he says. Restating the articles of indictment against a nation that has lost its capacity for outrage, he writes, "These are unpleasant things to realize. But it is the way things are, and it is always better to accept reality than merely wish it away. . . . There is no escaping the fact that Bill Clinton's Year of Lies — told and retold, not believed but accepted — has been an ignoble moment for a great people." In his book, Bennett spoke frequently about "we" — meaning we Americans. But at one point in the book he slips: "We — and by 'we' I mean in the first instance the political class itself — need to reclaim some of the high purpose of politics." There, I believe, he slips into a truth that deserved more attention in his diagnosis. The political class, including political intellectuals inside the beltway, should not be confused with the American people. The political class — notably congressional Democrats who unanimously and shamelessly defended a President whom, one must assume, most of them knew to be guilty of removable offenses — is deserving of Bennett's outrage. Of course, such politicians calculated that the voters would let them get away with what they did. But that is a somewhat different question, to which I will return. It may also turn out to have been a grave political miscalculation.

The Media Made Us Do It

It is not only conservatives who say that this has been a moment of truth revealing some unpleasant facts about the kind of people we have become. Since liberals generally defended Clinton, at least by opposing impeachment and conviction, they, unlike Bennett, do not take that as an indication of moral turpitude. Many blame the year of horrors on the media. The media made us do it. That is the suggestion of Lewis Lapham, the editor of *Harper's,* for example. His wrap-up reflection is portentously titled "Exorcism," and he begins with the line from *Troilus and Cressida:* "Take but degree away, untune that string. And, hark, what discord follows!" The electronic media, says Lapham, have untuned the string of public reason. Citing Marshall McLuhan as his authority, Lapham asserts that the habits of mind derived from the electronic media have deconstructed the texts of civilization founded on the print media, which leads him to the thought that "maybe the argument at the root of the impeachment trial was epistemological, not moral." Well, that's a relief, assuming we can get our epistemology straight.

But, of course, Lapham is on to something about the electronic media, and he puts it nicely: "Sympathetic to a pagan rather than a Christian appreciation of the world, the camera sees but doesn't think; it cares only for the sensation of the moment, for any tide of emotion strong enough to draw a paying crowd. A plane crash in the mountains of Peru commands the same slack-jawed respect as Mick Jagger in a divorce court, Monica Lewinsky eating Belgian chocolate, cruise missiles falling on Baghdad." And there is more: "Because the camera doesn't know how to make distinctions — between treason and fellatio, between the moral and the amoral, between an important Senator and an important ape — its insouciance works against the operative principle of a democratic republic. Such a government requires of both its politicians and its citizens a high degree of literacy, also a sense of history, and, at least in the American context, an ethics derived from the syllabus of the Bible. None of those requirements carry any weight in the Kingdom of the Eternal Now governed by the rule of images. Bring narrative to Jay Leno, or hierarchy to Howard Stern, and you might as well be speaking Homeric Greek."

Lapham covers his political backside by describing the impeachment as an "attempt at political assassination dressed up in the rhetoric of high-minded conscience." Yet he seems to be not entirely without sympathy for the congressional Republicans who "objected to the society's order of value and wished to overturn it." But in the kingdom of the camera and celebrity, it is simply too late for that. Since they couldn't impeach the electronic culture, it is understandable that conservatives turned on Clinton. "Who better to bear the blame for everything else that has gone so badly wrong in the once happy land of Christian print?" Henry Hyde's concluding speech was "a prayer for the safe return of an imaginary American past, and when he finished, the nearly perfect silence in the Senate chamber again brought to mind the ritual stillness of a world out of time. For a long moment none of the Senators moved in their chairs, and in the press gallery skepticism was temporarily in short supply. The evening news broadcasts cut the scene to what seemed like a very long twenty seconds." McLuhan was right. Get used to it.

Lapham's reading resonates with Neil Postman's amusing and depressing book on the electronic media, *Amusing Ourselves to Death*. Many commentators on the Clinton affair, on both the left and right, come back to the supposedly omnipotent media. Against that explanation, it is pointed out that the yellow and feverishly partisan papers of a century ago were hardly more conducive to calm deliberation. But the news came more slowly then, and the positions advocated, no matter how partisan, had a modicum of continuity. And surely there is a very big difference between reading and looking at the tube, a difference that I have no doubt does something devious to our minds. Yet the electronic media are not omnipotent, and we let ourselves off the hook by thinking otherwise. Were it up to the television networks — and almost all the prestige print media, for that matter — many things would have been very different in recent history; for instance, Reagan and Bush would never have been President, we would not have prevailed in the Cold War, and there would certainly be no pro-life movement.

In addition, the network audience is fast decreasing, and I am among those who believe that the Internet and the multiplication of cable channels, among other things, hold high promise also for public life. Those who fret about a fragmentation that precludes the possibility of a "national conversation" about great issues are usually those who thought they were in charge of national conversations. Apart from times of real crisis, such as a real war, the things that matter do not require a national conversation. To the extent there has been a national conversation about what to do with the miscreant in the White House, it has been pretty much controlled by the people who think they are in charge of national conversations. Had the conversation been more tightly controlled, things would have turned out more or less the way they did, except he would never have been impeached in the first place.

Who Is Responsible?

It is, I believe, dead wrong to reify (if I may borrow the Marxist term) "the media" as though it were a collective agent doing this or doing that. It compounds the wrong to identify the media with the culture. Of course, we fall into these errors because we want to talk about the culture and "the American people" but nobody can talk *with* the culture or *with* the American people. All of us have only ourselves and a handful of other people with whom we can talk, even if our friends are intellectuals who are forever talking about the culture and the American people. So people listen to the people whom people in the media have certified as experts on the culture and the American people. There is no doubt that in the last year there has been a further degrading of the media and what it excretes into the general culture. We did not before have prime-time discussions of fellatio, gropings, and semen-stained dresses. Referring to reports on what Clinton does in the office, a mother in my parish remarked, "I'm tired of my kids asking me about 'oval sex.'" Pornographer and (according to his daughter) child molester Larry Flynt, who pornographers complain has given pornography a bad name, appears on supposedly reputable talk shows to share his ponderings on the nation's changing mores. And it is surely no coincidence that in the same year

60 Minutes decides to broadcast a snuff film in which Dr. Kevorkian kills one of his "patients." That's not all. I am puzzled that there has not been more discussion of Bob Dole's commercials for Pfizer about how Viagra helps him cope with his erectile dysfunction. The poor fellow looks like he's restraining the impulse to unzip and show us the happy change. Longtime Senate majority leader, former presidential candidate. Does anyone remember the last time "statesman" was used with reference to a political leader? Dole's nervous claim that the subject of his "dysfunction" should not be embarrassing only increases the embarrassment.

Such things did not appear in the mainstream media before. They are a distinct contribution of the Clinton presidency. It is not the media, and certainly not the culture, that decided to define deviancy down. Individual people with names did that. Larry King and Peter Jennings invited Larry Flynt. Mike Wallace, a proponent of euthanasia, favored showing the snuff film, as did his producer, who calculated, correctly, that it would give the program a boost during ratings week. Bob Dole, and presumably his wife, decided to go public with his difficulty. A depressing thought is that, whether Clinton or Dole had won in 1996, the public might have been required to contemplate presidential private parts. Would Dole be publicizing his if Clinton had not publicized his? I don't know the answer to that. Perhaps there is a political purpose in the Dole commercials, aimed at demonstrating the relative innocence of Republican dysfunctions. In any event, while these vulgarities assault the public, they tell us little or nothing about the American character. They tell us a great deal about individuals in leadership sectors who have abandoned the canons of taste and decency, with Bill Clinton being the chief culprit. And of course they could, in time, have a significant effect on the American character as the country is dragged down to the level of its putative leadership.

On a certain afternoon twenty-plus years ago, somebody at *Penthouse* decided that the centerfold would exhibit the whole works. More recently on cable television, somebody decided that the f-word is now okay. This is known as the artistic creativity of challenging taboos. For decades Hollywood worried about popular backlash and used the Legion of Decency and the Hays Office to take the rap for prudery. But that was when the great majority of Americans went to movies at least once a month. Then a new movie was part of something like a national conversation; at least it seemed everybody was aware of it, just as they talked about Fibber McGee and Molly, or repeated the Jack Benny jokes from last night's show. That was a long time ago, when there were depressions, wars, and other crises concentrating the popular mind. Now there are peace (more or less), prosperity, two hundred cable channels, and the Internet, while less than 10 percent of the people go to movies regularly, and they are free to choose their elixir or their poison. Nothing is national, everything is niched. The office of the presidency, apart from the Super Bowl, is maybe the last popularly recognized "national thing." When Bill Clinton took the office of the presidency on MTV and answered questions about his underwear, that is something that Bill Clinton did. It was not done by the American people; it was done to them. Many Americans loved it. There have always been a lot of slobs. Clinton's innovation is in pandering to them. Earlier Presidents felt some obligation to maintain the dignity of a national office, even to exemplify national standards. Clinton has niched the national thing that was the presidency, and niched it very low.

As for what this tells us about the American character, remember the patient being given the Rorschach test and the psychiatrist tells him he has a dirty mind. "What do you mean?" he responds. "You're the one with the dirty pictures." In this case the patient is right. Michiko Kakutani on Andrew Morton's book, *Monica's Story:* "Its obsessive account of teenage shenanigans, its tiresome prattling about sex and self-esteem, its therapeutic jargon and Judith Krantz prose sadly sum up the sorry state of affairs our culture has reached," and so forth. As Tonto might have said to the Lone Ranger, "What do you mean *our* culture?" David Brooks of the *Weekly Standard,* to whose erratic analyses I will return, writes of Barbara Walters' interview of Monica: "The world we've been peering into is somehow beyond good and evil. It's a world of sentimentality, of makeovers, of people who tear up just before the commercial breaks, and then return with uplifting visions of a life with family by show's end." He cites the philosopher Vico, whom he says he does not understand, and who "maintained that each civilization gets the dramas it deserves." "The Greeks got terrifying and grand tragedies. We're more forgiving, more comfortable, and more bourgeois. And so we get, in the perils of Monica Lewinsky, a night of pretty engaging television, which we'll probably all have forgotten by next week." He's right about not understanding Vico, and wrong about this being the drama our civilization deserves. It is a subculture "we've been peering into." More accurately, people watch with fascinated disgust as an unstoppable toilet backs up into their living room.

There are those who know such things should not happen, and even plumbers who used to fix matters when they did. The *New York Times,* for instance, the old gray lady of public rectitude. But that was a long time ago. For some years now she has been telling us to get used to the backup — in the form of transgressive art, obscenity as free speech, gay sex, and, of course, the unlimited license to kill unborn children. But the Clinton eruption momentarily startled her into sobriety. She had some very severe things to say about his behavior. An editorial of September 12, 1998, declared that, until the Starr report, "no citizen — indeed, perhaps no member of his own family — could have grasped the completeness of President Clinton's mendacity or the magnitude of his recklessness." Clinton will be remembered "for the tawdriness of his tastes and conduct" and for producing "a crisis of surreal complexity." Then, most ominously, "A President without public respect or congressional support cannot last."

But, of course, the *Times* opposed impeachment, and when he was impeached, opposed conviction. How Clinton would be given a pass was signaled in the same editorial. "He and we must await not only the adjudication of Congress, but the even more potent process of public deliberation." Ah, yes, the venerable process of public deliberation, meaning the spin on tomorrow's news and the omnipotent polls. Why do people in the media so bridle when it is pointed out that 90 percent of them voted for Bill Clinton, and that it would be remarkable to the point of incredible if their political bias did not affect their reporting? The liberal commentariat, it is true, said harsh things about him. While there were other spins, such as a long *Newsday* story that told "a political parable" of Bill Clinton cast as Jesus persecuted by the Republican Pharisees, the media, more typically, took FDR's tack: "He may be an S.O.B., but he's our S.O.B."

The analogy with Shakespeare's Coriolanus is apt, except of course that he was a genuine hero. Like Coriolanus, Clinton contemptuously manipulated the hoi polloi: "I will practice the insinuating nod, and be off to them most counterfeitly; that is, sir, I will counterfeit the bewitchment of some popular man, and give it bountiful to the desirers" (Act II, iii). From 1992 on, the reporters were in on the game; they saw the wink and the nudge, and entertained one another with the feats of their man, "Slick Willy." Then, quite abruptly, in January 1998, they became the game. He was dealing with *them* most counterfeitly, and they were furious. Not furious enough, however, to abandon their S.O.B. Not all were prepared to go so far as Nina Burleigh of *Time* magazine. "I'd be happy," she said, "to give him [oral sex] just to thank him for keeping abortion legal." But most were prepared to circle the wagons against the attacking neo-Puritans, while letting Clinton know in no uncertain terms that they were not at all happy about his forcing them to defend the indefensible.

The battle metaphor is no exaggeration in describing the never to be underestimated hysteria of the left. Mrs. Clinton set the tone when, immediately after the Lewinsky scandal broke, she went on television to talk about a "vast right-wing conspiracy" that has long been out to get them. Ken Starr is a "politically motivated prosecutor who is allied with the right-wing opponents of my husband. . . . It's — it's not just one person, it's an entire operation. . . . I don't think there's any doubt that there are professional forces on the right at work for their own purposes and profit. There are just so many curious relationships among a lot of people, and various institutes and entities. And I think that that deserves thorough investigation. . . . There's just a lot going on behind the scenes and kind of under the radar screen that I think the American public has a right to know."

A vast conspiracy requiring thorough investigation. McCarthyism, anyone? But, unlike any public figure who might allege a vast left-wing conspiracy, she was not asked to name names, to put up or shut up. Bennett observes, "Mrs. Clinton's charges are either intentionally preposterous or unintentionally paranoid." Undoubtedly they were calculated, and, while I don't know how intentionality enters into it, paranoid is an apt term for a large number of people on the left who seem earnestly to believe that they are the last and desperate defense against Fascist jack boots and the midnight knock on the door. McCarthyism would get mentioned quite a bit in the subsequent months, but it was the "sexual McCarthyism" of the neo-Puritan Fascists. (Terminology tended to get awfully muddled in "the potent process of public deliberation.")

At impeachment time, artists and intellectuals rallied at New York University. The persecution of Clinton has "all the legitimacy of a coup d'état," said novelist E. L. Doctorow. Toni Morrison, Elie Wiesel, Arthur Miller, that most distinguished historian Arthur Schlesinger, and hundreds of others cheered. "Vietnam is almost the last moment I can think of until now when intellectuals, writers, and artists have really raised their voices in a chorus of protests," said novelist William Styron. Happy days are here again. "There's the smell of brimstone in the air," warned legal philosopher Ronald Dworkin, sending a frisson of terror through the crowd. Todd Gitlin, loyal archivist of radicalisms past (but not past enough), opined, "For years, the intellectual left has been deeply divided over identity politics. Here's an issue on which they can agree, and there's relief."

Harvard's Alan Dershowitz had his own distinctive contribution to the solemn process of public deliberation: "A vote against impeachment is not a vote for Bill Clinton. It is a vote against bigotry. It's a vote against fundamentalism. It's a vote against anti-environmentalism. It's a vote against the right-to-life movement. It's a vote against the radical right. This is truly the first battle in a great culture war. And if this President is impeached, it will be a great victory for the forces of evil — evil — genuine evil." Then there was actor Alec Baldwin on *Late Night with Conan O'Brien:* "I'm thinking to myself if we were in other countries, we would all right now go down to Washington and we would stone Henry Hyde to death! . . . And we would go to their homes [Congressmen who vote for impeachment] and we'd kill their wives and children. We would kill their families." The usual sources warning us against the horrors of "hate speech" were strangely silent.

Back at the NYU rally, feminist intellectual Blanche Wiesen Cook declared: "We are looking at theocrats. We have to mobilize like we mobilized against the war in Vietnam, like we mobilized against slavery. This is about race! This is about crack cocaine in the neighborhoods!" Right. By the time retired Episcopal bishop Paul Moore got his turn, one might have thought that all the apocalyptic imagery had been used up, but the bishop rose to the occasion: "I think of the millions and millions of people who will suffer and die because the Republicans want to get President Clinton for a personal sin." Writing in the *New Republic,* John B. Judis deplored the "extreme" language used by the proponents of impeachment who were "turning the factional struggle into a crusade." Conservatives, he observed, were like the Salem witchhunters and Joe McCarthy in their fanatical opposition to everything associated with the sixties and represented by Clinton — "feminism, free love, Unitarianism, bilingualism, drugs, abortion, and rock 'n' roll." Clinton's Unitarianism is a really big issue on the right.

But perhaps it was Elie Wiesel, the survivor of unspeakable horrors past and icon of moral gravity, who was most impressive. Told that Henry Hyde had argued that, when people abandon the rule of law, they invite tyranny, including terrors such as the Third Reich, Wiesel exploded: "My God, how dare he!" Clearly Mr. Hyde was infringing upon Mr. Wiesel's copyrighted piece of history. "What a comparison to make!" declared Wiesel. "Do you use the Holocaust to describe this affair?" Well, as it turns out, yes you do. It seems that people such as Mr. Hyde who insist upon the letter of the law are the real Nazis. "It *was* the law to put Jews in concentration camps, to kill them," Wiesel expostulated. And so continued "the potent process of public deliberation."

Empty from the Start

Moral bankruptcy is an overused term, but nothing better comes to mind to describe the circumstance of the left in its Faustian bargain with Bill Clinton. The rhetoric of moralistic excitements is there, but it is devoid of substance. From the beginning it was not only the feminists turning a blind eye to "bimbo eruptions." Remember the remarkable case of Rickey Ray Rector, a young black man in Arkansas who killed a policeman and then turned his gun on himself, blowing out part of his brain. In early 1992, then-Governor Clinton, in order to show that he was tough on crime, flew home from New Hampshire just in time to deny him a stay of execution. Rector, who functioned with the mind of a five-year-old, had to be lifted to his feet to walk to the death chamber.

With no trace of irony, Rickey Ray asked the guards to say hello to Gov. Clinton, whom he had just seen on television, and said they should save the piece of pecan pie which he planned to eat when he got back. A young black man. A mentally disabled young black man. All of this was well publicized at the time. The left, overwhelmingly and passionately opposed to capital punishment, was quiet. After all, what choice did they have? It was either Bill Clinton or the Fascists.

Terms such as preposterous and paranoid are appropriate. But the fact is that much of the left does believe that conservatives are but the cat's-paw of the Gestapo waiting in the wings. Many conservatives hate Bill Clinton. Liberals, generally speaking, hate conservatives. Dennis Prager puts it well: "Conservative hatred for President Clinton has often been ugly, and I for one have never taken part in it. But it was directed primarily against one man. Liberal hatred is directed toward millions of fellow Americans — non-liberals, especially religious ones. Indeed, it is almost impossible to debate important issues with many liberal spokesmen because opposing the liberal position opens a person to charges of evil: opposition to race- and sex-based affirmative action means one is racist and sexist; opposition to abortion renders one a misogynist; opposition to same-sex marriage means a person is homophobic; and on and on." "Where is the outrage?" asked Bob Dole in 1996. It was there. But it was outshouted by the outrage directed against those outraged by Bill Clinton. The loudest shouters with the biggest bullhorns belong to the left that has largely succeeded in its "long march through the institutions." The winners of Nobel and Pulitzer prizes rally at NYU, not in Colorado Springs, Colorado. They have nothing but contempt for the "process of public deliberation." How could you trust a public that includes millions upon millions, perhaps even a majority, of conservatives? They elected Reagan, didn't they? There's no telling what they would do next time, if given half a chance.

Some conservatives have remarked that the one good

thing to come out of all this is the total demolition of radical feminism. I would not bet on it. True, Gloria Steinem was not bothered by Clinton's groping of a distressed supporter in the Oval Office because, she explained, Clinton finally took No as an answer. This became known as Steinem's One Free Grope Rule. And true that Betty Friedan said that, even if Clinton did everything he's accused of doing, and more, "It's no big deal." The rape charge did shake some loyalists such as the *Washington Post*'s Richard Cohen: "Take the rape charge. It is that — get it? I feel I have to emphasize it: the President of the United States is accused of raping a woman back when he was attorney general of Arkansas. An account of this alleged rape ran on *Page 1* of the *Washington Post*. Get it? Page One! The *Washington Post!* Do you want to know what happened next? Nothing." He concludes, "The Clintons play by no rules. They have vanquished outrage." But what could outrage do, even if there were more and undeniably credible charges of this nature? He can't be impeached again, and statutes of limitation have a way of running out. Feminism's hypocrisy is exposed, but feminists' letting Clinton off the hook does not undo feminism's damage. Ideologically skewed sexual harassment laws are still harassing thousands of men in the courts and military tribunals. And maybe it is not fair to speak of feminist hypocrisy. They have not disguised the fact that, at the end of the day, their cause is about one uncompromisable, don't-give-an-inch thing: "reproductive rights." On that one thing Bill Clinton has kept his word. He is their S.O.B.

This You Will Not Believe

I will not go into detail about the dishonesty and confusion about the polls. Cohen reflects the conventional wisdom: "How can it be . . . that with every outrage, Clinton rises higher and higher in the polls? The rape charge ought to put him about where Roosevelt was for ending the Great Depression and beating the Axis powers." I don't believe it for a minute. Of those familiar with the rape accusation by Juanita Broaddrick, 62 percent said it is likely true and 20 percent said it is likely not true. By the end of February, 40 percent had a "generally favorable" view of Bill Clinton, the lowest number recorded to date. But even if that falls to 20 percent, what are those who hold him in understandable contempt supposed to do? Storm the White House and throw him out physically? In his public appearances he is carefully distanced from protesters by all the security that becomes the majesty of his august office. Anyway, as Dale Bumpers would undoubtedly say, it's only a matter of another year and a half. Plus, storming buildings and disrupting meetings is not what conservatives ordinarily do.

As to what "The American People" really think, read again Robert Jenson's article of that title in the April issue. The American people have been and, God willing, will be around for a long time. They are not instantiated in responses to a telephone poll that interrupted the watching of a basketball game, or by a question asked as they're leaving the mall. Yes, it is objected, but the polls are generally accurate about many things, such as predicting whom people will vote for. Good for the polls. What does that have to do with what people think about marital fidelity, adultery, lying under oath, rape, and the meaning of "high crimes and misdemeanors"? About some of these things people think very deeply in ways that cannot be caught by a polling question; about others they have not thought at all, which does not prevent them from having an "opinion" to be registered. Take your own poll. How many fathers (apart from Monica's) think it is okay for a fifty-year-old man to do that with their twenty-one-year-old daughter? How many wives would put up with their husbands doing it? Of course Clinton and his claque have defined deviancy down, but is there really any evidence that a substantial number of people have in their own lives bought into that definition? Among the more egregiously delinquent, there are no doubt some who are pleased to know that the President is no better than they are. Many others have come to expect less of this President, and maybe of politicians in general, which is not all bad.

It is not true that The American People "knew what they were getting" when they elected him in 1992 and again in 1996. Richard Cohen of the *Washington Post* again: "Here is a President who has been like no other. If I told you three years ago — even two years ago — that the President was having sex in the Oval Office with a young intern, you would not have believed me. In fact, I would not have believed it myself. The rumors, I thought, were the work of his worst enemies — crazies, mentally unstable." And so with sex-stained dresses, and keeping Yassir Arafat waiting or chatting with Congressmen on the phone while being serviced by Monica. And now rape. If he had reported such things, says Cohen, "You would have called me deranged, a perverted pundit. No one does that." Yet it all happened. "You can look any of this up. But you could not make any of this up." Cohen is being slightly disingenuous. He is paid to pay attention, and anyone who paid attention knows that Clinton lied about Gennifer Flowers back in 1992. It's on the tape. But that was followed by *60 Minutes* with Clinton's admission of troubles in the past; he and Hillary eyed each other lovingly and promised ever so earnestly that they would be worthy of the high office to which they aspired. It is not to the discredit of the minority of Americans who voted for him that they wanted to give him the benefit of the doubt. They turned out to be wrong, of course. They did not know what they were getting.

Pulpit Prophecy and Pandering

A question persistently asked through all of this, especially by Clinton opponents, was, "Where are the voices of religious leadership?" I was asked that again and again, and was a little puzzled about what people expected from religious leaders. I would quote my bishop, John Cardinal O'Connor, who said on several occasions that he really did not think there was much public suspense about where the Catholic Church stood on adultery and lying. But that never satisfied those who pressed the question. They apparently thought clergy should be leading the outcry against presidential perfidy, issuing jeremiads that rattled the rafters and brought the miscreant to book. There is no way of knowing for sure, but I expect that in most of the hundreds of thousands of local pulpits in America the subject of presidential misconduct was addressed more or less directly, and probably more than once. In many instances, no doubt, to illustrate the point that we are all sinners in need of forgiveness, in many others to underscore that we should not be "judgmental," and in yet others to emphasize the general decadence of the culture. Most clergy likely thought it was not their business to prescribe what ought to be done about the prodigal President; that was a job for the politicians. From many black pulpits and from the more overtly political pulpits of white liberals, of course, the President was vigorously defended against his alleged persecutors.

Shortly after the Lewinsky ignominy was exposed in January 1998, and before Clinton partisans were able to organize the spiking of the initial outrage, Peter Steinfels of the *Times* put the question this way: "When it comes to questions of morality and public life, sex and power, honesty and the law, friendship and trust, personal conduct and political responsibility, the right to know and the right to privacy, why do the views of historians, psychologists, political scientists, lawyers, lawyers, lawyers, and, of course, the news media's pundits so overshadow those of religious leaders?" Steinfels offered a number of possible explanations. For one thing, clergy understand themselves to be more in the business of forgiving than condemning, and are especially reluctant to condemn when all the facts aren't known and there is strong skepticism about the media that is reporting the facts.

"Clergy want to keep their distance from politically partisan preachers and super-righteous [he means self-righteous] radio hosts. It could be that the aggressiveness of the religious right has actually made it harder rather than easier for many religious leaders to address politically charged moral issues." Then, too, says Steinfels, clergy may have plenty to say but reporters and editors aren't asking them to say it. Or it may be that, despite the vitality of religion in the private lives of most Americans, "it has lost its institutional power as a social force."

An important factor in the relative absence of clerical expressions of outrage is that there was no real public dispute about the gross immorality of what Clinton had done. It was not necessary to call in moral experts to certify that his behavior was outrageous. Even many of his sycophants were outspoken in deploring his shamelessness, recklessness, infidelity, habitual mendacity, and related moral deficiencies. The question of what was to be done about it quickly became a political and legal question. Part of the political equation was to determine whether Clinton was appropriately contrite, at which point the clergy were invited in to certify the state of his soul.

Not all the sycophants, of course, were candid about the President's wrongdoing. The Rev. J. Philip Wogaman, a very liberal Democrat, professor of Christian ethics, and pastor of Foundry Methodist where the Clintons attend, wrote a little book, *From the Eye of the Storm* (Westminster). There it is suggested that Clinton is the victim of a Western history deeply conflicted about sexuality. Maybe our outrage should be directed not at Clinton but at, for instance, St. Augustine. "Augustine's own sexual history may also have contributed a discordant note to our culture today. He may have made it more difficult for subsequent generations to see the intrinsic goodness of sex when it is expressed in loving commitment," etc. Or perhaps the buck stops even higher up. With respect to sexual ethics, Wogaman asks, "Was Jesus placing an utterly impossible standard before us?" He answers, "Maybe so." But then, letting Jesus off the hook, he adds, "Somehow I do not think Jesus was so much asking us to struggle against feelings that are built into our human nature as he was reinforcing the message about hypocrisy. Do not be so quick to condemn people for doing what you have *wanted* to do!" Somehow I think the Rev. Wogaman has overlooked, among other distinctions, the difference between being tempted to sin and surrendering to temptation.

But "the deepest question of all," says Wogaman, is this: "Do we ultimately define ourselves as a community based on law, or is there a deeper sense in which we are a community of mutual caring?" If we are a nation defined by law, Wogaman allows, Clinton "must be removed either through forced resignation or impeachment." But "we are a society that should understand itself more deeply as a community of love than as a community of law." Not that law and love are "incompatible," but insisting upon obedience to the law is "the spirit of legalism [that] is at odds with community and love." One must sympathize with the theology students, as well as the congregants of Foundry, who are exposed to a steady diet of such sentimental drivel. And be grateful that the Constitution of laws given us by the Framers has not yet been replaced by liberalism's Constitution of Mutual Caring.

A religious voice heard regularly during the past year was that of the Rev. Joan Brown Campbell, general secretary of the National Council of Churches (NCC). That near-moribund institution was partially resuscitated in the nineties by its much publicized "access" to the Clinton White House, where most of its statements over these months might as well have been, if in fact they were not, drafted. The NCC's endless refrain was that the country should "move on" and let the President "get on with the job he was elected to do." Between that repeated refrain were imprecatory incantations against the horrible conservatives who were violating the Constitution of Mutual Caring.

After the defeat of the impeachment effort in the Senate, Ms. Campbell joined with others, including the ordinarily sensible Senator Sam Brownback of Kansas, the ever-anguished acquitter Senator Joseph Lieberman of Connecticut, as well as Archbishop Justin Rigali of St. Louis and Rabbi Yechiel Eckstein, who has his own interfaith organization, in discussing the merits of a national "Day of Reconciliation." Lamenting the divide between liberals and conservatives, Ms. Campbell said, "It's hard for us to be the ambassadors of reconciliation if we're locked into these camps." After her camp had, with exquisite mutual caring, trashed the other camp, she invites the vanquished to come on over. Reconciliation means promising not to gloat, or at least not very much.

Another old reliable was Father Robert Drinan of Georgetown Law School. Drinan is in some circles a hero of the Watergate episode in which, unlike the Democrats this time around, Republicans urged their President to do the decent thing and resign. In testifying to the House Judiciary Committee, Fr. Drinan lifted up the easily overlooked fine point of constitutional law that says that God will judge very harshly anybody who votes to impeach President Clinton. In a September 1998 article he argued that "no President has ever before spoken of his wrongdoings in such an impressive manner." In fact, no President has ever had occasion to speak about wrongdoings such as these in any manner at all. Like so many other Democrats noted for their fiscal frugality, Drinan was deeply distressed by the Starr investigation costing forty million dollars. And all it produced was "a tawdry tale of a President who, after at least twice trying to disengage himself from a star-struck intern, succumbed to temptation."

Were Clinton to resign or be removed, "the consequences would be enormous." Specifically, "It would imply that the Democrats not once but twice elected a very unworthy person to the White House." Clearly, the thought is simply not to be entertained. The "entirely new" thing in all these events, says Drinan, is "the President's public contrition." "It is gripping, it is astonishing, it resonates of Old Testament sinners who return to God. One commentator has suggested that a parent should not punish a child who has the level of repentance manifested by Clinton." Unfortunately, the people who want to punish the child President are "political animals who are most interested in their political survival and advancement." Thus did Fr. Drinan play the dual role of prophet consigning the persecutors to perdition and of priest welcoming home the prodigal son.

In February 1999, Clinton addressed the National Prayer Breakfast, an annual orgy of civil religion in devotion to Americanism and a mostly unnamed God. He told the congregation of thousands that they should pray "for yourselves," that we all be "purged of the temptation to pretend that our willfulness is somehow equal to God's will." He enjoined them to listen well to all the good things that had been said at the breakfast. Writer Peggy Noonan was there. "I thought: He's talking to us as if he is a moral leader and we are the nice people being led. He's providing moral instruction to a room full of ministers. Then I thought: And this is Bill Clinton!"

Noonan was not the only one who had doubts about Clinton's contrition. After his disastrous televised "apology" of August 17, Clinton convened a clutch of clerics in the White House to testify to his being truly sorry. The National Association of Evangelicals declined the invitation, explaining: "NAE leadership decided no representative would attend the breakfast because there would not be an opportunity to express a prophetic voice. The paradigm of the Old Testament prophets was that they went to the palace to speak God's word to the King with a call to repentance. . . . NAE did not relish the distinct possibility that it would be considered by the media as part of the President's 'amen corner.'" The amen corner at the breakfast, however, was chock full of others who did not suffer such pangs of scrupulosity in certifying the sincerity with which the President felt his pain.

Andy Warhol said everybody gets fifteen minutes in the

spotlight. Really big history-making events get half an hour. Clinton tries to look presidential as he stumbles through the rubble, and it is easy to forget that nine months ago and a year ago many thought he was finished. He is less "the comeback kid" and more the Energizer bunny that just keeps on going, more or less. More than 150 newspapers, some of them quite influential, had called for his resignation by last fall. But then the entire drama changed, turning to the impeachment hearings and Senate trial. That revised script had him either losing or winning, but he had already lost. Religious publications, for the most part, pulled their punches. The liberal *Christian Century* fretted about the quality of his contrition; the evangelical mainline *Christianity Today* said Clinton's actions had "rendered this Administration morally unable to lead," but stopped short of calling for resignation or removal; *America,* the Jesuit weekly, was in Clinton's corner and expressed satisfaction that the bishops had remained largely silent during the entire affair.

In September, Bishop Anthony Pilla, then President of the National Conference of Catholic Bishops, noted that what Clinton had done was wrong, but he "has indicated his sorrow over his behavior, his acceptance of blame, and his desire for healing." As to his "accountability in terms of public office," Pilla said, "it is up to the constitutional process to determine the appropriate response." Among Catholic moral theologians, Fr. David Hollenbach of Boston College was in the distinct minority calling for resignation or removal.

Robert Schuller of Crystal Cathedral in California was perceived to be close to Clinton in recent years in the White House, and in December concluded he should resign. "I ask that you look within your conscience and summon the will and strength to end this agony. By stepping aside, you can spare our nation weeks, perhaps months, of divisive debate and repulsive testimony. Your action can help restore public confidence in the moral fabric that sustains our form of government and the moral standards we have a right to demand in our leaders." Already by October the heads of the Southern Baptist Convention, the Reformed Church in America, and other denominational leaders, including some liberal Methodist bishops, had publicly called on Clinton to resign. On October 9, I was pleased to join many others in a most respectful letter to Clinton from religious leaders coordinated by the Institute on Religion and Democracy and laying out the reasons why he should resign. In sum, hundreds, if not thousands, of clergy of some national prominence publicly called for resignation or removal. This received almost no attention in the media and, of course, no response from the White House.

Resignation was, literally, unthinkable. All those who were thinking about it apparently did not exist in Bill Clinton's mind. Once again, the autism kicks in. In the March 31, 1999, *60 Minutes II* interview, Dan Rather asks, "Did you ever consider resigning?" "Never." "Never for a second?" "Never, not a second, never, never." "Never entered your mind?" "Never entered my mind. . . . I wouldn't do that to the Constitution. I wouldn't do that to the presidency. I wouldn't do that to the history of this country. I would never have legitimized what I believe is horribly wrong with what has occurred here over the last four or five years." Note the time span — the last four or five years. We are back to the vast right-wing conspiracy that has been trying to get the Clintons all along.

That is the overarching explanation of what has happened, with Clinton being sorry that he made some personal mistakes that the conspirators were able to exploit. How does Clinton understand his role in all this? "I do not regard this impeachment vote as some great badge of shame," he tells Rather. "I am honored that something that was indefensible was pursued and that I had the opportunity to defend the Constitution." He alludes to "the great figures of the Bible" who also "did things they shouldn't have done." The Bible teaches that "everyone sins, but everyone is held accountable, and everyone has a chance to go on." That, he says, is what our children should learn from the past year and more. "Kids are pretty smart. And they — this is a good lesson, not a bad lesson for them."

Not only is he honored to have had an opportunity to defend the Constitution and to teach morality to America's children, but he also bears no grudges against his persecutors. "I realized that particularly in the last year, if I wanted people to give me forgiveness, I had to extend forgiveness. . . . And I have worked very hard at it. I have had very powerful examples. I look at a man like Nelson Mandela who suffered enormously." And so forth. This takes the breath away. It is crazily Christian in a surreal way, a moral ju-jitsu whereby he is more sinned against than sinner, but is prepared to forgive those who tried to hold him accountable for what he does. "Forgive them their trespasses as we forgive ours."

Judgment Day

In December, more than two hundred university and seminary teachers of religion signed a "Declaration Concerning Religion, Ethics, and the Crisis in the Clinton Presidency." This became the basis of a book, edited by Gabriel Fackre of Andover Newton, that will be an invaluable document for the study of this period, *Judgment Day at the White House* (Eerdmans). Essayists include Jean Bethke Elshtain, Max Stackhouse, Stanley Hauerwas, Fr. Matthew Lamb, and Don Browning. The declaration and most of the essayists did not explicitly call for Clinton's replacement, but did offer incisive criticism of the political manipulation of Christian themes of contrition and forgiveness. The book also has Wogaman-like opposing views by Nicholas P. Wolterstorff, Lewis Smedes, and Donald and Peggy Shriver. Also in opposition to the declaration is Glen Harold Stassen, who invokes the political wisdom of his father, the perennial presidential candidate, in understanding the role of morality in public life.

Of particular interest is an essay by Edward P. Wimberly of the Interdenominational Theological Center, Atlanta, from the viewpoint of "African-American pastoral theology." The overwhelming black support for Clinton, he observes, is similar to the pattern of "settling" among black women. That is, they don't expect much from a man and are glad to settle for what they can get. The "almost unanimous" support for Clinton, Wimberly says, is reinforced by his sharing "a small-town, folksy, rural style with black preachers and Southern white politicians." Nor does it hurt that he, too, depicts himself as a victim. He may be an S.O.B., but . . .

Judgment Day reprints a notable essay by Shelby Steele of Stanford University, "Baby-Boom Virtue," which is, I believe, helpful in understanding the moral confusions surrounding the Clinton debacle. His generation, says Steele, won its rebellion against parents who defined virtue in terms of personal responsibility, largely in the sphere of family, work, and religion. The boomers subscribe to "virtue-by-identification." He quotes Senator Tom Harkin of Iowa who said last fall that "Clinton is a failed human being but a good President." Virtue-by-identification means virtue is not a matter of who you are but of what you stand for. Of the boomers Steele writes: "Thus, in the name of virtuousness that could redeem society and allow for our fulfillment, we created a new 'good' in which private moral responsibility was secondary, if not passé. . . . We created a virtuousness that could be achieved through mere identification."

It is a matter of identifying with the right causes and with those who identify with the right causes. "But iconography of this sort," Steele writes, "is even more effective in its negative mode." "Because it represents virtue, it also licenses demonization. Those who do not identify are not simply wrong; they are against virtue and therefore evil. Any politics of virtue is also a politics of demonization, and this has been a boomer specialty since the 1960s. . . . We could not have had a Bill Clinton without the generational corruption that allowed virtue to be achieved through mere identification."

And, of course, there are elders who should know better but pander to the boomers.

Generational generalizations such as Steele's are suggestive, but I continue to be disinclined to blame Bill Clinton or the failure to remove him from office on the American people, or even on the boomer generation. The liberal claim that conservatives in their disappointment have turned anti-American does not, Paul Weyrich and a few others notwithstanding, bear close examination. The January issue of *Commentary* asked seventeen prominent conservative thinkers whether, "read as a barometer of the national temper," the November elections and the reaction to the Clinton scandal tell us much about America. Among the questions asked was this: "What is your own sense of where, on moral matters, the public stands?" Six (including William Bennett) thought we had received bad news about the American character, one was undecided, and the ten others put the blame elsewhere, mainly on the ineptitude of Republican leaders. A month later, the *Weekly Standard* ran a similar symposium with twenty-one participants (two overlapping with the *Commentary* symposium), and the blame-America count, as I read it, is no more than five out of twenty-one.

There were so many things that went wrong, including the decision not to have a full trial with witnesses in the Senate. Earlier, there was Robert Livingston, on the eve of taking over as Speaker of the House, resigning because of his sexual misdeeds and calling on Clinton to do likewise. Livingston's resignation was honorable, but the suggested parallel with Clinton undercut the Republican case that the question was not sexual misdeeds but the rule of law. Nor, most important, can one overlook the spectacle of Senate Democrats, some of whom were on record saying Clinton is guilty, many, if not most of whom, had made it clear they thought he should not be removed, and all of whom took the solemn vow to judge his case impartially. In brazen lockstep they voted to acquit. In *The Death of Outrage*, Bennett makes much of the fact that "we" were the kind of people who twenty-five years earlier forced Nixon to resign, but the "we" then included a large number of Republicans who put the integrity of the office before party. This time around, bolstered by the polls, Democrats felt no need to temper their partisanship.

"The System Worked"

In some quarters it is said that, at the end of the day, "the system worked." Maybe so. In 1787 when the impeachment provision of the Constitution was being debated, Benjamin Franklin proposed that the President should be impeachable when he has "rendered himself obnoxious." Had Franklin prevailed, we would have been spared all the talk about high crimes and misdemeanors. In a similar vein, British cousins such as Andrew Sullivan and James Bowman argued that in the parliamentary system Clinton would have been long gone. The American Framers, says Bowman, wanted a system that would, as much as possible, obviate the need for virtue, honor, and trust. The result is a President without virtue, honor, or trust. Bowman writes: "T. S. Eliot observed that the Socialist project was to design a system so perfect that no one would have to be good. The Socialists were anticipated by the Founders of the American Republic, whose aim was to design a system so well that honor would not have to be relied on. But, it turns out, we have to rely on it still." That judgment of the constitutional order is not quite right. Washington, John Adams, and other Founders repeatedly said the system could not work without virtue, honor, and trust. They were so urgent in their warnings precisely because the system provided no remedy for the absence of those factors that cannot be secured by law.

While on the subject of honor, one cannot fail to mention Representative Henry Hyde, maybe the only politician who comes out of this with his stature enhanced. He was the adult on the Judiciary Committee while juvenile delinquents such as Barney Frank and John Conyers variously clowned and postured, making themselves and, they hoped, the proceedings look obnoxious. At one point Hyde said that he would catch hell no matter what he did, so he might as well do what is right. Apart from the clowns, even his opponents acknowledged, albeit sometimes grudgingly, his integrity. Paul Gigot got it right: "As for Henry Hyde, he likes to joke that when he first came to Washington he wanted to change the world; now he just wants to leave the room with dignity. By impeaching a law-breaking President, he did both."

The national character, however, was left with little dignity, according to some. Roger Kimball of the *New Criterion* thought Paul Weyrich was a bit overwrought. "But by and large I think it must be admitted that his unhappy diagnosis is right. At the deepest level — at the level of the culture's taken-for-granted feelings and assumptions about what matters — the hedonistic, self-infatuated ethos of cultural revolution has triumphed to an extent unimaginable when it began." He is especially exercised by an article by the erratic David Brooks in the *Weekly Standard,* arguing that the past year has demonstrated that American culture is in pretty good shape. "Today's moral attitudes are anti-utopian," Brooks wrote. "They are utilitarian. They are modest. They are, in fact, the values of the class the counterculture hated most. They are the values of the bourgeoisie." Kimball calls Brooks' article "an unashamed paean to philistinism," and reminds Brooks that "what conservatives have traditionally championed were bourgeois *values,* not bourgeois vices." What Brooks espouses "is not conservatism but a cheerful, buttoned-down version of the moral vacancy that Mr. Weyrich rightly laments."

It Has Never Happened Before

Bennett, Weyrich, Kimball, Gertrude Himmelfarb, and a good many others have drawn such doleful conclusions, but

I am not persuaded. So what have we learned from all this? One thing we have learned is what might happen if we had an MTV President. We never had one before. The political philosopher Leo Strauss liked to say that the American system was built on foundations that are low but solid. The Clinton presidency was built on foundations that are low and sordid. For all his successes in life, it seems that Bill Clinton as a person never rose above his origins. That is a difficult subject not untouched by the delicate question of class, but the fact is that Clinton plays to the pit. Maureen Dowd of the *Times,* who nonetheless opposed the impeachment, writes: "He campaigned and governed using lowbrow forums of popular entertainment . . . and now the lowbrow culture he cultivated has engulfed his presidency and, most likely, his legacy. Just as movie and television comedy is permeated with the ill-mannered, self-indulgent mentality of adolescent boys, Mr. Clinton has reversed the usual pattern of the presidency, switching from a paternal model to an adolescent model. He expects us to clean up, ignore, or forgive his messes. . . . You might call it a vast gross-out conspiracy."

Lowbrow. As in lower class. It is a term deemed dangerously incorrect today, but it is a reality that cannot be denied. Here it means not the economically poor but the morally impoverished. In the past we were more candid about the fact that a large number of people in any society, including this one, are moral slobs. That recognition is key to Edward C. Banfield's brilliant 1968 analysis of social policy, *The Unheavenly City.* Once upon a time there were "our kind of people" and other kind of people. The better kind of people felt an obligation to help uplift the lesser breeds. Today the lesser breeds are victims and the better kind of people are the victimizers — or at least so our academic and media elites would convince us.

Of course the old way was marred by snobbery and hypocrisy, the inevitable attendants of any effort to maintain standards. It is not that people used to be more moral than they are now. Moral slobbery is, I expect, pretty evenly distributed through time and societies. In the nineteenth century, the better kind of people were aghast at the manners and mores of the immigrant hordes, mainly Catholics and Jews. But Banfield notes: "In Boston, which in 1817 had only about four hundred Catholics, the native American residents must have patronized the city's two thousand prostitutes (one for every six males above the age of sixteen), hundreds of liquor shops, and the gambling houses open night and day. It must also have been the native Bostonians who denied the mayor, Josiah Quincy, reelection after he waged a vigorous war on vice." Nothing daunted, Quincy and those like him embraced the unending task of elevating public standards.

Like none who held the office before him, the MTV President has exulted in playing to the pit in a populism not of policy but of appetite. In an orchestrated slander against a woman on whom Clinton tried to force himself, and with whom he later settled out of court for a huge sum, a Clinton media lackey spoke of the trash that turns up when you trawl money through a trailer park. It is a fitting image of this presidency, and the trailer park is not just Arkansas, for every state and every community has a subculture that wallows in being pandered to, even as the panderer wallows in their gratitude for his being one of them. Ronald Reagan started in Hollywood and lived it down by living up to the presidency. Bill Clinton's achievement is to be accepted by a Hollywood responsible for a meretricious popular culture to which he has defined down the presidency. With a wink and a nudge, the media and politics junkies went along with it for a long time, declaring him a political genius. Until it became evident that he viewed them, too, as trash to be trawled — and casually discarded when they would no longer play the game.

Over the year, as noted above, puzzlement was regularly expressed at Clinton's high ratings in the opinion polls. Playing low can keep the ratings high. A majority was agreeing with Senator Harkin that Clinton is a failed human being but a good President — or at least that he is not so bad a President that he should be removed, or at least that he should not be removed for an adolescent sexual indulgence, or at the very least that he should not be forced out of office by those whom the nightly news portrayed as vicious partisans out to get him.

Moreover, put together the numbers: feminists and those intimidated by them, for whom the only issue is abortion; die-hard liberal Democrats and leftists on the commanding heights of culture for whom conservatism is pure evil; big labor, especially in education and other parts of the public sector, for whom the alternative to Clinton is catastrophe; and blacks who are pitiably grateful for the assurance that Master feels their pain. Add in the very large number of sensible Americans who found the whole thing repugnant and just wanted it to go away, and you ended up with those high "approval" ratings.

This, at least, is my reading of the Clinton squalor that consumed much of the attention of the nation and the world for more than a year. Now attention has turned to what I believe is the grievously misguided U.S. – NATO war in Serbia (see "The Clinton Era, At Home and Abroad" in last month's "Public Square"), and God only knows how that will end up. But the one thing we must not do is follow the counsel of those who say we should put behind us the impeachment and the events that precipitated it. It was a moment of important truth not just about this President and not chiefly about what is called the American character, but about the ways of public discourse, so to speak, about who we are and how we live now.

What happened beginning in January 1998 does not tell us much that is worth knowing about "the American people." The fact is that nothing like this has happened to us before. If it is allowed to happen again any time soon, we might have to reconsider the dark ponderings about the American character that have gained such currency. The most hopeful thought is that enough Americans have learned from this experience never again to entrust the presidency to a person of such reckless habits and suspect character. But that hope comes with no guarantee.

Meanwhile, we have a President who is guilty of perjury, witness tampering, the obstruction of justice, and sexual predation, including, it seems, at least one rape. Very likely there will be further charges, and possibly further crimes, in the months to come. But, in what is presented as the clinching argument of his loyalists, it's only for another year or so. Until somebody comes up with a better idea, the course of wisdom is to pray for the nation while averting our eyes as much as public duty permits from the sorry spectacle of a man stumbling through the rubble of what remains of a ruined presidency.

Why "Hate Crimes" Are Wrong

It is a sad story, and what they did to him was despicable. These guys were drinking in a Laramie bar and University of Wyoming freshman Matthew Shepard reportedly made a pass at one of them, whereupon two young men took him out, brutally beat him, robbed him, and left him tied to a fence. A few days later, he died in hospital. It immediately became a nationwide cause celebre for gay and lesbian groups agitating for hate crime laws that include "sexual orientation." Mr. Shepard's father expressed the hope that nobody would exploit his son's death in order to push an agenda, but the agitators knew when they had come across a good thing. The lead editorial in our establishment paper was titled "Murdered for Who He Was."

The editors remind us that African-Americans, Asians, Jews, Italians, Irish, and others have been victims of hatred.

"Gradually, crimes motivated by hate have come to be seen as a category of their own." It apparently took the editors some time to recognize that few such crimes are motivated by love. As to "Who He Was," the editors describe young Shepard as being "slight, trusting, and uncertain how well he would be accepted as an openly gay freshman." They add that he had spent time in Europe and "spoke three languages or more." The point being made, it seems, is that this is not just another black or Puerto Rican kid who was brutally beaten and killed. The editors are saying that he is one of us. This is a young man with whom we can, as it is said, identify. This is a murder that matters.

The editors continue, "He died in a coma yesterday, in a state without a hate-crimes law." It is hard to know what to make of that. He might have pulled out of it if Wyoming had a hate-crimes law? "Hatred can kill," the editors portentously announce. Noted for the record. Observing with satisfaction that the killers will be tried for first-degree murder, the *Times,* which is otherwise adamantly opposed to the death penalty, adds, "But his death makes clear the need for hate-crime laws to protect those who survive and punish those who attack others, whether fatally or not, just because of who they are." Apparently it needs to be made clear that beating people up and killing them is against the law. And, if it is done because of "who they are," maybe the perpetrators should be executed more than once?

The admitted purpose of gay agitation for hate-crime laws is to have homosexual acts (which in the real world define "sexual orientation") put on a par with religion, race, gender, and age as a legally protected category. There are many good reasons for thinking that a bad idea. But the very idea of "hate crimes" is highly dubious. Hate is a sin for which people may go to Hell. It is quite another thing to make it a crime for which people should go to jail. The law rightly takes motivation into account; for instance, whether someone is killed by accident or by deliberate intent. In the latter case, malice of some sort is almost always involved, but it is not the malice that makes the killing a crime. A murderer may have nothing personal against someone whom he kills for his money.

It is generally wrong to disapprove of people because of their religion, race, or gender, but it is not a crime. (An exception may be disapproval of someone whose religion includes committing terrorist acts.) The purpose of the gay movement and its advocates, such as the *Times,* is to criminalize disapproval of homosexual acts, or at least to establish in law that such disapproval is disapproved. Most Americans, it may safely be assumed, disapprove of homosexual acts. It is not within the competence of the state to declare that they are, for that reason, legally suspect. In a sinful world, sundry hatreds, irrational prejudices, and unjust discriminations abound. The homosexual movement is notable for its venting of hatred against millions of Americans whom it accuses of being "homophobic." In whatever form it takes, hatred toward other people must be deplored and condemned. But it is utterly wrongheaded to try to make hatred illegal.

David Morrison, writing in the *New York Post,* offers a further reason for thinking more than twice about laws against hate crimes. He notes *Newsweek's* report that Mr. Shepard seems to have had a history of approaching "straight" men for sex. There is, says Morrison, who describes himself as a "former gay activist," a substantial subculture of the gay subculture that goes in for "rough trade" — cruising in public places for sex with straight or semi-straight toughs. He writes, "Yet the fact that a significant number of men strongly desire and pursue public sex under occasionally dangerous circumstances should influence the ongoing conversation, spurred by Shepard's death, about the necessity or wisdom of including sexual orientation in hate-crimes laws. . . . Americans should think long and hard about the making the feeling of repugnance at an unwanted sexual advance subject to additional penalties under the law. There is an old saying that hard cases make bad law. It seems to me that the 1990s have provided a corollary: Tragic cases can make bad laws more quickly. Americans should examine the calls for additional hate-crime legislation with extreme care. There is more at stake than any simple claim of human rights."

Martin Luther King, Jr. used to say, "The law cannot make you love me, but it can prevent you from lynching me. And, if you don't lynch me, you may eventually come to love me." We should certainly love our gay brothers, even as we disapprove of the acts that define them as gay. Loving them includes our saying, always lovingly, that they are wrong in trying to use the law to stigmatize those who disapprove of what they do, which is not, the *Times* to the contrary, the only or the most important thing that determines "who they are."

✴ It's fine and dandy to be tolerant, but some people really do go too far. For instance, Alan Wolfe reviews Nancy L. Rosenblum's *Membership and Morals,* a book on American pluralism put out by Princeton University Press, and has this to say: "Even as we pursue justice, equality, and diversity, we need to respect and to honor difference. That turns out to be a much harder task than most liberals recognize, for it also means that we need to accept a certain amount of discrimination, venality, religious orthodoxy, wrong-headedness, perversity, and snobbery. Since humans are human, politics is very hard." Venality and perversity maybe, but do we really have to put up with religious orthodoxy?

Encountered by the Truth

There is no point in arguing with the claim that Jacques Derrida is the most famous philosopher in the world today.

The most famous at least among those who set academic fashions and their camp followers in the popular media. He is commonly called "the father of deconstructionism," an ill-defined intellectual disposition that is thought to give carte blanche to the denial of "objective truth" in the service of making up whatever "truths" suit one's fancy. Deconstructionism has provided a capacious playpen for queer studies, radical feminisms, and a wide range of debonair nihilisms that have taken exuberant advantage of the last several decades' sabbatical from the tasks of clear thinking. Little wonder that Derrida — along with Nazi-tinged Paul De Man and the late celebrant of the culture of death, Michel Foucault — has become a byword of derision among conservatives. Children of Heidegger all, they are thought to vindicate the truth that evil ideas, too, have consequences.

Over the years, Derrida has returned regularly to Johns Hopkins University where thirty years ago his deconstructionist manifesto first excited the neophiliac professoriate. In between there have been more than thirty books in which Derrida has maintained his reputation for being at the cutting edge, or, in the view of his critics, for taking French intellectual life over the edge into terminal silliness. As so often happens, the master is just a bit embarrassed by what his epigones have done in his name. Just a bit, mind you. He is careful not to jeopardize his celebrity standing, but he does want it understood that he is not responsible for all the bizarre things perpetrated in the name of deconstructionism. This was evident in a recent interview at Johns Hopkins in which he said that those who assert it is not possible to determine what is right and wrong are operating with a "relativistic image of deconstruction." He did not provide a non-relativistic definition of deconstruction but appeared to suggest that his method, so to speak, was little more than the inculcation of modesty in what we claim to know for sure. There is a long tradition of French intellectuals sending signals through the medium of interviews, and there are no doubt books already in the works deciphering Derrida's enigmatic allusion to the existence of relativistic and non-relativistic deconstruction.

Also enigmatic but suggestive of something genuinely interesting in Derrida's thought is what might be viewed as a theological turn. Asked about his role as the world's most famous philosopher (a description he does not dispute), Derrida opined: "I have been given this image, and I have to face some responsibility, political and ethical. It is as if I am indebted to — I don't know to whom — to thinking rigorously, to thinking responsibly. I am in a situation of trying to learn to whom, finally, I am responsible. To discover . . . who is hidden, who gives me orders. It is as if I have a destiny which I have to interpret and decipher." It does sound as though Mr. Derrida is taking the long way around to the Big Question. Perhaps, he seems to be saying, the decipherer is himself a "text" being deciphered. The deconstructionist deconstructed is but a small step from the discovery of the One to whom he is responsible and by whom he is destined. If or when he publicly takes that step, watch for the announcement that Jacques Derrida, once celebrated as the world's most famous philosopher, has in his old age taken refuge in religious obscurantism.

Abetting Atheism

I will not be surprised if he does take that step toward the truth ever ancient, ever new. Reading the Derridadists, one gets the impression that many of them think they are being terribly innovative and radical in making what is usually the adolescent discovery that there is no "totalist" explanation of the truth about everything. Sophomores of all ages, many of them tenured, declare themselves "liberated" by the realization that there are other ways of viewing almost everything, and then concluding that no one way can be "privileged" as the truth about anything. Their rebellion against the pretentious certitudes of Enlightenment rationalism, often defined as modernity, is in large part warranted, and that is the kernel of truth in "postmodernism." Postmodernism can be a lower-case relativism that is not Relativism but simply a disciplined modesty in search of the way things really are. This is not relativism as a dogma but relativism in the service of truth.

The dismal truth is that generations of moderns were miseducated to think that religion, and Christianity in particular, claims to be "objectively" true in a manner that eliminates the subjectivity of experience and perspective. Regrettably, that miseducation was and is abetted by Christians who confuse orthodoxy with the exclusion of intellectual inquiry. In this habit of mind, the truth is an object, a thing possessed, which must be assiduously protected from any thought that is not certified by Christian copyright. The alternative is to understand that truth is personal, less a matter of our possessing than of our being possessed in service to the one who is the way, the truth, and the life. As St. Paul reminds the Corinthians, our apprehension of that truth is always partial, something seen through a glass darkly in anticipation of the time when we will know even as we are known.

Few things have contributed so powerfully to the unbelief of the modern and postmodern world as the pretension of Christians to know more than we do. In reaction to unwarranted claims of knowledge certain and complete, modern rationalists constructed their religion of scientism, and postmoderns, in reaction to both, claim to know that nothing can be known. Please do not misunderstand. Christians do know the truth, saying with St. Paul (Romans 8:38-39), "For I am persuaded that neither death, nor life, nor angels, nor principalities, nor things present, nor things to come, nor powers, nor height, nor depth, nor anything else in all creation, will be able to separate us from the love of God in Christ Jesus our Lord." As St. Paul goes on to say in Romans 11, "O the depth of the riches and wisdom and knowledge of God! How unsearchable are his judgments and how inscrutable his ways!" Christian thought is the open-ended adventure into searching the unsearchable and scrutinizing the inscrutable. Always, if it is authentically Christian, it ends up in doxology: "For from him and through him and to him are all things. To him be glory forever. Amen."

Unthinking Christian polemics against "relativism" play a large part in creating upper case Relativists. The objective truth of revelation is perceived as an alien intrusion (heteronomy is the technical word) that is the enemy rather than the end of honest inquiry. The great thinkers of an earlier era — from Justin Martyr through Athanasius, Augustine, and Aquinas — understood that all truth is the truth of Christ. "In the beginning was the Word," the *Logos* who is the universal wisdom in which all wisdom finds its source and end. The thought that any truth can violate that truth is a violation of the law of noncontradiction, which cannot be violated without self-contradiction. Faced with the apparent choice of following Christ or following a truth that we know to be true, the course of fidelity is to follow the truth, for only thus will we be following Christ, if, as we are persuaded, Christ is the truth.

The inquiring subject is not eliminated but encountered by the truth of the Word. Our apprehension of the objective is always relative. This is true in matters both trivial and cosmic. How far is Kansas City? The answer is relative to whether you're in New York or in Peoria. Each of us apprehends the truth from his own circumstance, which is *a* standpoint that is not to be confused with *the* standpoint. Only the one who is both Alpha and Omega occupies *the* standpoint from which all is known, comprehensively and without remainder. St. Paul again: "Now hope that is seen is not hope. For who hopes for what he sees? But if we hope for what we do not see, we wait for it with patience." If Christians exhibited more intellectual patience, modesty, curiosity, and sense of adventure, there would be fewer atheists in the world, both of the modern rationalist and postmodern irrationalist varieties. I have never met an atheist who rejects the God in whom I believe. I have met many who decline to commit intellectual suicide, and maybe spiritual suicide as well, by accepting a God proposed by Christians who claim to know more than they can possibly know.

Which brings me back to Jacques Derrida. I don't know whether he was just being cute in that interview. He does, unfortunately, have a record of posturing to put his devotees more off balance than they already are. But I would very much like to believe that he is resolved to think rigorously about to whom he is indebted, to whom, finally, he is responsible. That way, pressed honestly enough, lies the encounter with the truth that deciphers our deciphering and deconstructs our deconstructing. And, who knows, perhaps Derrida's disciples, too, will one day weary of their sophisticated knowingness and be opened to the truth that frees us from our poignantly compulsive liberations.

❧ Call it quixotic, but it brightens the day. The Phillip Morris company gave $40,000 to Belmont Abbey College, a small Catholic school in Belmont, North Carolina. The money was to fund an adult literacy program run by the college. Then college president Robert A. Preston came across an ad for Virginia Slims in *Time* magazine that in his judgment and that of others was clearly promoting premarital sex. He discussed the matter with the students in his ethics class. "Some of them argued that it would do more good for us to keep the money and use it for the literacy project, or that it was such a small amount that it wouldn't matter to a big company like Phillip Morris." But most of the students thought the money should be returned, as did the trustees, and so it was. Said Phillip Morris: "We regret their decision because our grant would have helped improve literacy in Gaston County." Dr. Preston's letter returning the money made it clear "that this action is in no way connected with the fact that Phillip Morris is in the tobacco business." Draw a line between those who would approve returning the money as a protest against the promotion of tobacco and those who approve it as a protest against the promotion of premarital sex and you get one way of understanding alignments in what some call the culture wars.

❧ So this junior at Winslow High School in Arizona brought to English class the cremated remains of her mother to show a friend. When she opened the box, some ashes fell on the floor, which set off a panic among many of the eight hundred students, more than half of whom are Navajos or Hopis. These tribes have very definite taboos about anything having to do with dead bodies, and more than a hundred students boycotted classes. Principal John Henling brought in a Navajo medicine man to conduct ceremonies removing evil spirits from the classroom, but it turns out he was not certified as a really traditional medicine man, so Henling had to get two others, one Hopi and one Navajo, to do additional ceremonies. The unidentified student was not disciplined, said Henling, "because we have a lot of things in our student handbook but we never thought about putting anything in about what happens to those who bring human remains." The Rev. Jack Miller of the evangelical Potter's House Church, however, threatened to sue the school district unless he was given equal time to conduct ceremonies cleansing the classroom of the effect of the pagan rituals employed by the medicine men. "We try to satisfy the cultural and religious needs of our community," said Dale Patton, attorney for the school district. "If they want to come in and do something roughly comparable to what was done by the other group, I don't have any problem with that." Ah, pluralism.

❧ St. Martin's continues to publish a distinctive, if not distinguished, list. There is, for instance, *The Pleasure Principle: Sex, Backlash, and the Struggle for Gay Freedom* by Michael Bronski, who writes: "For decades, conservative psychoanalysts, religious leaders, and politicians have charged that homosexuality is about nothing more than having sex; that homosexuals are 'obsessed' with sex; that homosexuality is a 'flight' from the responsibilities of 'mature' sexuality. And they are right." That's the point of the "pleasure principle" — pleasure for pleasure's sake. The reviewer in *Publishers Weekly* says Bronski takes on the question of homosexuals and children "forthrightly." I don't think you want to know what that means. The review concludes by noting that before matters of sexuality can be resolved, "sexuality itself and the concept of pleasure must be confronted head on." An editor might have suggested rephrasing that.

❧ Herewith another pronouncement from an elevated religious authority on the great evil of consumerism: "In a radically new world of unprecedented technological change, the media, and television in particular, have effectively deprived millions of people of their moral agency, programming them as passive consumers in the slave-like service of a vast economic machine that is out of control. Human beings have become means to the end of consumption." If true, this is truly alarming, and it has regularly worried me that I am not alarmed about it. Maybe, I thought, I am missing something. So the other evening I made notes of the commercials while watching *The Maltese Falcon* for the enteenth time. I was determined to have a record on how the television monster was turning my mind to mush and reducing me to a slave of consumerism. First, there was a pitch for a zippy BMW, but I live in Manhattan where sensible people don't have cars, so I resisted the impulse to run out and buy one. About a third of the commercials were for forthcoming television shows, aimed at persuading me this is a really neat channel. It's nice that the people there seem proud of their work. There were two pitches for mutual fund operators, both claiming they are good at making money. They would say that, wouldn't they? The Sears company wants me to buy a nifty new wrench they sell. I'll keep it in mind in the event I ever need one. I see there's a pill that relieves headache faster than aspirin, which is good to know. Apparently there is a veritable plague of stomach gas going around, but, fortunately, there are all kinds of new remedies for that. The effectiveness of one of them was conclusively demonstrated with scientific charts and the assurance that doctors recommend it. It didn't say which doctors. I'm told I can get a good price on a Caribbean cruise, and I suppose that would be of interest to people with time on their hands. As for me, I'm busy countering the dehumanizing effects of the consumerist beast. Oops, here's an ad for a pill that relieves genital herpes. What's that doing here? But then I recall reading that nine out of ten "sexually active" Americans have STDs — sexually transmitted (a.k.a. venereal) diseases. Back to Bogart. Nothing like that would happen to him. In the next break, American Express tells me I should be sure to take my card with me if I don't want a boy in Italy to steal my donkey, or something like that. Then there's Delta airlines saying they'll get me there on time, which I know isn't true, but I really didn't expect them to buy television time to fess up to that three hour delay on the flight to San Francisco. Next is an outfit called ACE hardware which has just the tool for digging in the garden, if I had a garden. That is followed by Xerox, which I am told has a color copying machine that works much faster than the competition's. After the deliciously wicked Sidney Greenstreet slips Bogart that mickey, Prudential life insurance delicately hints that a lot of people have not adequately provided for their families. Even the unsophisticated can see that this is in the sneaky service of getting people to buy more life insurance. There are two ads for alternative phone companies that, as best I can make out, will pay me for making all my calls with them. I'm sure there's a catch somewhere. Finally, there is a spot urging people to subscribe to the *New York Times*. I already get it, but I can see how the critics of our radically unprecedented, technology-dominated consumerist society might in this case be on to something when they claim advertising is a threat to public health. So that's it, one evening's notes on the dehumanizing assault by the corporate masters of consumerism. Of course, as I assume most people do, I ordinarily hit the mute button during commercials. After this one evening of careful scientific research, I do not say that ours is an age of innocence, but I am inclined to the view that moralists raising alarums about the insidious predations of television advertising turning us into ciphers of consumerism should maybe take a Caribbean cruise. I know where they can get one cheap. As for the movie: Don't trust fat men shopping for birds.

The Impertinence of Protesting Aggression

An editor at the *New York Times* recently remarked that the use of the term "culture war" is dangerously inflammatory. I think it's a useable and useful term. I do not use it as much as the *Times* does, and I think it should not be used in a way that precludes the conversation and persuasion that should be, but is not, the ordinary mode of public discourse. The prestige media are generally blind to their own belligerency in the culture war; they champion as courageous the exercise of free speech that is vituperative and slanderous while simultaneously calling for civility, and condemning as uncivil even the measured responses of those who are slandered. Perhaps because the remark of the editor was on my mind, I was struck by several items in just this morning's *Times*. Two cases illustrate the point.

In the arts section there is a long and laudatory profile by Alan Riding of the recent Nobel laureate in literature, José Saramago. The novels and other writings of this Portuguese writer have for years been noted for their strident atheism and attacks on the Catholic Church. When the Nobel was announced, the semi-official Vatican paper, *L'Osservatore Romano*, noted that, for the second year in a row, the Nobel in literature had been given to someone conspicuous for the virulence of his anti-Catholicism. Last year it went to Dario Fo of Italy, who is less a writer than a comedian in the music hall tradition of Benny Hill. He has, for instance, a routine in which an aged pope, hobbling on his cane, gropes young girls. Really hilarious stuff. The *Times* notes that the Vatican is not happy that the Nobel has again gone to "someone it perceives to be antireligious." That "perceives" is a nice touch. You know how thin-skinned those Catholics are.

Saramago was a staunch Stalinist and is still an unreconstructed member of the Communist Party. That doesn't faze Mr. Riding. He writes, "Perhaps most intriguing is this atheist writer's fascination with religion. In [his book] *The Gospel According to Jesus Christ,* it is apparent that he knows his Bible, and he treats the figure of Jesus with compassion, as a victim of a power struggle between God and the Devil. But his underlying message is that religion has turned man against man in wars, massacres, exterminations, autos-da-fe and the like, 'all in the name of God.' " It is presumably very creative to point out that terrible things have been done in the name of religion, and to depict the Church as being on the side of the Devil against a God in whom the writer does not believe. According to Saramago, Jesus is of course the representative of the revolutionary proletariat, and of course there is no mention of the horrors perpetrated in the name of atheism by the Soviet Union, Maoist China, and others. Alan Riding finds this cliché of agitprop hack-writing "most intriguing."

In response to the Vatican displeasure with the award of the Nobel to Fo and Comrade Saramago, the *Times* quotes the latter: "Why does the Vatican get involved in these things? Why doesn't it keep itself busy with prayers? Why doesn't it instead open its cupboards and reveal the skeletons it has inside?" In sum, how dare the Vatican interfere in the elevated world of literature just because the Catholic Church is viciously traduced? What business is that of the Vatican? The Nobel laureate mugger is offended by the impertinent protest of the muggee. Perhaps it would have been wiser if *L'Osservatore Romano* had not commented and thus inadvertently bestowed a certain status upon the Nobel Prize for Literature. But, despite its history, the Nobel, like the *New York Times,* should not be excluded from the circle of conversation by the friends of civility. Attention should be paid, in the hope that their incivility is not incorrigible.

Pushing the Hot Buttons

The second item this morning is the *Times'* editorial on the narrow (seven to six) vote by which the Miami–Dade County Commission in Florida approved a "gay rights" law. Of course the *Times,* which is undoubtedly the most influential voice of the gay movement in the country, is pleased by the vote, but the editors note that their victory is fragile. The popular defeat of a similar law twenty years ago under the leadership of actress Anita Bryant "spurred the rise of the religious right," the editors observe, and the same thing could happen again. By passing the ordinance, the civic, business, and political leaders show how much they have "grown" in the interim, but there is a problem with the people. The editors note that, since the ordinance exempted religious organizations, it was not opposed by the Catholic archdiocese. But there is still the Christian Coalition and other obstacles to progress.

"The population of the county has shifted in ways that could lessen support for gay rights," the editorial observes. "Its residents are poorer, fewer of them are Jewish or middle class, and many more of them are socially conservative Roman Catholic Hispanic immigrants than a generation ago." If there is a referendum on the ordinance, "it will be a pitched battle that could charge the national political atmosphere once again." "With the next presidential election in sight, neither the Christian Coalition nor gay activists who felt they played an important role in Bill Clinton's victory will want to lose the second battle of Miami." Talk about inflammatory. The editors push the hot buttons: liberal Jews; the famously poor, uneducated, and easily led "religious right"; culturally benighted Hispanics; Catholicism and immigration. It is a potent mixture for the anticipated conflagration that is "the second battle of Miami." The editors may well be right in their political analysis of what is happening in Miami, and the paper is legally entitled to applaud the antireligious ravings of unrepentant Stalinists, but it would become the editors to refrain from lecturing others about the incivility of speaking about the culture war which their paper is so aggressively waging.

❧ Some years ago I had a friendly correspondence with a *New York Times* columnist who regularly used "righteous" as an adjective of denigration. For instance, she would criticize "righteous political leaders." I suggested that surely she meant "self-righteous," to which she responded that righteous and self-righteous are today synonymous. I thought of this again when working on a Sunday homily. The text was Luke 18, and the New American Bible (NAB), which is, regrettably, the most widely used in Catholic parishes, renders verse 9 this way: "Jesus spoke this parable addressed to those who believed in their own self-righteousness while holding every one else in contempt." The KJV, RSV, NIV, and other standard English translations all speak of those who trust in their own righteousness, correctly translating the Greek *dikaioi*. It is of more than passing interest that the NAB translators seem to agree with the above-mentioned columnist that righteousness today means self-righteousness. Rome's response to the joint declaration with the Lutherans on justification by faith emphasized the need to find fresh language with which to communicate the good news of justification in contemporary culture. The need is highlighted by the NAB treatment of Luke 18:9. Presumably we do not want to say that the sinner is justified in appropriating by faith the self-righteousness of Christ. Behind this apparently small linguistic quibble is a larger cultural shift in which necessary distinctions are erased in a process of denigrating any appeal to the normative. Righteousness becomes self-righteousness, a moral argument becomes a moralistic argument, and reference to objective truth is absolutism. Although it goes largely unnoticed, it is a change in language that changes how people think. Of course the ideologues of relativism know perfectly well what they are doing, and feel very righteous about it — as in "self-righteous." It must immediately be said that this is not to suggest that the NAB translators are part of a conspiracy. The deficiencies of that hapless translation can be explained quite satisfactorily in terms of insouciance toward the original text, deafness to verbal grace and clarity, and easy acquiescence in cultural drift. The parties responsible for the NAB should not be accused of more than they are guilty.

❧ This is simply for the record. Every time I mention New York City's being the prolepsis of the New Jerusalem, it provokes a protest from a reader or two who wonder how we can live so deprived of "nature." Of human nature there is plenty, needless to say, but also of other kinds. For instance, I rather enjoy all the birds. Birds in Manhattan? You bet. Amy, who lives next door and is more avid about matters avian, gave me a list the other day of birds sighted this past year in our adjoining back yards: American robin, cardinal, purple finch, dark-eyed junco, black-capped chickadee, tufted titmouse, blue jay, house sparrow, field sparrow, starling, crow, pigeon, and mourning dove. Of tree-clinging birds there was the hairy woodpecker, downy woodpecker, and common flicker. And one day I saw a falcon, ravenously eating a mouse it had killed. I'm not trying to prove anything, mind you, but I wouldn't be surprised if that list compares quite favorably with the sightings of those who, for whatever strange reasons, deliberately live somewhere other than New York City.

❧ A reader possessed of a perhaps terminal measure of individual creativity sends me the product of what he describes as three years of "Christian Research": "THE NEW REFORM THEOLOGY OF THE CHRISTIAN FAITH" (caps are his). He says the Catholics, Arminians, Calvinists, Lutherans, and others have got it all wrong. "I have revised the Nicene Creed, as set forth by the early Church leaders, to reflect the 'true sense and meaning' of Scriptures." "This New Reform Theology of the Christian Faith is THE WAY OF SALVATION FOR THE TWENTY-FIRST CENTURY AND THE MILLENNIUM." Clearly, this is important. But it is the ending of the letter that I especially liked: "I just thought I would share this with you." Considering what is at stake, I should hope so.

Minding the Mind

The word-mavens — William Safire, for instance — routinely complain about the use of "intriguing" when "engaging," "fascinating," or just plain "interesting" would do as well. The complaint is justified. But intriguing is the right word to describe current discussions about the relationships between brain, mind, knowing, and consciousness. These discussions engage one's attention to a marked degree, and edge into the realm of mystery. At least they engage my attention and open my mind (using that word in the ordinary sense) to wonder. On these questions there are two new books that are to be warmly welcomed: John R. Searle, *Mind, Language, and Society: Philosophy in the Real World* (Basic) and Edward Pols, *Mind Regained* (Cornell University Press). There are basic agreements between them but equally basic disagreements, making the two in combination an excellent introduction to a set of questions of considerable significance for philosophy, ethics, religion, and theology. Both are written in a manner accessible to the educated reader with no specialized training in those several fields.

John Searle of the University of California at Berkeley is surely among the most respected philosophers of our time and writes regularly on science and philosophy in the *New York Review of Books*. Against the academically trendy postmodernists and deconstructionists, he declares himself to be a philosophical "realist." "Just to put my cards on the table at the beginning," he writes, "I accept the Enlightenment vision. I think that the universe exists quite independently of our minds and that, within the limits set by our evolutionary endowments, we can come to comprehend its nature." On the major philosophical issues, he subscribes to what he calls, borrowing a computer metaphor, "the default position," meaning by that the views we hold so naturally ("pre-reflectively") that it takes mind-bending effort to let oneself be argued out of them. The default position includes the belief that we have direct perceptual access to the world that exists independently of us; that words such as *tree* and *rabbit* typically have clear meanings that make it possible to talk about real objects in the world; that statements are typically true or false, depending on whether they correspond to determinable "facts in the world"; and that there are real relations in which one phenomenon, called the cause, accounts for another, called the effect.

Such views may seem pretty obvious, indeed commonsensical, to the sane reader. Searle, however, doesn't like the word commonsense, in part, it seems, because he doesn't want to insult those who disagree with him by suggesting they don't have it. But I'm not sure it helps to speak of the "default position," since the computer metaphor may suggest that there is something very wrong with their mental hardware. In any event, Searle's defense of human reason — what he calls the Enlightenment vision — is a salutary antidote to the fashionable irrationalities of Derrida, Foucault, Rorty, and a host of others who in various and implausibly ingenious ways contend that "reality" (in quotes) is something that we are making up as we go along. Most of *Mind, Language, and Society* is devoted to exposing the incoherence and frequent fatuities of the enemies of the Enlightenment vision.

Why does the "default position" of realism have so many enemies? "I do not believe that the various challenges to realism are motivated by the arguments actually presented," Searle writes. "I believe they are motivated by something much deeper and less intellectual." People resent being "subject to and answerable to a dumb, stupid, inert material world. Why shouldn't we think of the 'real world' as something we create, and therefore something that is answerable to us? If all of reality is a 'social construction,' then it is we who are in power, not the world."

Upon Closer Examination

Searle's is an interesting suggestion, but I am not sure it bears close examination. If the will to power is present in almost everything, and it is, it may help to explain the antirealist impulse. It probably does, at least in part, but a little further thought leads to the recognition that such power is itself a delusion and pretense — my fiction with which I contend against the fictions of others. If my supposed power has no relation to a real world independent of myself, I am totally powerless. What I call my socially constructed power is just whistling in the dark, and all my contentions with the constructions of others are finally no more than a whistling contest.

But in proposing this further consideration I may be assuming that the postmodernists are more self-critical than Searle thinks they are. He may have the more realistic assessment of their capacity for clear thinking. In any event, Searle recognizes that his psychological explanation of antirealism is not sufficient. "Pointing out the psychological origins of antirealism is not a refutation of antirealism. It would be a genetic fallacy to suppose that by exposing the illegitimate origins of the arguments against realism, we somehow refute the arguments."

Searle makes a bracing case for philosophical realism understood as the "Enlightenment vision." But like many, perhaps most, of those whom he calls "the educated members of our civilization at the turn of the millennium," intellectual inquiry stops at the edge of certain dogmatic boundaries. When it comes to some truths about "*how things really are* in the world" (emphasis his), we "are no longer dealing with matters of philosophical analysis" but with "the results of modern science." "As far as we know anything at all about how the world works, there are two propositions of modern science that are not, so to speak, up for grabs. They are not optional. . . . These are the atomic theory of matter and the evolutionary theory of biology." He does not make an argument for these propositions or dogmas; they are simply assumed by "the educated members of our civilization at the turn of the millennium." But of course these propositions have everything to do with "philosophical analysis," as we shall see in discussing Edward Pols' *Mind Regained.* The two dogmas as asserted by Searle determine his philosophical materialism, his understanding of cause and effect, and his atheism.

On these questions, Searle's is an engaging but thoroughly unconvincing instance of "beyondism." He says we are beyond the conflict between materialism and what he calls dualism, and then he opts for the default position of materialism. He says we are beyond the debate between atheism and theism, and then he opts for the default position of atheism. He even has a section titled "Beyond Atheism" in which he notes that earlier philosophers of his disposition, such as John Stuart Mill and Bertrand Russell, thought it necessary to mount "polemical and eloquent attacks on traditional religion." That was then, this is now. "Nowadays nobody bothers, and it is considered in slightly bad taste to even raise the question of God's existence. Matters of religion are like matters of sexual preference: they are not to be discussed in public and even the abstract questions are discussed only by bores."

What the "Educated" Can Believe

Impatience with abstract questions might be viewed as a deficiency in a philosopher, especially one who proposes to explain *how things really are* in the world. The fact that Searle dismisses abstract questions about God as boring no doubt explains why he has not given serious attention to such questions, which he manifestly has not. The smugness and insularity of a world of discourse in which the following passage is presumably thought to be intellectually coherent would be cause for astonishment, were its kind not so frequently encountered. Searle writes:

> For us, the educated members of society, the world has become demystified. Or rather, to put the point more precisely, we no longer take the mysteries we see in the world as expressions of supernatural meaning. We no longer think of odd occurrences as cases of God performing speech acts in the language of miracles. Odd occurrences are just occurrences we do not understand. The result of this demystification is that we have gone beyond atheism to a point where the issue no longer matters in the way it did to earlier generations. For us, if it should turn out that God exists, that would have to be a fact of nature like any other. To the four basic forces in the universe — gravity, electromagnetism, weak and strong nuclear forces — we would add a fifth, the divine force. Or more likely, we would see the other forces as forms of the divine force. But it would still be all physics, albeit divine physics. If the supernatural existed, it too would have to be natural.

"For us, the educated members of society." What a fine ring of invincible complacency that has. It is a phrase that

Schleiermacher used almost two hundred years ago in describing "the cultured despisers of religion." Note also Searle's assertion that, no matter what turns out to be the case, it "would have to be a fact of nature like any other." That certitude has already been determined by the aforementioned dogmas that, as he says, are not up for grabs, and indeed are not subject to intellectual challenge or inquiry. The word "God" in Searle's discussion, needless to say, has nothing to do with what serious thinkers from Plato to Aquinas to Balthasar have meant by "God." But then, Searle has told us that those who think seriously about such questions are bores. Which presumably gives him license to be supremely unserious, as in the above paragraph that may kindly be described as non-sense.

I know nothing about John Searle's history, but there is a deep and evident animus at work here. Religion is no more than superstition and deserving of unbridled derision. His tone is that of the village atheist of yesteryear, now, one might have thought, almost an extinct species. For us, the educated members of society (if I may borrow a phrase), the vulgar exhibition of ignorance and hostility is an embarrassment. It is disconcerting to watch a distinguished professor of philosophy at a leading university as he thinks he is clinching an argument by pointing out that human credulity has played a part in religion. In Italy he lived near a church where a statue of Mary was found buried in a garden, and people used to believe (hee-hee) that it had fallen from heaven. That was then, this is now.

"Even if the statue were found in the gardens of the Vatican," Searle writes, "the church authorities would not claim it had fallen out of heaven. That is not a possible thought for us because, in a sense, we know too much." The "in a sense" is a nice qualifier, but it does not seem to qualify anything. Obviously, the statue's falling from heaven is "a possible thought" because John Searle thought it — not seriously, of course — in order to reject it. But his real clincher is the Shroud of Turin, the dating of which, according to radioactive tests, is still disputed. Whatever the right date, Searle concludes with this: "But, and this is the point, why do we assume the tests are more to be believed than the miracle? Why should God's miracle be answerable to carbon 14?" Simply at the level of Logic 101, it seems not to occur to Mr. Searle that the point of the tests is to determine whether it is a miracle, for if it is not a miracle there is no miracle to believe in or not believe in. Of course, we could have an interesting discussion about what is meant by a miracle. But we have already been told that people who discuss such things are bores, except, presumably, when Mr. Searle discusses them. If I understand him correctly, he believes he has the advantage in understanding such matters because he knows they are undeserving of serious thought. I think I mentioned that he is professor of philosophy at Berkeley, a school of no little renown.

Thinking About Our Thoughts

But I do not take back what I said earlier. *Mind, Language, and Society* is an intelligent argument for philosophical realism and a telling polemic against the antirealists, crippled only by an "Enlightenment vision" of a relentlessly dogmatic and reductionist force. The reductionist belief system within which Searle is constrained could not be more explicitly stated. In an intellectual world far removed from Searle's, the theologian Dietrich Bonhoeffer wrote witheringly about a "God of the gaps" in which the word "God" is no more than a placeholder until we get a better explanation. John Searle subscribes to what we might call "philosophy of the gaps." Philosophy, he says, "is concerned with questions that we do not yet have an agreed-on method of answering." When science provides an answer, we will no longer need philosophy. "A good example of this is the problem of the nature of life. This was once a philosophical problem, but it ceased to be so when advances in molecular biology enabled us to break down what seemed a large mystery into a series of smaller, manageable, specific biological questions and answers. I hope that something similar will happen to the problem of consciousness."

For all the interesting things that John Searle has written about mind and consciousness, both here and elsewhere, his dogma so cripples his thought that, in principle, he cannot explore possibilities other than those with which he begins. His "Enlightenment vision" is, in fact, an iron cage. It would seem that his demystification has to end up in the mystification that all our thinking can in fact be broken down into something less than thought, which means we only think we think, or, more precisely, we have neither mind nor consciousness. There are neural firings in the brain that we call thoughts, but, if there are only neural firings, it becomes exceedingly difficult to know who or what are the "we" who call them thoughts. As Stephen M. Barr recently wrote in these pages, we should pay close attention to the best minds of our time, but we may be permitted to ignore them when they tell us they have no minds. It would seem that it is only by virtue of his inconsistencies — inconsistencies that, for the sake of his sanity, we may deem felicitous inconsistencies — that John Searle does not explicitly say that he has no mind at all. When, as he hopes, the mystery of mind and consciousness is broken down by science into a series of smaller, manageable, specific biological questions and answers, how would we know whether they are the right questions and answers, and what in this context would "knowing" mean? Mr. Searle's well-intended defense of realism finally evaporates into the mists of unreality.

Another Realism

A very different treatment of these questions is offered by Edward Pols, longtime professor of philosophy at Bowdoin College, in *Mind Regained.* His essay is marked by a breadth of vision, clarity of expression, and unembarrassed humility before what we do not, and perhaps cannot, understand. Against postmodernist fashions, Pols, too, is a determined realist. His previous book was *Radical Realism: Direct Knowing in Science and Philosophy*. His realism, however, is not confined by the iron cage of dogmatic reductionism. He urges us to pay close attention to the phenomenon of the mind as we actually experience it in discerning and thinking about reality. The mind *as experienced* should be admitted as evidence in our thinking about the mind. For Searle and many others, the story of philosophy really begins with Descartes and systematic skepticism about the relationship between mind and reality. Everything prior to and counter to the Cartesian starting point is, with varying degrees of insouciance, dismissed as obfuscation — or more simply, as boring.

Pols takes very seriously the moment in human thought that began with Descartes in the seventeenth century and reached its climax in the exchange between Hume and Kant at the end of the eighteenth. But he views it only as that, a moment in the much longer and larger history of human reflection on the nature of the world and our part in it. Pols treats Descartes with great respect, even reverence, and in *Mind Regained* offers a marvelously lucid exposition of the *Meditations*, making the point that moderns who take their Descartes without what he had to say about God and infinity are simply not taking Descartes seriously. Descartes, Pols suggests, would not recognize his thought in what many contemporary textbooks present as the Cartesian turning point.

Pols begins his story at the beginning. "For the West, the conceptual shape of this study of mind was formed by such great philosophical doctrines as those of Plato, Aristotle, Plotinus, and Thomas Aquinas. That doctrinal tradition culminates in the medieval notion of the mind of a creative God, a notion whose power in the West is hard to overstate. For a long time the notion was as important in science as in religion and morals; and although its importance for science gradually diminished after the eighteenth century, it remained a vital force for our culture in general all through the nineteenth century." The perception of the human mind as participating in the mind of an "other" is deeply entrenched in our culture, and careful reflection upon that perception leads to a consideration of "causes" — material, efficient, formal, and final — that cannot reduce the mind to something less than we "know" it to be. "From antiquity until the present," Pols writes, "certain highly complex entities have seemed so impressive that their functions do not seem to be adequately accounted for if they are regarded as mere assemblages of more basic entities." That perception undergirds and is essential to the idea of human beings as rational and moral agents.

Playing Billiards with Mozart

I cannot do justice to the elegance of Pols' argument in this space, but he contends that reason compels the conclusion that "*there is an ordering power intrinsic to nature that cannot be adequately explained in scientific terms*" and that "*the ordering power intrinsic to nature works also in human purpose*" (emphasis his). These are, admittedly, bold assertions, but they are derived from close attention to the mind itself. By the mind itself, Pols writes, "I mean the *full concreteness*, the *full actuality*, the *wholeness* of mind, the *lived reality* of mind." He illustrates his point by an imaginative but convincing reconstruction of what was happening when Mozart was playing billiards and taking time out from the game to write down musical passages he was composing in his head, and what is happening in our minds when we read about Mozart doing that. One can abstract what is undeniably a piece of what is happening, such as the central nervous system or neural synapses in the brain, but one has not thereby captured what is happening. "Although the central nervous system is a thing of flesh and blood and so concrete enough, it is then being considered in abstraction from the full concreteness of mind itself." It is simply arbitrary to declare that this piece, separated from all the other pieces of what is happening, is the explanation of the whole.

Much of modern philosophy, says Pols, has made a "negative judgment" about the mind. But there is a curious incoherence in this judgment. "In short," he writes, "the negative philosophical judgment about the powers of the human mind was reached by the study of mind itself — a study conducted of course by mind itself. I call the judgment negative because its most profound claim is that the mind cannot get at reality, at what is the case, at what is independent of mind's own capacity to believe or to construct. It needs to be emphasized that the negative judgment still hovers over science itself, even as it did in the days of Hume and Kant. If that judgment is taken seriously, science cannot be exempt from it. An incapacity on the part of the mind to know what is real in independence of the mind's own construction is a general incapacity. It is thus a paradox that the negative judgment has turned attention away from the study of the mind itself to the scientific study of the infrastructure of mind." Pols' contention is that the mind's study of the mind must pay attention to the mind itself. The alternative, although he does not put it quite this way, is that we tell ourselves we are studying the mind while determinedly ignoring, or even denying, the mind that is being studied and, most important, the mind that is doing the studying.

Pols is deeply respectful of science, and of the scientific method as conventionally defined, and he is also keenly aware of its limitations. In one section he spells out the eight steps, or principles, in the received scientific doctrine of causality, concluding with these: "6. Causality has no telic [purposeful] feature, although human beings tend to attribute teleology (final causality) to nature. 7. Causality has no form-creating feature, other than that expressed in the laws of nature. 8. Agency as such, whether divine or human, forms no part of a scientific causal explanation: although human agency is often appealed to in commonsense causal explanations, agency itself is subject to causal explanation in the sense of the preceding principles. Agency is thus something to be explained, not something that is in itself explanatory." The last point is crucial. What agent is to explain that there is no agency? Which brings us back to some of the best minds of our day telling us they have no mind.

The Knower and the Known

With respect to the "negative judgment of the mind," Pols sums up his case with the observation that it is futile and incoherent to try to achieve an absolute separation of the knower from the known:

> With this phase of our reflective turn we overcome the negative philosophical judgment about the power of our minds which has gradually developed in the course of the epistemological era that is coincidental with modernity — including that last jaded period of modernity which now masquerades as postmodernity. The negative judgment led to the dismal conviction that we can know neither other beings nor ourselves directly and so cannot know any causal significance they may have. It contributed to the gradual discrediting of a complex and nuanced doctrine of causality which, whatever its limitations, left some explanatory room for morality, art, and religion. It left us with a scientific doctrine of causality for which it is impossible to provide a satisfactory philosophical justification. To speak more precisely, it condemned us to oscillate between the conviction that the scientific doctrine is a thoroughly adequate replacement for all the older views of causality and the suspicion that it is a useful pragmatic device whose writ must be carefully circumscribed. It is time to set aside the negative philosophical judgment once and for all.

Between the arguments of Searle and Pols a decision must be made. Pols' is the more aesthetically and intellectually attractive, in that it is marked by modesty, a seriousness that eschews flippancy, a readiness to engage alternative explanations, and a refusal to take refuge in fundamentalist dogma — whether religious or scientific — that is finally a form of fideism. The subtitle of Searle's book is "philosophy in the real world," but it is Pols who attends to the mind as we actually experience it in the real world. He is the uncompromising realist in refusing to accept less than a conclusive argument that that experience is delusory. (And it is impossible to imagine what such an argument might look like.) Most important, Pols can understand and explain the intellectual moves made by Searle, while Searle steadfastly ignores the moves made by Pols.

Thus Pols' argument is able to give an account of Searle's argument, whereas Searle refuses to engage the argument of Pols — and of Plato, Aristotle, Augustine, Aquinas, and a good many contemporary philosophers. What Mozart thought he was doing as he played billiards and what you think you are doing as you read these words have, for Searle, no explanatory force. Your thinking is the object to be explained, but there appears to be no explaining subject. Put differently, the explaining subject, the rational agent, disappears into the fundament of the (as yet to be scientifically determined) explanation. Those who think that this poses metaphysical puzzles deserving of careful exploration are for John Searle and "the educated members of our civilization at the turn of the millennium" to be dismissed as "bores."

Three final points. I do not know what religious conclusions, if any, Edward Pols draws from his argument. He does not say. His essay is, at most, a prolegomenon to theological reflection, just as Searle's is intended to preclude such reflection. Second, it is not adequate to say, as Pols does, that the realism he champions leaves "some explanatory room for morality, art, and religion." This sounds once again like morality, art, and religion that is "of the gaps" — for the time being, until we achieve a fuller explanation. Pols' argument, it seems to me, not only invites but demands the explanatory employment of morality, art, and religion — in short, attentiveness to the mind as experienced in the real world. Morality, art, and religion are not short-term expedients until some better explanation of the real world comes along. They are irreplaceable and irreducible in the real world as experienced, as well as in any world we can imagine, recognizing that our imagining is part of the real world as experienced. I am not sure whether Pols would disagree with that. Third, one should not leave this subject without noting that the caricature of religion and theology offered by thinkers such as John Searle is too often a caricature handed them by religious thinkers who, as we are reminded by the recent encyclical *Fides et Ratio* (Faith and Reason), do not respect the imperatives of thinking clearly. But that is another big subject, also aptly described as intriguing.

❧ Charles Colson of Prison Fellowship approves of John Paul II's appeal that all the world's bishops should visit a prison during the Jubilee Year. But then, so many evangelical Protestants respond favorably to this Pope. As a Southern Baptist official remarked fifteen years ago at the beginning of the pontificate, "You guys sure got a Pope who knows how to pope." In this instance, however, even the *National Catholic Reporter* approves of the Pope's suggestion: "This is the kind of imaginative gesture John Paul has made all too seldom. Too preoccupied with keeping the lid on doctrine and discipline, he failed to use his vast popularity to act rather than react, to enable rather than control. Yet it's never too late." So apparently there is still time for him to learn how to pope. On the other hand, who would have predicted that twenty years of unimaginative repression and reaction would have produced such "vast popularity"?

❧ For years Northern High School in Calvert County, Maryland, had student-led prayer at commencement. Earlier this year the ACLU protested, and the school ruled that the student who wished to pray could call for a silent "time for reflection," but without mentioning God. Come the commencement and the time for reflection, a voice in the crowd intoned "Our Father who art in heaven" and soon at least half the crowd of four thousand was joining in the Lord's Prayer. The ACLU stated, "The real loser here is the Constitution and the right of people to express dissent." I expect that some of the people thought that is exactly what they were doing.

❧ To paraphrase the title of an old movie, "They kill old people and cripples, don't they?" Mention the Netherlands and that's the question that comes to mind. For decades the Dutch have been in the vanguard of nations allowing euthanasia and doctor-assisted suicide. What was previously allowed is now to be formally legalized. A bill proposed to the parliament also allows children aged twelve and over to make their own euthanasia decisions, even against their parents' objections, if a doctor consents. The aptly named Dr. Ben Crul of the Royal Dutch Medical Association supports the measure, noting that children with terminal illnesses are "a lot more grown-up than many adults." An official of the Justice Ministry says it's a matter of consistency, since teenagers can already get contraceptive devices and abortions without their parents' consent. It makes a kind of sense. Why shouldn't those who have a right to kill also have a right to be killed? The culture of consistency, also known as the culture of death.

Science, Matter, Spirit, and Three-Card Monte

Watch very carefully now. There are three cards: one named Spirit, one named Matter, and the other Science. The dealer shuffles them quickly and places them face down. Now, which is Spirit, which Matter, and which Science? It's illegal, of course, but three-card monte is regularly played by young hustlers on the streets of New York (less regularly since Giuliani). They set up a cardboard box for a table and can count on gathering a crowd of locals and tourists, the former enjoying the gullibility of the latter who invariably lose the dollars they put down in the misplaced confidence that their eye is faster than the dealer's hand.

Most of us are tourists, so to speak, when it comes to the great debates among scientists and philosophers about the nature of reality. But it's marvelous fun to listen in. There is, for instance, this continuing confabulation about the connections between brain, mind, and consciousness. It seems that at least two new books on the subject appear every week. This week there is Colin McGinn's *The Mysterious Flame: Conscious Minds in a Material World* (Basic Books). McGinn, a British philosopher currently at Rutgers, argues that the existence of consciousness in a material world is a deep mystery that we will never unravel. It is, he insists, an entirely natural phenomenon that emerges from the physical brain ("a hunk of meat"), but we don't know how that happens and we never will know. And that for the simple reason that, as I have written elsewhere, our minds are not complex enough to understand our minds, and, if our minds were more complex than they are, our minds would have to be that much more complex in order to understand our minds. And so forth ad infinitum.

Galen Strawson of Jesus College, Oxford, has also produced a book on mind and consciousness. Writing in the *New York Times Book Review,* he is not unsympathetic to McGinn's claim that consciousness is an unfathomable mystery. McGinn's mistake, he writes, is to think that consciousness is unusual in this respect. McGinn thinks that, unlike matter, which we can understand, consciousness is a mystery. The truth of the matter, contends Strawson, is that we can't understand matter either. "Current physics thinks of matter as a thing of forces, energy, fields. And it can also seem natural to think of consciousness as a form or manifestation of energy, as a kind of force, and even, perhaps, as a kind of field. You may still feel the two things are deeply heterogeneous, but you really have no good reason to believe this. You just don't know enough about matter." Those who know enough about matter know that it, too, is a deep mystery.

Here's where the three-card monte comes in. Strawson opines that maybe Bertrand Russell was right when he conjectured more than seventy years ago that "we know nothing about the intrinsic quality of physical events except when these are mental events that we directly experience." Strawson writes: "It is not easy to hold onto this line of thought (it requires a kind of meditative effort), but it's the way to go. . . . It shows that there is nothing to be surprised about when it comes to consciousness, although there is a very great deal we don't understand. It deepens one's feeling for the material world — the only world there is."

The last five words clearly indicate where the card marked Matter is, right? Just as clearly, in this variation of the game, Matter is trump and therefore materialism wins, right? But think again. Remember that matter is "a thing of forces, energy, fields." It is all mystery, says Strawson. It sounds very much like "being," which many philosophers (knowing this line of thought requires intense meditative effort) say is that which you cannot think not to be. Strawson presents himself as a materialist. When people do that, it usually means they don't want to get into the God question and all that. But he is already into it, and possibly over his head. The trick of the game is that the Matter card is now the Spirit card, and the Science card is Philosophy, which can also be used in a variation of the game, called Theology. To speak of reality as infinite mystery, as many scientist-philosophers now do, is to say that we can only speak of it analogously (analogy being a much more sophisticated concept than Russell's "mental events").

Analogy goes like this: "A is to B as C is to D." So, for example, "God is to the world as the artist is to his painting."

Theological language — and philosophical language that addresses how things really are — is necessarily analogous, and that because we can only speak of ultimate reality (a.k.a. God) in terms of the created things that we know. The Fourth Lateran Council (1215) declared that "No similarity can be found [between God and His creatures] so great but that the dissimilarity is even greater." Strawson is surely right; the distinction is not between matter, which we understand, and consciousness, which is a mystery. Rather, it is, so to speak, mystery all the way down and all the way up. Nor does "mystery" denote the terra incognita beyond the limits of our present understanding; that way of speaking makes mystery synonymous with a puzzle that we may one day come to understand. Mystery is not what is left over after our understanding fails. Rather, it is the case that we have come to *understand* that it is mystery all the way up and all the way down. Put differently, matter, too, is spirit. (In the first volume of his *Systematic Theology,* Wolfhart Pannenberg very suggestively discusses the Holy Spirit in terms of what contemporary science calls the universal force field.)

Tainted Science

For very understandable historical reasons, as distinct from logical reasons, most scientists dealing with questions such as the brain-mind-consciousness connections have a powerful aversion to anything hinting of religion or theology. In scientific circles, to be known to be a believer is to be vulnerable to the suspicion that your science is tainted by your religion. This goes way back to Hume's divorce of "fact" and "value," with science addressing the former and religion (along with poetry, literature, and other private indulgences) addressing the latter. For a long time, most scientists and theologians have been content to play on their side of the divide between fact and value, with theologians frequently wanting to treat the divide more as a net in a game of table tennis. (See Basil Mitchell, *How to Play Theological Ping-Pong: Essays on Faith and Reason,* 1990.) Scientists typically were not interested in playing that game.

One way for scientists to avoid being bothered by pesky theologians or by philosophers who want to take on the big questions was to adamantly declare themselves to be materialists. The material world, asserts Strawson, is "the only world there is." The late television astronomer Carl Sagan delighted in concluding his programs with the pronunciamento that matter is all there is, all there ever was, and all there ever will be. But what to do when the most rigorous scientific thought about the hardest evidence leads to the conclusion that matter and spirit are not antithetical, that at the deepest level matter is spirit, and maybe even Spirit? Galen Strawson is right in saying that this line of thought is the way to go. But the perduring aversion to religion, theology, and serious philosophy is such that we should not expect most scientists to advance quickly or directly in this line of thought. Be prepared for decades to come in which some scientists will persist in the sleight of hand by which they switch the cards marked Matter, Spirit, and Science. Three-card monte is a mug's game, but we can understand why some people think they need it.

It is mystery all the way upward, all the way downward, and all the way backward. It is the last direction that was addressed twenty years ago by astronomer Robert Jastrow in *God and the Astronomers.* In trying to discover the origin of the universe, he wrote,

> We would like to pursue the inquiry farther back in time, but the barrier to further progress seems insurmountable. It is not a matter of another year, another decade of work, another measurement, or another theory; at this moment it seems as though science will never be able to raise the curtain on the mystery of creation. For the scientist who has lived by his faith in the power of reason, the story ends like a bad dream. He has scaled the mountains of ignorance; he

is about to conquer the highest peak; as he pulls himself over the final rock, he is greeted by a band of theologians who have been sitting there for centuries.

The danger of that well-known passage is that it can contribute to smugness among theologians, and it can be used to perpetuate the old idea that theology is unrelated to reason. As so powerfully argued in the 1998 encyclical *Fides et Ratio,* faith that does not think is no faith at all. But Jastrow's observation does underscore the end of an older form of scientific reason — sometimes called scientism — that was relentlessly constrictive and reductionist in what it permitted people to think. Now the best of science opens toward wonder, and the opening toward wonder can be an opening toward wisdom. It is not equivalent to, but neither is it unrelated to, the words of the psalmist, "The fear of the Lord is the beginning of wisdom."

Watch very carefully now. The cards are quickly shuffled and placed face down. Which is Matter, which is Spirit, and which Science? What if each is all and all each? The next time you meet someone who declares himself a materialist, you might want, if he is an intellectually serious person, to encourage him. Perhaps he is not materialist enough. As Galen Strawson says, it's the way to go. And, I would add, to keep on going, ever deeper into the mystery, at the heart of which — or so it has been discovered by most of the most thoughtful of our species — is Wisdom.

❧ What a beautiful brouhaha. The Brooklyn Museum of Art scheduled a British show called "Sensation" and featuring, among other items designed to shock, carved-up animals floating in a tank of formaldehyde and the bust of a man made from his own frozen blood. Most attention was fixed on *The Holy Virgin Mary,* a painting by a young man by the name of Chris Ofili, which has clumps of elephant dung pasted on Mary and a background of bottoms and genitalia cut out of pornographic magazines. The papers played up

Catholic protests against the exhibit, almost as though other Christians worship a Lord born of a different mother. But things really heated up when Mayor Rudolph Giuliani said taxpayers shouldn't pay for blasphemous schlock and threatened to cut off city funds for the Museum. The usual alarums about artistic freedom were raised, although from some surprising corners the point was made that nobody should be surprised if shock art elicits the reaction of shock politics. Hillary Clinton, who is presumably running against Giuliani for U.S. Senate, criticized the mayor's threat to cut funds, but indicated that she was personally opposed to the porno and dung depiction of the Blessed Virgin. She said she would not go to see the show. Other museum directors in the city were strangely subdued because, it was said, they feared for their own city funding or, as others said, because they realized that the Brooklyn Museum had recklessly gone one outrage too far. Art critics at the *Times,* not surprisingly, defended the exhibit. It was repeatedly noted that Ofili is a Catholic and therefore the painting cannot be anti-Catholic. In addition, he is of African background, and in some parts of Africa, or so they claimed, elephant dung is a symbol of fertility, and Ofili has also used it on other paintings. They did not claim that there is a distinctively African symbolic understanding of pornography. Carol Vogel of the *Times* tried to set straight opponents of the show: "While news reports have described his paintings as being splattered with dung, the clumps are actually carefully placed on each canvas." So there. Carefully placed dung is an entirely different matter. Back in London, Ofili says he is mystified by the controversy over the painting. "There's something incredibly simple but incredibly basic about it. It attracts a multiple of meanings and interpretations," he said. Incredible is the word. He is currently working on a painting called "Magic Monkey" that tries "to capture the three powerful elements of life: sex, money, and drugs." These are represented by separate (and carefully placed) clumps of elephant dung and colored tops that he buys at the grocery store. Ofili's paintings are selling briskly. One went for $36,000 last year, and it is expected that prices will soar as a result of the current row. Says noted collector Dean Valentine, "Of all the young British painters I think he's by far the best. The paintings have a depth of expression. He has something to say." This is artistic self-parody and political soap opera of rare quality. From Paris 1914 and Stravinsky's *Rite of Spring* to dung art in Brooklyn, one may be permitted to hope that this is the way a misguided inspiration ends, with a political bang and an artistic whimper.

❧ From an aerial view, the human population looks like a cancerous growth on planet Earth. Or so says physician and epidemiologist Dr. Warren M. Hern, who, perhaps not incidentally, is big in the abortion business. Considering that the developed world, notably Western Europe, has a birth rate that assures a declining-to-disappearing population in the future, this gloomy observation comes as something of a surprise. It was popular fare, though, at a meeting of the American Anthropological Society in December 1998, where the ideas of the Rev. Thomas Robert Malthus were enthusiastically bandied about. This too comes as something of a surprise, since Malthus predicted two hundred years ago that imminent overpopulation beyond the planet's capacity would lead to mass poverty, misery, and destruction, and, as far as we can tell, that hasn't happened. There has been more than enough misery in this century that John Paul II calls "a century of tears," but overpopulation is not among the chief culprits. In fact, population growth rates are beginning to trail off, even in apparently overpopulated areas such as Bangladesh. But the theory's being devastatingly falsified does not deter Malthusians any more than the collapse of communism deters some Marxists. Thus in the symposium entitled "Is the Human Species a Cancer on the Planet?" one Dr. Lynn Margulis — known for her "Gaia Hypothesis," which postulates that Earth is one giant organism herself — solemnly asserted, "For millions of years, the

Earth got along without human beings, and it will do so again. The only question is the nature of the human demise that has already begun." In agreeing with her, anthropologist Dr. Kenneth Wise insists he is not necessarily supporting human extermination on the record, since, after all, "facing up to dangerous ideas is not the same as advocating them." The conference participants don't expect that the great unwashed overpopulated masses will take them seriously anyway. "You don't seem to realize the problems created by population pressures until you get old, and then nobody listens to you," complained another anthropologist, Dr. Bernice A. Kaplan. In some instances, that is probably a very good thing.

To Be a "Normal" Society

For a number of years now, I have been involved in the *Centesimus Annus* Seminar in Krakow, Poland. In that seminar we bring together young academics and clergy from Poland and other Central and Eastern European countries to study Catholic teaching regarding the free and just society. Since the Revolution of 1989, I have noticed a striking change in the attitudes of Central European students toward democracy, and more particularly toward the American version of democracy. In the first few years, everything American was thought to be good. We had to caution the students against an uncritical admiration of everything American.

More recently, a certain disillusionment has been evident. In Poland, the Czech Republic, Hungary, Ukraine — and especially in Russia — people have discovered that democracy is not easy. After the Communist era, these societies declared their determination to be "normal" societies. Now they have discovered that normality is difficult. It is difficult in Poland as it is difficult in the United States, as it is difficult in Italy, Zimbabwe, Brazil, and everywhere else in the world. Our seminar students have learned that they cannot simply imitate things American but must find their own way to democracy. And yet — as the largest, the most influential, and arguably the oldest and most vital democratic experiment in world history — America remains both model and warning. In Central and Eastern Europe today, the question of American democracy and the question of American power get entangled in confusing ways. There is a sometimes latent but nonetheless strong streak of anti-Americanism in many European minds. That is in part a leftover from Marxist ideological influences, in part an understandable envy of America's preeminence on so many scores, and in part a justifiable resentment of the imperious, if not imperial, ways the U.S. throws its weight around. (International affairs are not, and probably cannot be, conducted democratically.)

There is no dispute that the U.S. is the only remaining superpower in the world. Some go further and say that America is the world's "lead society," meaning that what happens in America will, sooner or later, mutatis mutandis, happen elsewhere. There is a strong element of truth in this. As we have had frequent occasion to observe, the world deserves a better "lead society" than the U.S., but this is what the world is stuck with, at least for the foreseeable future.

Catholic social teaching in the past, I think it fair to say, has been somewhat indifferent to the American experience. When Rome addressed questions such as democracy and church-state relations, it was usually with the French Revolution of 1789 chiefly in mind. In recent years, and most impressively in the pontificate of John Paul II, that has changed dramatically. It seems to me, however, that in the United States and elsewhere Catholic intellectuals have hardly begun to internalize the impressive teaching initiatives of the pontificate. As George Weigel contends in his magnificent *Witness to Hope: The Biography of John Paul II* (HarperCollins), coming to terms with the arguments of John Paul is a great task for years to come. We are dealing here with what is called, following John Henry Newman, the development of doctrine. That development will be clearer if, as with *Centesimus Annus,* we give the Revolution of 1776 at least equal billing with the Revolution of 1789 in addressing democracy, church-state relations, and related questions.

❦ Bats in the belfry are a venerable phenomenon, but in the thirteenth-century All Saints Church in the village of Mattersey, England, 150 miles north of London, bats are pretty much wherever they want to be. The same is true all over the country. Britain has sixteen species of bats and seven prefer to reside in churches. Bat-protection laws prevent their being removed, or even disturbed. Bats are terribly messy creatures, but the conservation group English Nature reminds worshipers of the "significance of the church for bats," and suggests that works of art and other valued objects be moved to areas that receive what it terms "a low rate of deposition." Parishioners are cautioned not to remove bat droppings just because they want to sit there. Rather, they should "count the number of spots of urine or droppings" in order to provide better "baseline data on the disposition of bat excreta." Politics frequently requires hard choices, and at some point Parliament may have to consider which is the more endangered species, bats or people who go to church. If it is forced to choose between the two species of churchgoers, observers are not sure that people would win. With old barns and other farm buildings dwindling in the English countryside, bats need new roosts, and cold, drafty churches suit them best. They need the churches. For people, church is optional. It makes sense, in an eccentrically English way.

❦ *The Kissinger Transcripts,* just out from New Press, provide insights on Kissinger's and Nixon's secret meetings with, among others, Chairman Mao. At Mao's residence on February 21, 1972, Kissinger engages in diplomatic flattery, telling

Mao that he assigned his writings in his Harvard classes. Mao responds, "Those writings of mine aren't anything. There is nothing instructive in what I wrote." Nixon protests, "The Chairman's writings moved a nation and have changed the world." No, says Mao, "I haven't been able to change it. I've only been able to change a few places in the vicinity of Beijing." Mao talks about his impending death. "Anyway, God has sent me an invitation." In a 1975 meeting, Mao expands on that. "I am going to Heaven soon. And when I see God, I'll tell him it's better to have Taiwan under the care of the United States now." Kissinger says he is astonished to hear him say that. "No," answers Mao, "because God blesses you, not us. God does not like us because I am a militant warlord, also a Communist. That's why he doesn't like me. He likes you." Kissinger, apparently embarrassed by this turn in the conversation, says, "I've never had the pleasure of meeting him, so I don't know." Astonishment is in order.

❧ The new edition of Wilson Follett's *Modern American Usage,* revised by Erik Wensberg and published by Hill and Wang, says "good usage is what people who think and care about words believe it to be." Exactly. I am of the prescriptive rather than descriptive school, the chief prescription being that you think and care about how something is written, and then test it by whether it sounds right. There are right and wrong ways of saying things. The descriptivists speak of "standard" and "nonstandard" English, the latter being a weasel word for substandard. John Simon reviews the new Follett's and thinks it very good. Rules of good usage, he writes, are like good manners. "One can muddle through without them, but they make the world infinitely more civil, efficient and livable in." Surely "immeasurably" would be the better word. But it is with "livable in" that Mr. Simon indulges his sense of mischief. Better, and less pedantic, to say "more civil, efficient and livable." (I will not even mention the missing comma before "and.") Livable — as in tolerable, bearable, enjoyable. Livable in? Really. Put it to the sound test.

American History and Theological Nerve

We begin the new millennium without millennialism. At least in our public life there is little talk about the unfolding of a providentially directed plan for the world, with America cast in the leading role. It was very different in the beginnings of the American experiment. The framers of the Constitution declared this to be a *novus ordo seclorum* — a new order for the ages. Those words appear on the Great Seal of the United States and are printed on the back of every dollar bill. The idea of newness, of progress, has always been at the heart of the American experience. Also in our political life of more recent decades we have had Franklin Roosevelt's New Deal, John F. Kennedy's New Frontier, and Ronald Reagan's "It's morning in America." Although it may now be hard to remember, Bill Clinton ran in 1992 on the promise of a New Covenant, meaning a renewed relationship of mutual trust and obligation between leadership and people.

Such political slogans are weak echoes of an understanding of history that was once given powerful expression in the public life of "Christian America." The millennialist (or millenarian) vision is grounded in Judeo-Christian tradition, notably in the Old Testament's Book of Daniel and late Jewish apocalyptic literature of the pre-Christian era. The main source of the teaching and its subsequent impact on history, however, is the New Testament Book of Revelation, especially chapter twenty. Christian millennialists fall into two camps, premillennialists and postmillennialists. Premillennialists believe that the second coming of Christ will precede the millennium, which is a thousand-year period in which the world will know perfect peace, justice, and general blessedness. Postmillennialists believe that Christ will return after we have succeeded in establishing such a happy circumstance on earth.

Most Christians of both the past and present are not millennialists of any variety. What the Book of Revelation means by a thousand-year reign of the saints on earth is, in the mainstream of Christian orthodoxy, taken to be a deep mystery about which the greatest reticence is in order. On this question, too, St. Augustine (354-430) prevailed, especially in the Christian West, with his antimillennialist reading of history. In Augustine's view, the "city of God" and the "city of man" would continue in ambiguous tension and conflict until the final judgment when Christ returns in triumph and brings history to a definitive end.

The Augustinian view discourages excessive excitements about the possibilities of history. Millennial excitements erupted from time to time, as with the twelfth-century Joachim of Fiore, and exploded in the sixteenth century among Anabaptists, Bohemian Brethren, and other groups belonging to what is called the radical Reformation. Postmillennial convictions, however, were by no means limited to a radical fringe. In this country, the belief that America is God's instrument for establishing the millennium and thus ushering in the Kingdom of God was, with varying degrees of theological explicitness, the official faith of Christian, and very Protestant, America. Postmillennialism dominated public thought and speech well into the twentieth century.

Putting Reason on Alert

The Enlightenment of the American Founders was not that of Voltaire or Rousseau but of an Anglo-Scottish stream of thought that put reason on alert to what was thought to be the unfolding of Providential purpose in history. John Adams, who would become the second President of the United States, wrote ten years before the Declaration of Independence about the Protestant Reformation liberating the world from the evil "confederacy" of Romish religion and political tyrants who had for centuries held humankind in thrall.

Thus, as long as this confederacy lasted, and the people were held in ignorance, liberty, and with her, knowledge and virtue too, seem to have deserted the earth, and one age of darkness succeeded another, till God in his benign providence raised up the champions who began and conducted the Reformation. From the time of the Reformation to the first settlement of America, knowledge gradually spread in Europe, but especially in England; and in proportion as that increased and spread among the people, ecclesiastical and civil tyranny . . . seem to have lost their strength and weight.

It was in the world of the American Founders a conventional trope that, as with the course of the sun, enlightenment, liberty, and empire moved from East to West. From the Near East to Greece, from Greece to Rome, from Rome to England, and now, with wondrous consistency, across the Atlantic to America. In this vision, world history and spiritual destiny were unbreakably joined. Mark Hopkins, the preeminent nineteenth-century educator, gave voice to the common understanding:

Christianity has, indeed, always proposed to herself the subjugation of the world; but she had practically fallen back from her undertaking, not knowing the extent or character of her field. Gradually these were opening upon her, until about the commencement of the present century, when the command of Christ, interpreted by modern discoveries, began to work in the heart of the Church. This, though as yet far from assuming the place and creating the movement it ought, is still to be regarded as the central idea. Everything tends to show that this is to be the ultimate result of God's plan.

The idea that Christ's command to evangelize the world awaited implementation until the Protestant Reformation and the development of America may strike us as somewhat implausible, but it was from the seventeenth through the nineteenth century a commonplace in Christian America. In this context, "modern discoveries" such as the telegraph, transoceanic cables, and transcontinental railroad were all integral to the unfolding of Divine purpose. J. Downell, a representative Congregationalist minister, declared in 1869: "We must see a Divine adaptation and harmony in all this — a fitting together of means and ends, a playing of material instrumentalities over into the objects of the spiritual kingdom. Not a railroad is swung by God into its orbit, that he does not put to work on this upward mission." The upward mission of America, said Hopkins, is nothing less than "that triumph of Christianity in which alone the perfection of society is involved." Science and progress do not operate by their own momentum but are God's instruments for fitting the human being to "receive those influences of Christianity through which alone our perfect manhood can now find its consummation."

The Israel of Our Time

The much later Herman Melville of *Clarel* would become disillusioned and even bitter, but in *White Jacket,* the book that came just before *Moby Dick,* he powerfully summarizes the doctrine of his time in Christian America. A representative passage deserves to be quoted in full:

> Escaped from the house of bondage, Israel of old did not follow after the ways of the Egyptians. To her was given an express dispensation; to her were given new things under the sun. And we Americans are the particular, chosen people — the Israel of our time; we bear the ark of the liberties of the world. Seventy years ago we escaped from thrall; and besides our first birthright — embracing one continent of earth — God has given to us, for a future inheritance, the broad domains of the political pagans, that shall yet come

and lie down under the shade of our ark, without bloody hands being lifted. God has predestined, mankind expects, great things from our race; and great things we feel in our souls. The rest of the nations must soon be in our rear. We are the pioneers of the world; the advance-guard, sent on through the wilderness of untried things, to break a new path in the New World that is ours. In our youth is our strength; in our inexperience, our wisdom. At a period when other nations have but lisped, our deep voice is heard afar. Long enough have we been skeptics with regard to ourselves, and doubted whether, indeed, the political Messiah had come. But he has come in *us*, if we would but give utterance to his promptings. And let us always remember that with ourselves, almost for the first time in the history of earth, national selfishness is unbounded philanthropy; for we cannot do a good to America, but we give alms to the world.

Heady stuff, that. And it would live on through the stream of American consciousness, sometimes repressed and flowing underground, only to erupt again in moments of crisis or national exuberance. After World War I, a failing Woodrow Wilson took his case for ratifying the League of Nations to the American people. In Oakland, California, on September 18, 1919, he declared: "I wish that they [opponents of ratification] could feel the moral obligation that rests upon us not to go back on those boys, but to see the thing through, to see it through to the end and make good their redemption of the world. For nothing less depends upon this decision, nothing less than the liberation and salvation of the world." Something of the same intuition about the American possibility resonates in Martin Luther King's "I have a dream" speech of August 28, 1963, and the distance between John Winthrop's 1630 anticipation of a "a city upon a hill" and Ronald Reagan's "morning in America" is not so far as many seem to think.

While it is important to recall the vision of what Ernest

Lee Tuveson, in an engaging book by the same title, called the "Redeemer Nation," there is no denying that it is not the dominant vision in our public life at the beginning of a new millennium. Many changes in society and the political culture have worked transformations in the way we think of America and its role in world history. But perhaps more fundamental is the different way in which we think about progress, and especially moral progress. (See my article, "The Idea of Moral Progress," August/September 1999.) From John Winthrop and John Adams up through the present, there have been frequent bombast and boosterism — and no little measure of sinful pride — in the ways people have talked about America's "destiny" and its meaning for world history. Current enthusiasms marching under the banner of "multiculturalism" are, in part, motivated by the fear of a revival of national arrogance. In very small part, I should add, since the more aggressive forms of multiculturalism represent an attack on Western culture across the board, including its moral injunctions against arrogance.

There are many ways to explain the absence of millennial excitements today. Some might say that we have learned from history the tragedies produced by such excitements, as so thoroughly documented in, for instance, Norman Cohn's admirable book, *The Pursuit of the Millennium.* That may be part of it. But it is at least worth considering that our disinclination or inability to speak about God's purposes in history, and of America's part in His purposes, may reflect a failure of theological nerve. The modesty on which we pride ourselves may, in fact, be a lack of faith, or at least an unwillingness to let faith think in public about what God may be up to through time. Thinking about what God may be up to is not unrelated to what Christianity, from the New Testament through the Second Vatican Council, has meant by "reading the signs of the times." Such thinking need not be marked by hubris or apocalyptic excitements, as is amply demonstrated by St. Augustine and other worthies. Such thinking does assume that there are signs to be read and, in full awareness of the risks entailed, to be acted upon in faith.

❧ Seldom does headline hype soar so wondrously over the top. I confess to having choked on my breakfast Cheerios when confronted by this headline on the front page of the *Times:* "Mass Found in Elusive Particle: Universe May Never Be the Same." Wow! The universe may never be the same! The story continued: "Among other things, the finding might affect theories about the formation and evolution of galaxies and the ultimate fate of the universe." I love that, putting the ultimate fate of the universe into the category of "among other things." These excitements are occasioned by physicists announcing that they have discovered the existence of mass in an elusive subatomic particle called the neutrino. Malcolm Browne, the paper's excitable science writer, may be right that this is a very important discovery indeed. But it means the universe will never be the same? If the neutrino has mass today, didn't it have mass yesterday or, say, a billion years ago? Or maybe like Bishop Berkeley's falling tree in the forest, things are not unless we perceive they are. The headline's embrace of a radical theory of the social, in this case scientific, construction of reality seems somewhat overheated. I'm no authority on neutrinos; for all I know the little buggers do have mass, but I expect the universe is sublimely indifferent to our discovery of the fact. At the risk of sounding like an old-fashioned philosophical realist, I think we should be careful about assuming that our consciousness creates reality. A measure of modesty is in order, especially when the ultimate fate of the universe is at stake.

❧ The new norms for implementing the 1990 document *Ex Corde Ecclesiae* could be "disastrous" for Catholic higher education in the U.S., say the editors of *America.* The norms require that presidents of institutions, teachers of theology, and a majority of the boards of trustees be "faithful Catholics." *America* opines: "For Catholic colleges and universities that live in a world of accrediting associations and government regulation, the adoption of such norms would reverse three decades of development." Precisely.

Forget the Bilderbergers

Who will guard the guardians? That question, variously expressed, is among the oldest in political theory and practice. Jeremy Rabkin, professor of government at Cornell, has written an important book, *Why Sovereignty Matters* (1998), that addresses that old question in a way both thoughtful and provocative. It's not that national sovereignty is sacred. It's not. The sacralized nation-state is one of the great idols of modern history. At the same time, our ideas of political and legal legitimacy in "politics among nations" (Hans Morgenthau) assumes the sovereignty of the nation-state. And some nation-states, the United States among them, are founded on the premise of the political sovereignty of the people, as in government by "the consent of the governed." The guardians are guarded by their accountability to the sovereign people of the nation. These ideas of democratic legitimacy are gaining ascendancy in the world, but they do not go unchallenged.

Such challenges come from conventional despotisms and dictatorships and, increasingly, from Islamist versions of a divine right to rule. But the challenge also comes from the United Nations, or, more precisely, from the forces surrounding the UN known as Non-Governmental Organizations (NGOs). Forget the Bilderbergers, Masonic conspiracies, the Trilateral Commission, and black helicopters. Fevered fantasies about sinister plots to enslave the world only get in the way of trying to understand what is happening and what might be done about it. There are numerous organizations, including certain NGOs at the UN, that explicitly contend that the nation-state is the enemy, or at least is obsolete and an obstacle to global progress. Proposals for transcending the nation-state with a world government have been around for centuries, and gained many adherents following the catastrophic breakup of the world system in World War I.

World government proponents were deeply ambivalent about the formation of the UN after World War II, recognizing that in important respects it entrenched the nation-state by creating a General Assembly based on national representation and a Security Council reflecting the conventional notion of Great Powers. Advocates of world government were at the time divided about the UN, some saying it was a step in the right direction, others pointing out that you don't leap a great chasm by taking one step at a time. As things are turning out, the former view may have been more prescient.

I confess that I, too, have been ambivalent about the UN. The more gossamer stuff about a worldwide transcendence of differences and the establishment of universal and perpetual peace always struck me as what it is fairly called — globaloney. Perpetual peace and justice await the coming of the Kingdom, which I fully expect in God's good time, which is not yet. That being said, truth and human nature are, ultimately, universal, and there do need to be institutions for the accommodation of differences and containment of conflicts. One cannot help but be impressed also by the strong support the Holy See has given the UN from the start. Although very different, the UN and the Catholic Church share the distinction of being global institutions of moral-political influence. For reasons strategic as well as moral-theological, Rome has an interest in checking the absolutist claims of national sovereignty. As a participant in the UN, however, the Holy See today frequently finds itself allied — notably on population, development, and family issues — with that organization's sharpest critics.

The UN's Moral Right

In the early nineties I was a presidential appointee to a commission charged with reexamining U.S. policy toward the UN. I embarked upon that with an open mind, eager to learn and ready to have my prejudices corrected. The experience, I must admit, left me depressed about that institution. For one thing, I had not appreciated the pervasiveness and scale of the waste and corruption. Bureaucratic duplication, endless international conferencing, and quota systems in employment that are tantamount to graft and nepotism are pervasive and powerfully resistant to remedy. Much is made in some circles about the fact that the U.S. was for a long time in arrears in paying its dues. The bookkeeping behind that complaint is highly dubious and, in my judgment, the U.S. is right to insist upon fiscal and other reforms rather than pouring billions more dollars into a bottomless hole.

More important, I was struck by the prevailing assumption in UN leadership that it had, by moral right, replaced nation-states as the legitimate governor of the world. I recall a long meeting with then Secretary General Boutros Boutros-Ghali in which he complained that member states, and especially the U.S., were morally culpable in not providing the UN with the means to fulfill its role as global policeman, global doctor, global tutor, and global everything else. He seemed to be sincerely puzzled when I and others suggested, ever so respectfully, that his expansive view of the UN mandate was warranted neither by the charter nor by the consent of its members.

As one has too frequent occasion to remark, history has many ironies in the fire, and they surely are not lacking here. One irony is that some member nations actually sense that their status is enhanced by supporting the inflation of the UN's claims to govern. Of the 188 member nations, some are so very small that membership in the UN plays a key part in their claim to nationhood. Middling countries that tend to feel marginalized by the dominant players in international affairs can also feel that they are playing in the major leagues by inflating the importance of the UN and their role in it. Canada and the Scandinavian countries are notable in this respect; they are in the forefront of encouraging NGOs to assume the lead in pressing the UN organization to override national sovereignty. Thus we have the curious circumstance in which sovereign nations seek to enhance their importance by curtailing national sovereignty.

"Civil Society" from the Top Down

A further curiosity is that the NGOs now present themselves as the champions of "civil society." Current enthusiasm for civil society is usually traced to the arguments of Vaclav Havel, the Czech president, and others who posited the claims of civil society against the totalitarian claims of communism, and, earlier than that, to the *To Empower People* manifesto authored by Peter Berger and myself in order to lift up the crucial role of non-governmental "mediating institutions" in public policy. The whole idea of civil society was to distinguish sharply what is public and what is governmental, and thus to make government more accountable to the "people-sized" institutions of society. The irony is that, in the name of civil society, the NGOs at the UN are determined to expand the scope of government — under the auspices of the UN, its auxiliary organizations, and international law — in a manner that would make government accountable to the NGOs, which, in turn, are accountable to nobody but the philanthropies that fund them and their own, typically very small, memberships. The combination of small and middling nations curtailing national sovereignty to enhance their own sense of importance and of NGOs using the idea of civil society to undermine political accountability makes for a fine muddle in trying to understand what is going on.

The listings in the *World Government Address Book* give some idea of the hundreds and hundreds of NGOs that make no bones about their dedication to, well, world government. Some are very handsomely funded indeed; for instance, the Open Society Institute, which is bankrolled by billionaire George Soros. The Commission on Global Governance (CGG) is a major player, and its cochairman Shridath Ramphal, former Secretary General of the British Commonwealth, puts its goal this way: "When we talk about 'governance' and 'democracy,' we have to look beyond governance within countries and democracy within states. We have to look to Global Governance and Democracy within the Global State." The CGG, it has been observed, has a board of directors that looks like it could be the first cabinet of the United States of Earth, including Jacques Delors, former president of the European Commission, and Canada's Maurice Strong, long a ubiquitous power in the networks of one-worldism.

In the setting of organizational priorities, the drafting of documents, and public advocacy for "internationally approved" policies, the NGOs have dramatically increased their role in recent years. "Global Governance and Democracy within the Global State" means that small groups are able to make rules affecting the domestic affairs of countries that it would have been difficult or impossible to achieve democratically in those countries. Global Democracy is, in fact, an end run around democracy. In this respect, the UN-NGO nexus is becoming an instrument as useful to some activists in advancing their causes as are the courts in their own countries. Whether through the UN or through judicial lawmaking, the result is the usurpation of democratic politics.

A "People's Assembly"

Nobody should doubt the sincerity and determination of those who back these developments that others find troubling. Hillary Clinton has called this version of civil society "the vanguard" of a new international order in which NGOs will be more nearly equal with nation-states. UN Secretary General Kofi Annan says that NGOs are "not only disseminators of public information or providers of services, but shapers of policy, too." They are, he says, "the new superpower" which "information technology has empowered to be the true guardians of democracy and good governance everywhere." Of course there is a measure of ideological hype in such statements, but one cannot help but be impressed with, for instance, the proposal that there should be a second chamber of the UN's General Assembly — a People's Assembly. This proposal is backed by, inter alia, the World Federation of United Nations Associations and former UN Secretary General Jávier Pérez de Cuellar.

UN observer Lorne Gunter comments: "Rather than the People's Assembly being comprised of members or deputies from around the world, elected by and accountable to the people they represent [as is at least theoretically the case with the General Assembly], it would likely be made up of the heads of civil society NGOs, and, under most scenarios, only those NGOs accredited by the UN. In other words, the government would elect the voters." Along with the People's Assembly, there is also a drive to place taxes on international financial transactions, airline flights, and properties deemed global in ownership in order to give the UN a source of funding independent from its member nations — especially from the U.S.

These are not simply ideas being tossed around by a few enthusiasts. At the fiftieth annual meeting of NGOs, Kofi Annan called for a People's Assembly by the year 2000. A Millennium People's Assembly Network (MPAN) is at work drafting a "People's Agenda and Vision for the 21st Century" and planning regional People's Assemblies around the world. A first-ever World Civil Society Conference (WOCSOC) was held in Montreal in December 1999. When the NGOs are challenged as to who are "the people" whom they represent, a conventional response is that their goals are the goals the people would choose for themselves if conservative governments and transnational corporations did not hide from them what is good for them, and good for the world. The intention is thoroughly democratic: the UN-NGO combine has such a high estimate of the wisdom of "the people" that it anticipates the consent of the governed to being governed by those who know best. This is government by anticipatory consent. Admittedly, the people as presently constituted are slow to understand their own interests.

A Formula for Despotism

The aforementioned Jeremy Rabkin notes that the ambitions of the NGOs and the proliferation of dubious international agreements, agencies, and regulations aimed at overriding national sovereignty are "mostly just straws in the wind right now. But people in the movement have big plans and have gained a fair amount of momentum. Mostly this has gone on unchallenged, but the longer it goes on, the harder it will be to put an end to it later." And again, one must underscore that national sovereignty should not be defended uncritically. International agreements and modest institutions to enforce them are necessary, but they should be established and controlled in a manner that is, as much as possible, accountable to the people through their representative political institutions. Of course great inequities and injustices will persist, but they are a lesser evil than "Global Governance and Democracy within the Global State," which is a formula for the despotism of a self-appointed elite. Nobody should deny that most in that elite believe in their own good intentions. Historically and at present, despots typically believe in their own good intentions.

A curious twist in this story is the World Trade Organization (WTO). At its riotous meeting in Seattle last December, President Clinton nearly torpedoed the proceedings by saying the U.S. intended to impose upon other nations American-style labor, environmental, and other regulations. The poor countries understandably revolted against a proposal that would effectively exclude them from the global market. There were reportedly more than five hundred organizations protesting the WTO at Seattle, many of them the same NGOs that gravitate around the UN. Suddenly the WTO rather than the UN was where the action was. This, it was said, is where real power, meaning economic power, is located. Some of the protesting world government groups said they were against the WTO undemocratically making the rules for the world. The reality in most cases is that they want the WTO to impose their rules. Quite predictably, out of Seattle came proposals for various instrumentalities that would give NGOs a permanent decision-making role in the WTO. Advocates of world government are not particular about whatever institutions will advance their dream.

In the *New York Times Magazine,* David Rieff takes up related concerns in "The Precarious Triumph of Human Rights." He says that the human rights movement is in trouble because, by its manipulation of the UN and other international organizations, it has lost touch with any constituency that gives it democratic legitimacy. Rieff writes: "Human rights workers sometimes talk of their movement as an emblem of grassroots democracy. Yet it is possible to view it as an undemocratic pressure group, accountable to no one but its own members and donors, that wields enormous power and influence. For example, would there have been a war in Kosovo without the human rights movement? As a supporter of the war in Kosovo, I applaud the result. As a democrat, I worry. It was a moral decision, but it was arrived at undemocratically." He asks a good question. As an opponent of that "humanitarian intervention," I worry not only about the undemocratic factor but, even more, about the way in which human rights are now being exploited as a justification for war. In many parts of the world, and in this country as well, such a development reinforces the cynical view that human rights is little more than a slogan invoked by the U.S. to justify whatever we and whomever we can get to go along with us want to do. And, of course, such cynicism flourishes when the U.S. declines to impose even the most modest penalties on egregious violators of human rights such as China and Sudan.

Rieff draws an interesting parallel. If the human rights movement does not attend to political accountability, he says, "there is a great chance that the human rights paradigm will backfire the way affirmative action did. Affirmative action was also well meant. It drew popular opposition not, for the most part, because it was wrong, but because it was sneaked in, with no serious effort made to win people over. Convinced that their cause was right, its advocates saw no reason to campaign for it among the public at large. Instead, they relied on the courts, the law, and legislation. And eventually, the whole project came undone." Leaving aside whether affirmative action (a.k.a. quotas) is right or wrong, Rieff seems to assume that the people could have been won over, as they can be won over to the globalist push for international courts of justice and other instruments designed to override national sovereignty. That is, it seems to me, a very doubtful assumption in both instances.

In any event, big ambitions are afoot. Forget about the Bilderbergers, the Masons, the Trilateral Commission, and the black helicopters. While keeping our eyes on the NGOs and the human rights movement of international "civil society," we can be grateful that there are also countervailing forces. For instance, the Holy See, some more sensible NGOs, and some third world countries that resist being ruled by George Soros, the Ford Foundation, and allied New York–based globalists. They, soon reinforced, we may hope, by a more clear-eyed U.S. policy, may succeed in recalling the United Nations to its former and more modest self — a necessary, if frequently irritating, instrument of sovereign states in search of cooperation without abdication.

❧ It's really true. Some of my best friends, plus one sister, live in Florida. But I confess it's the one state in the Union that I've never been able to warm up to. (All right, so there are two or three I haven't been to.) A while back I spoke at the annual convention of the American College of Surgeons held in Orlando. I stayed in a hotel with a grotesque swan stuck on the top of it. Across the way was a hotel with a grotesque Something Else. There came a moment when I surveyed the entire scene from the hotel window and could not see one thing that was not ugly, as in vulgar. But now *Christianity Today* reports that Orlando is becoming *the* center for evangelical Protestant organizations. Years ago there was Wheaton, Illinois, then Colorado Springs, and now Orlando. What is it with this herd instinct among evangelicals? My friend Bill Bright is building a $42 million headquarters for Campus Crusade near Orlando airport, close to new campuses of Asbury Theological Seminary, Reformed Theological Seminary, Ligonier Ministries, and a host of others. And of course my very dear friend Chuck Colson lives in Florida, when he doesn't have to be in Washington, Buenos Aires, or wherever. I don't get it. But then, I've never understood why so many people, including very intelligent people of my acquaintance, choose not to live in New York City. Be assured, however, that the exit to Florida will not get in the way of projects such as "Evangelicals and Catholics Together." Christian unity is worth an occasional flight to Orlando. Nobody said this would be easy.

1984 and Now

The Association of Christians in Political Science was launched some years ago, mainly by evangelicals, and is today a lively and ecumenical group that recently held its annual meeting at Calvin College in Grand Rapids. I was invited to give a public lecture on the subject of President Clinton and the American character (you know what I have to say on that) and the next day there was a special session to mark the fifteenth anniversary of the publication of *The Naked Public Square: Religion and Democracy in America.*

In preparation for that, I went back for the first time to reread *The Naked Public Square.* For a writer, it is both encouraging and discouraging to recognize the continuity in one's thinking; encouraging to see how arguments have held up, discouraging to see how little the basic arguments have changed. But that, too, is vanity. Only the writer is inside his own head, and he should not assume that others will see all the continuities he sees. I conceive of writing as engagement in a conversation, and the reader's questions and challenges are essential to the conversation continuing. After we have fallen into silence, as we inevitably shall, we may hope that others will take up the conversation where we left off.

While it does not seem to me that my mind has been greatly changed with respect to the basic arguments, the circumstance at the beginning of a new century is very different. Upon rereading *The Naked Public Square,* I was struck by how taken I was with the Italian social theorist Vilfredo Pareto and his idea of "the circulation of elites" in social change. Put too briefly, I posited that what was in the early 1980s called "the new religious right" was positioned to succeed, over time, the liberal Protestant mainline in giving moral-cultural definition to the American experiment. That may still happen, it may in fact be in the process of happening. The prospect has subsequently been reinforced by developments such as "Evangelicals and Catholics Together," in which evangelical Protestants and Roman Catholics join in acknowledging one another at the deepest level as brothers and sisters in Christ, and also embrace together the great tasks of cultural reconstruction.

This convergence was anticipated in *The Catholic Moment,* a book published three years after *The Naked Public*

Square, in which I speculated that Father John Courtney Murray may have been right in the 1950s when he foresaw a time when Catholics, picking up a fallen banner, would take the lead in publicly articulating the constituting truths of the American order. Murray could not then imagine that this would be done in cooperation with evangelical Protestants, who were then easily dismissable as a band of self-isolated "fundamentalists" quite content to let America go to Hell in a handbasket of its choice while they awaited the Rapture.

The kinds of major reconfigurations of social forces discussed in those two books take a long time to work themselves out, and I am certainly not prepared to say that what I anticipated then has been falsified by subsequent events. On the contrary, the convergence of evangelical and Catholic dynamics in giving religio-cultural redefinition to American life continues to be the only believable game in town. But such a redefinition is not going to prevail any time soon. On the Catholic side, the episcopal and intellectual will is still flabby and undecided. The mindless rush to prove that Catholics are "good Americans" and "just like everybody else" has slowed down, but has hardly been reversed. The greatest disappointment, at almost all levels of Catholic leadership, is the failure to seize upon the comprehensive program of renewal proposed in the social teaching of the pontificate of John Paul II.

And, as I said at Calvin College, I have been sobered by the evidence of the apparently incorrigible individualism of so much of evangelical Protestantism that simply does not see the connection between God's salvific purposes and the tasks of cultural engagement. This is underscored by, for instance, Christian Smith's *American Evangelicalism,* in many ways an excellent book but one that is resigned to evangelicalism being forever a loosely linked network of subcultures providing individuals with "sacred umbrellas" while evidencing little interest in the "sacred canopy" (Peter Berger) of public meanings. (For a discussion of Smith's argument, see

"Those Unsecular Evangelicals," Public Square, August/September 1999.) But, as I say, these things take time, and I am by no means prepared to withdraw what I have proposed as the promise of both Catholicism and evangelical Protestantism, and of evangelicals and Catholics together.

The Fading of Secular Humanism

Upon rereading *The Naked Public Square,* I was also struck by how seriously I and others took the arguments of those who were then described, and described themselves, as "secular humanists." The band of supremely confident secular intellectuals who gathered around figures such as John Dewey to issue proclamations such as the 1933 "Humanist Manifesto" appeared as a force to be reckoned with. In 1984 I noted that that kind of assertive secularism seemed to be no longer so confident, and maybe was going on the defensive. Today it seems that species is almost extinct, although it is more likely that they now present themselves in a different guise. In public education, from grade school through graduate school, there is less frequently a frontal assault on Christianity and the Judeo-Christian moral tradition. Almost nobody today is explicitly proposing, as John Dewey did, a "religion of secularism" or "a common faith" to replace biblical religion. But the religions and quasi-religions of "multiculturalism" are pervasive and they provide a more insidious replacement. The newly imagined religions of Native Americans and devotions to Mother Earth and her pantheon of nature gods and goddesses are a commonplace in school curricula. The currents of thought that now run under the banner of "postmodernism" are a major factor in undermining the former confidence of secularists who opposed religion in the name of Enlightenment rationality.

In going back to what I wrote in 1984, I am impressed by how powerful was the remembered presence of the Vietnam War, and the real presence of the Cold War of which Vietnam was part. I proposed then that a crucial dividing line in the culture war is between those who do and those who do not agree with the proposition that "On balance, and considering the alternatives, America is a force for good in the world." That formulation caught a lot of flack from liberal critics who condemned it as "simplistic." I thought it rather carefully nuanced. No doubt there are still many who would deny that proposition today. But they do not now make such a big issue of it. Agreement or disagreement with the proposition does not now, as it did then, go a long way toward answering the question, "Whose side are you on?" The reason for that, of course, is the disappearance of the totalitarian alternative of the evil empire. That is perhaps the biggest difference between then and now.

Fifteen years later, and ten years after the end of the Cold War, there are signs that elements of the left and right are coming together in opposition to what is widely recognized as a kind of American imperium in maintaining world order. The fecklessness of the Clinton policies — from Haiti to Somalia to Kosovo — has precluded any clear definition of the imperium, but that will likely change in the years ahead, resulting in some curious realignments in response to the proposition that "On balance, and considering the alternatives, America is a force for good in the world."

Confusing the Cities

In important respects, our circumstance at the beginning of the twenty-first century is more promising than we had any right to expect fifteen or thirty years ago. The argument about the dangers of the naked public square is not thought to be so controversial today as it was in 1984. Perhaps because the dangers have become more evident. There are other factors as well, such as the way in which the courts, including the Supreme Court, are backing off somewhat from a rigidly secularist understanding of "the separation of church and state." Yet one also notes today the growing habit of writers, both religious and secular, to speak of America as a post-Christian society. Among some Christians, this way of speaking reflects disappointment that, after two decades of their full bore political activism, the nation has not been returned to the paths of righteousness.

Talk about post-Christian America typically assumes a necessary connection between Christianity and civic righteousness, and of course that connection cannot be denied. Christianity, however, is also very much about sin and sinners, and how to cope in an earthly city that is not to be confused with the city of eschatological promise. Some conservative Christians who have turned against what they call post-Christian or neo-pagan America have learned one right lesson: that most of what ails our culture cannot be fixed by politics. Unfortunately, they have also drawn from that a wrong lesson: that political engagement is futile.

Even more than I did in *The Naked Public Square,* I would today draw attention to the Jewish-Christian connection. Most Christians simply do not understand why Jews — who are, after all, about 2 percent of the population — should be so important to reconstituting the civil public square. Today we must address that puzzlement in a way that will provoke a new way of thinking about these matters among both Christians and Jews. In 1984 I cited a friend, a Reform rabbi, who asserted, "When I hear the phrase 'Christian America' I see barbed wire." He reflected what was then an almost unanimous sentiment among American Jews. Fifteen years later, there are important Jewish voices, even a few Reform voices, saying that it is in the interest also of Jews that American culture reassert its Christian identity, always remembering that such an identity is grounded in a Judeo-Christian moral tradition in which the "Judeo" is by no means incidental.

Toward the end of *The Naked Public Square,* I took up the contention of those who then said that the day of liberal democracy is past. There were many who said that, as there are still some who say it today. Most of those who said it then — in the churches, the universities, and the media — held the view that America was "on the wrong side of history." In their passionate support for "liberation struggles" in Cuba, Nicaragua, Angola, and elsewhere they left little doubt about what they thought — "on balance, and considering the alternatives" — was the right side. The conclusion of the book considered the "dour prospect" of the end of liberal democracy. The hazards in the new century now under way will be different of course, but America will continue to be an experiment, and it will continue to be an experiment that is sustained by an intelligent anxiety about what it would mean were it to fail. In short, I am not persuaded by Francis Fukuyama's "end of history" argument. We have to consider the prospect of the experiment's failure, and what I said about that in the concluding passage of *The Naked Public Square* I would still say today:

> It makes little difference whether the successor regime is of the right or of the left or unclassifiable. By whatever ideology the idea, this audacious democratic idea, would be declared discredited. By whom, where, under what circumstances, by what conception and what dedication could it ever be tried again? Yes, of course, life would go on and God's purposes will not be defeated, not ultimately. But the world would be a darker and colder place. That it can happen is evident to all but the naive and willfully blind. That it will happen seems probable, if we refuse to understand the newness, the fragility, the promise, and the demands of religion and democracy in America.

A World of Our Own Making

Born in February 1997, Dolly is two years old now, or maybe eight years old, because the cell used in cloning her was six years old at the time. Since Dr. Ian Wilmut announced Dolly to the world, some scientists have expressed skepticism about whether she really is a clone, though apparently most experts now concede she is. In any event, the announcement set off an enormous uproar in the media, and also occasioned reflection in more serious circles about the prospect of cloning not sheep but human beings. Two of the most notable reflections were by James Q. Wilson, "The Paradox of Cloning" in the *Weekly Standard,* and by Leon Kass in a long essay in the *New Republic,* "The Wisdom of Repugnance." Those articles, with a brief additional exchange between the authors, have now been brought together in an excellent little book, *The Ethics of Human Cloning* (American Enterprise Institute, 100 pp., $16.95).

Wilson of UCLA, author of books such as *The Moral Sense* (see FT review, November 1993), is a social scientist of rare moral attentiveness, and Kass of the University of Chicago, who has written frequently also in these pages, is simply one of the wisest and most morally serious people I have ever known. In his initial essay, Wilson concluded that, all things considered, we should not be alarmed by the prospect of human cloning. He acknowledged some dangers but wrote, "Provided certain conditions are met, the gains will turn out to exceed the risks." The chief condition is that "Cloning should be permitted only on behalf of two married partners, and the mother should — absent some medical condition that doctors must certify — carry the fertile tissue to birth." The intention is to make sure that the offspring "belong to the parents" and to prevent various misuses of cloning technology. He recognizes that "many devout Christians or Jews" will disagree: "I would ask of them only that they explain what it is about sexual fertilization that so affects God's judgment about the child that results."

Kass's "The Wisdom of Repugnance" is an article both much longer and more complex in its argument that we should respect and learn from our intuitive recoil at the separation of sex from fertility, and the replacement of procreation with the manufacture of children as a "product." (Wilson is a Catholic and Kass, by no means incidentally, is a Jew.) Both original essays are very much worth a careful reading, but I will confine myself to the further exchange in the new book. Kass writes that he does not think that the practice of cloning could be limited in the way that Wilson suggests, but his objections go further than that. "I regard cloning to be *in itself* a form of child abuse, even if no one complains, and a deep violation of our given nature as gendered and engendering beings."

There is a critical methodological difference between the two thinkers. Kass notes that Wilson has elsewhere written perceptively about the importance of a "prearticulate human moral sense," but in this case Wilson does not trust "his own sense of moral disquiet and sets out to explain it with reasons." As any parent knows, the child's question "Why not?" is often hard to answer. Wilson asks "Why not cloning?" and cannot come up with an answer that he finds convincing. Kass writes: "Whether he intends it or not, that move places the burden of proof on those who object to cloning rather than on the proponents. Worse, it requires that the reasons offered be finally acceptable to utilitarians who measure only in terms of tangible harms and benefits but who are generally blind to the deeper meaning of things." Kass, too, employs utilitarian — or what might be called consequentialist — arguments, but he wants to keep our attention fixed on "the deeper meaning of things."

Wilson's initial essay was impatient with such ponderings, and he was particularly dismissive of theologians who would worry about whether a cloned baby would have a soul. Kass is equally impatient with what he views as Wilson's "superficial" treatment of philosophical and religious considerations. "No thoughtful theologian," Kass responds, "objects to assisted reproduction because it limits God's power to inculcate a human soul; theologians worry not about the impotence of God but about the hubris of man." He cites Anglican Oliver O'Donovan's *Begotten or Made?*, Methodist Paul Ramsey's *Fabricated Man*, and the Vatican's instruction on "The Dignity of Procreation" as representative of the kind of thinking to which Wilson might pay attention.

In favor of cloning, Wilson had noted that in vitro fertilization had also been viewed as "ethically suspect" at first, but is now socially accepted. Kass responds: "Does the growing social acceptability of sodomy or adultery constitute a refutation of Leviticus 18:22 or the Seventh Commandment?" (That's the sixth for you Catholics and Lutherans.) "The arrival of cloning, far from gaining legitimacy from the precedent of in vitro fertilization," Kass writes, "should rather awaken those who previously saw no difficulty with starting human life in petri dishes." It is notoriously difficult these days to make an argument from what is "natural," but Kass urges that we attend to nature's "possibly normative pointings."

Is the Issue Sex or Marriage?

A friend suggested to Kass that the difference between him and Wilson on these matters is that he is chiefly concerned about human sexuality while Wilson's main concern is with marriage and family. Not quite, responds Kass. "[That] difference is more apparent than real, especially if one understands the generative meaning of sexuality and, even more, if one sees that one will be increasingly incapable of defending the institution of marriage and the two-parent family if one is indifferent to its natural grounding in what I call the ontology of sex. Can we ensure, even in thought, that all children will have two parents if we ignore, in our social arrangements, the *natural* (hetero) *sexual* ground of parent-hood?"

In his original article, Kass said that a clone, because asexually reproduced and lacking two parents, is a single-parent child. He now writes that "it would be more accurate to say that, since it is the twin rather than the offspring of its 'source,' it has *no* parents, biologically speaking — unless its 'parents' are the mother and father of the person from whom it was cloned." There are other real-world consequences. "Virtually no parent is going to be able to treat a clone of himself or herself as one does a child generated by the lottery of sex. The new life will constantly be scrutinized in relation to that of the older copy. The child is likely to be ever a curiosity, ever a potential source of déjà vu." And what about the look-alike copy of one parent when there are tensions in the marriage or the parents divorce? "Will mommy still love the clone of daddy?"

Kass does not hesitate to invoke the slippery slope, an image much mocked by those who hold that one thing does not usually follow from another. Prenatal screening, sex selection, the normalization of deviancy, and the eugenic implications of new reproductive technologies — cloning in particular — are all upon us. But Wilson says not to worry, so long as we hold fast to marriage and family. "Given the state of our culture," observes Kass, "it is rather late in the sexual day for Professor Wilson's call to rally the family wagons to protect the little beloved clone."

Kass' conclusion is nothing if not definite: "Even if human cloning is rarely undertaken, a society in which it is tolerated is no longer the same society — any more than is a society that permits (even small-scale) incest or cannibalism or slavery. It is a society that has forgotten how to shudder, that always rationalizes away the abominable. A society that allows cloning has, whether it knows it or not, tacitly said yes to converting procreation into manufacture and to treating our children as pure projects of our will. Indeed, the principles here legitimated could — and will — be used to legitimate the entire humanitarian superhighway to *Brave New World*. Professor Wilson's sweet reasonableness of today will come back to haunt him, once he sees what he has unknowingly said yes to. Better he should trust his immediate moral sense."

Professor Wilson gets the last word in this exchange. The "essential difference" between them, he says, is that Kass views the meaning of children in relation to sexuality while he views it in relation to the family. However the child is brought into being, Wilson's concern is whether "the child is likely to do well." "If Dr. Kass thinks that sexuality is more important than families, then he would object to any form of assisted reproduction that does not involve parental coition." One notes that the choice between sexuality and families is a false one, and Kass has already said that cloning should occasion long second thoughts about assisted reproduction in general. Wilson cites a number of studies indicating that children conceived by artificial means (although not, of course, children who have been cloned) do, in fact, generally do well. And that's the only thing that matters.

Arguments and Preferences

Well, not quite. In a somewhat marginally relevant discussion of surrogate motherhood and a case where the woman bearing the child refused to give it up to the couple with whom she had contracted, Wilson disagrees with the court that awarded the child to the couple. "The central fact was that she was the baby's mother. . . . The child belonged to its mother, period." He continues, "Some critics of my view would say that surrogacy is appropriate if the birth mother receives both egg and sperm from the parents who are to own the child. That mistakes genetic similarity for the birth effect." These things are asserted but not argued. I agree with the assertions but am impressed that Wilson seems to take them as self-evidently, dare we say "naturally," true, when in fact the crucial questions in such a dispute are over the meaning of "mother" and connections between genetics, contract, and what Wilson calls "the birth effect."

Wilson does not argue so much as he simply expresses preferences. To Kass' concern about the source of the egg in cloning, Wilson responds, "Nor do I much care for the idea of taking eggs from a Nobel Prize-winner." That establishes that James Q. Wilson does not much care for the practice, but does it tell us anything about what should be done about cloning? Later he writes, "We do not want families planning to have a movie star, basketball player, or high-energy physicist as an offspring." That "we" do not want it is undoubtedly true, but, just as certainly, many people might want it, and who are "we" to tell them they can't have it? Wilson goes on to say, "I am not clear as to how those limits might be drawn, and if no one can solve that puzzle, I would join Dr. Kass in banning cloning." He suggests, however, that the "puzzle" can be solved by allowing selection only for race, ethnicity, and sex. But by what moral reason or principle of justice should people be compelled to abide by such limited choices? If all the parties are agreeable, why should a couple be prevented from having a clone of Michael Jordan, Madonna, or — the preference is imaginable — Bill Clinton?

Wilson says that "Dr. Kass is right to stress the mystery and uncertainty of sexual union." But he gives no indication of understanding what Kass means by the mystery or its relationship to uncertainty, and he clearly thinks that Kass is wrong to stress these considerations as they might impinge upon the legality of cloning. Matters such as mystery, it appears, are in the private sphere of aesthetics, or maybe even theology. In the real world, cloning, legalized within the limits that Professor Wilson prefers, will remain, he says, "quite rare." That is because, he concludes on a note of high insouciance, "Sex is more fun than cloning. . . . Procreation is a delight."

Ironic Liberals

One is reminded of Richard Rorty's anti-foundational formula for sustaining a decent and democratic society: "We must hope there will continue to be enough ironic liberals like ourselves." Were the world populated only by eminently decent people such as James Q. Wilson, I am sure Leon Kass would not be as worried as he is. In the real world, however, some people, if not prevented, will do bizarre, destructive, and evil things. Nobody knows for sure what the consequences of human cloning would be, but in his original essay and in his response to Wilson's original essay, Kass offers a very plausible and sobering description of the *probable* consequences. To most of Kass' particulars Wilson does not respond at all. With respect to others, he thinks that very few people would want to do such things, he strongly prefers that they not do such things, and maybe "we" can translate our preferences into legal limits against doing such things. But finally, we are assured, the benefits of cloning human beings outweigh the risks.

The benefits, according to Wilson, are for a very small number of people, namely, couples who cannot conceive a child, either in the uterus or the petri dish, and who choose not to adopt, use a surrogate mother, or receive cells from an unknown donor for in vitro fertilization. Once again, choice is trump. Neither in principle nor in common sense is there any reason to believe that choice could be denied to those who choose what they see as other benefits in human cloning, such as owning the clone of a Nobel Prize physicist. Kass understands this. In his rosy view of the likely consequences of cloning, says Kass, Wilson is "playing Dr. Pangloss," and Wilson maybe believes that Kass is playing Cassandra. They both may be right, but when choice is trumps, Cassandra wins. The exchange, however, goes beyond who has the more adequate reading of our cultural moment and of cloning's probable consequences.

It is a matter of the "ontology" of human sexuality. Are

marriage, procreation, and family all of a piece within the ontology of sex? The alternative is a bricolage or tinkertoy approach in which these and other aspects of sexuality (e.g., love, pleasure, loyalty, obligation) can be taken apart and re-assembled according to diverse desires. Polymorphous perversity is the technical term for the infantile sexual state in which the child is confused about the purpose of genitals and does not understand coitus as the goal of erotic desire. A large part of civilization's work is the overcoming or containment of polymorphous perversity. In recent decades we have witnessed a vast civilizational undoing; not a sexual revolution but a sexual regression in which millions have been infantilized, encouraged to pretend that they do not know what they do know, and to call the resulting confusion choice.

Delicate Ground

Here we touch on delicate ground. Sexuality as bricolage inevitably raises the issue of contraception. Kass touches on it delicately, noting that in the 1960s the Supreme Court ruling that allowed the sale of contraceptives *(Griswold v. Connecticut)* was in support of *marital* privacy, but it almost immediately became an *individual's* right to *sexual* privacy, married or not *(Eisenstadt v. Baird)*. The right to privacy, the right to marry, the right to define marriage, the right to reproduce, the right to the child of one's choice. The ontology of sexuality lies shattered under a barrage of rights. Such was the prognosis offered with almost eerie (some would say prophetic) exactitude by the 1968 encyclical *Humanae Vitae*. The civilizational undoing is a moral undoing, and in the realm of sexuality, said the encyclical, it begins with the separation of the sexual act from its unitive and procreative end. To which the infantilized respond with the cunning appearance of innocence, "*Which* sexual act?" Our public debates move smartly along: from the sale of contraceptives to easy divorce to abortion to same-sex marriage to cloning human beings. And all in only thirty years.

The polymorphously perverse blame their confusion on the rapidity of technological change, and there is something to that. Not much, but something. The discovery of buggery and baby-killing did not have to await the dawn of the space age. Cloning is different. It is not the cause of our confusion but the result of our confusion. The source of confusion is in heeding the commandment that thou shalt not resist temptation, and cloning is but one more temptation. The results of the sexual regression, more and more people are coming to recognize, have been disastrous for everyone — except, in a superficial way, for rutting males, who have always known how conveniently detachable is sex from its attendant responsibilities. Women and children, of course, have been the chief victims of the liberation from the ontology of sex. In the discussion of abortion, more and more women are saying what all women must know, that it is a phony liberation that is purchased by the death of their children.

Sex seemed such a pretty tinkertoy, and so maddeningly complex. Telling ourselves that we did not know what it was for, we took it apart to find out how it works, and could be made to work in different and exciting ways. After the deconstruction, this part of the anatomy was stuck into that part, and this kind substituted for that kind, until all memory of design was lost in the immeasurable expanse of desire. "Sex is fun," it was said ever more insistently, ever more desperately. Of course there were the spoilsports among us. They remembered, and they mumbled about the nature of the thing, and how it was somehow and inseparably tied up with the nature of us. "Ontology" they called it. They were tolerated, so long as they didn't get in the way of our doing what we wanted to do, even though we had grown tired of wanting to do nothing more than what we wanted to do. Then the prospect of cloning came along, the prospect of making others who would be just like us. The realization dawned that, in talking about clones, we were not talking about them but about ourselves. The debate was not about what we can do or even about what we should do. The debate was about who we *are*. And it turned out that there was a revolution after all, and, as is the way with things that revolve, it came full circle to an understanding of the way things are, and are meant to be.

Imagine some years from now when people started being happy again, and being happy about being happy. Adults took great pleasure in watching children growing up and saying, "Oh, so that's how it's meant to be!" Of course there were also the very young and some slow learners who were always imagining how things could be otherwise and asking, "Why not?" But the adults were neither flustered nor intimidated now. The cloning debate had taught them to do some hard thinking about these things. They spoke confidently, persuasively, and winsomely about how things are and are meant to be. Some of them even talked about ontology. They still had problems of course — coping with temptations, keeping promises, forgiving betrayals of the way things are and are meant to be. But, all in all, they were very happy not to be lost in a world of their own making. Until they began to take things for granted again; until they began to think that that's just the way things are, and forgot the part about things being meant to be. And after they had been going on that way for a long time, somebody had what seemed like a really bright idea and asked, "Why not?" And the whole thing started all over again.